Power, Authority,
and the Anabaptist Tradition

CENTER BOOKS IN ANABAPTIST STUDIES

Donald B. Kraybill
Consulting Editor

George F. Thompson
Series Founder and Director

Published in cooperation with the Center for American Places
Santa Fe, New Mexico, and Harrisonburg, Virginia

POWER,
AUTHORITY,
AND THE
ANABAPTIST
TRADITION

Edited by Benjamin W. Redekop
and Calvin W. Redekop

The Johns Hopkins University Press

Baltimore and London

Chapter 5, "The Abuse of Power among Mennonites in
South Russia, 1789–1919," by Jacob A. Loewen and Wesley
J. Prieb, was published in *The Journal of Mennonite Studies*
(vol. 14, 1996, pp. 17–44) and is reprinted by permission.
The cartoon in Chapter 7 is used by permission of *Sword
and Trumpet*.

2   4   6   8   9   7   5   3   1

The Johns Hopkins University Press
2715 North Charles Street
Baltimore, Maryland 21218-4363
www.press.jhu.edu

Library of Congress Cataloging-in-Publication Data

Power, authority, and the Anabaptist tradition / edited by
Benjamin W. Redekop and Calvin W. Redekop.
p. cm. — (Center books in Anabaptist studies)
Includes bibliographical references and index.
ISBN 0-8018-6605-7 (hardcover : alk. paper)
1. Anabaptists—Doctrines.   2. Power—Religious
aspects—Christianity.   3. Authority—Religious aspects—
Christianity.   I. Redekop, Benjamin W., 1961–   II.
Redekop, Calvin Wall, 1925–   III. Title.   IV. Series.
BX4931.2 .P69 2001
230'.43—dc21

00-011273

A catalog record for this book is available from the British Library.

Contents

Contents

Introction

Anabaptism and *power?* What do these terms have in common? Did not the Anabaptist movement, the "left," or "radical," wing of the Reformation, reject clerical abuse of power as well as collusion between church and state? Did not Anabaptist/Mennonite groups become a peaceable people who rejected military service and practiced a communal ethic of love and *Gelassenheit* (yieldedness) toward each other?

One can answer a qualified yes to these questions, but therein lies a paradox that goes to the heart of this volume. On the one hand, the movement represented a break with the inherited system of intermingled religious and political power, a break in keeping with broader historical trends. As noted in Chapter 2, Mennonites may have more to do with Machiavelli than they think. On the other hand, as some of the other chapters in this volume demonstrate, this radical and innovative stance has the potential to yield its opposite, and even worse, can provide a deceptive, benign cover behind which naked power may operate as though invisible. This paradox, in which mundane power is renounced yet not in truth forsaken (and is perhaps even strengthened), is of course not restricted to Anabaptism. Philosophers long before Nietzsche identified a similar dynamic at work in the Christian tradition as a whole. A focus on the Anabaptist tradition provides a particularly vivid and poignant example of both the promise and the dilemmas of the Christian faith vis-à-vis the exercise of earthly power.

Even though "power is a universal phenomenon in human societies,"[1] no topic is as little understood or confronted. Even though the idea of power has occupied the thoughts of philosophers and theologians throughout history and numerous social philosophers (for example, Thomas Hobbes) made it the central hinge of their theories, power remains a mysterious and often-avoided topic. Kenneth B. Clark suggests that "perhaps its very pervasiveness leads to the attempt to avoid it—even to repress it psychologically—as a problem deserving serious and systematic theoretical analysis and empirical study."[2] According to Charles Page, "Like *love*, power is open territory for all: moralist or analyst, poet or scientist. No work can grasp the whole of it, even within the perspective of a single discipline."[3] Thus, the difficulties of understanding power are daunting. According to Robert Bierstedt, "We can truthfully say that power is a 'fundamental entity of society' but [with that] we are not saying very much. Our relative ignorance of the nature of power is itself a curious phenomenon. The word has been in our vocabularies for as long as we can remember and we frequently use it, but we find ourselves unable to define it. We here confront the dilemma of St. Augustine, who confessed that he knew perfectly well what time was—until someone asked him."[4]

When it comes to power in relation to other human beings, most people seem to accept a Weberian definition in which exercising power involves getting someone else to do what you want whether they would like to or not; it is authoritative when they comply willingly, dominating when they do not. But what are power's dynamics? How can we tell when someone has it, uses it, abuses it? Is it primarily a function of systems or of personalities? Preeminent philosophers of power like Nietzsche and Foucault, for all their similarities (and Foucault saw himself as a follower of Nietzsche), seem to come at the issue from opposite ends: Nietzsche ever emphasizing the heroic individual, Foucault focusing on systems, networks of a power that flows like blood through the body, operating perhaps most significantly at the capillaries.

It will not do to simply follow a particular *theory* of power; rather, what is needed is empirical, interdisciplinary analysis and reflection on the issue. And this is particularly the case when it comes to the question of power in the context of religion and religious practice. Most critical reflection on power and religion has come from the outside, from dissenters who, by stepping outside religious beliefs, have been able to see through the "veil of illusion" and diagnose the underlying workings of power. Such diagnoses have been salutary, if at times overblown. Yet so great and telling (and threatening) has been the critique that those who have remained "within the fold" have tended to avoid the topic. And those who seek sympathetically to understand religion in scholarly terms have not progressed very far in analyzing the subject. As Meredith McGuire notes, "Power is a pervasive theme in the sociology of religion. It was certainly a focus point in classical theories in the field. Yet we have not progressed much beyond these formulations . . . We need to make a theory of power explicit in the field and to focus much more closely and carefully on research which will shed light on the phenomenon."[5]

In one of the few recent substantive theoretical analyses of religion and power, Richard Schoenherr states unequivocally that "all religious belief systems assume the absolute necessity of a concentration of power. Religious collectivities are engaged in the relentless process of developing organizational power and authority sufficient to guard and preserve access to the definitive religious experience."[6] Schoenherr proposes that this critically important topic must be studied both from fideistic and empirical perspectives if we are to make progress in understanding religion and power.

There have, in fact, been some researches into the use of power in American Christian denominations. Joachim Wach was something of pioneer in the field, devoting a considerable part of his life to studying the types of religious leadership in various historical cultures.[7] Another early attempt to analyze the dynamics of power in American Christian denominations was Liston Pope's *Millhands and Preachers*. Among Pope's many conclusions about the dominant religious denominations in Gaston County, North Carolina, was that the churches, and especially the clergy, conformed to the power relations within the community and were very reluctant to disturb them.[8] In *Religion and the Struggle for Power*, J. Milton Yinger analyzed the numerous dilemmas Christian denominations face as religious interests and loyalties compete with one another. He concluded that economic factors basically informed the movement of religious groups from sectarian to "established church" status as they accrued wealth and power in the community.[9]

One of the first significant studies to thematize the study of power in a specific American denomination was Paul M. Harrison's *Authority and Power in the Free Church Tradition: A Social Case Study of the American Baptist Convention*. Harrison used the Weberian power-authority framework in his study of the American Baptist Convention, a congregational and democratic denomination, and concluded that "no group can function without leadership, and when leaders are divested of authority they will necessarily seek and gain power in order to meet their responsibilities; the power they acquire may exceed that which ordinarily accrues to leaders in nontotalitarian hierarchical institutions."[10] Schoenherr argues that a central implication of such studies is that problems associated with the exercise of power are basically linked to the power of the clergy: "Concentration on the priesthood and ordained ministry provides an important theoretical and methodological bridge toward understanding the link between the key living beliefs and the extant power structures of the churches."[11] A conclusion to be drawn is that one reason for the paucity of helpful studies of power and Christianity is that most groups' beliefs and ecclesiastical structures are dependent on the centrality of the ordained and elevated clergy.

Students of Anabaptist/Mennonitism have only recently begun to confront the issue of power and authority within their own faith communities; indeed, the present volume is the first to explicitly thematize the issue. J. Lawrence Burkholder (author of Chapter 1), a philosopher, has been at the forefront of thinking about power and Anabaptism.[12] In the early 1970s James Stayer (author of Chapter 3) published the first comprehensive historical analysis of Anabaptist thinking on pacifism, or "nonresistance," entitled *Anabaptists and the Sword*. In that book Stayer charted Anabaptist thinking about a "perennial problem," "the relation of coercion to ethical and religious values."[13] An edited collection that included chapters on contemporary Mennonite institutions, organizations, and power was *Kingdom, Cross, and Community* (1976).[14] In a 1996 study entitled *Wise as Serpents, Innocent as Doves: American Mennonites Engage Washington*, Keith Graber Miller examined Mennonite attempts at influencing Congress in the interests of peace. The establishment of a Mennonite Central Committee Peace Office in Washington, D.C., marked the first time Mennonites in America were involved in mixing religion and politics on an official level.[15] Perry Bush's *Two Kingdoms, Two Loyalties: Mennonite Pacifism in Modern America* (1998) peripherally raises issues of power and authority via study of Mennonite pacifism. Bush deals with the problem of Mennonite acculturation following World War II and its implications for the two-kingdom ideal of traditional Anabaptism.[16] Taken together, the studies of Miller and Bush problematize the idea that modern Anabaptist/Mennonites have been able to hold themselves aloof from the worldly exercise of power, and they indicate that traditional Mennonite "nonresistance" has come under fire in a world where boundaries between Mennonite churches and the state are becoming increasingly blurry.

Speaking more directly to the exercise of power within Mennonite communities, Fred Kniss has recently published *Disquiet in the Land: Cultural Conflicts in American Mennonite Communities*. Covering the period stretching from 1870 to 1985, Kniss studied a number of religious controversies and conflicts within the Mennonite Church. Kniss proposes that Mennonite conflict "revolves around two key paradigms, 'traditionalism' and 'communalism.'" In traditionalism the "locus of moral authority is the collective tradition," whereas the paradigm of communalism "holds that the primary moral project is the community, the maximization of the public good."[17] Studying internal conflict begins to bring us into the heart of the power question, and Chapter 7 in the present volume analyzes intra-Mennonite conflicts as struggles for power within the religious community.

We are thus still in the early stages of understanding the exercise of power, authority, and domination within the Christian tradition as a whole and within the Anabaptist/Mennonite tradition in particular. The present volume is aimed at making a contribution to this very important question, and we hope that it will be of use not only to those interested in Anabaptism but also to all students of religion. While we cannot claim that this book is comprehensive, we do believe it provides a wide-ranging introduction to the topic, beginning with the roots—historical, theological, philosophical—of the Anabaptist movement. As an important outgrowth of the Reformation, Anabaptists proposed that power and authority were not vested in traditional and inherited political power or in the ritually sanctioned offices of the ecclesiastical hierarchy, but rather only in the individual will and the community of the faithful. This signally explosive confrontation with power was immediately understood by the contemporary religious and political authorities and institutions, and it helps to explain why there was such ruthless extermination of early Anabaptists through martyrdom and exile. Its significance has also been recognized among non-Anabaptist scholars, who have rightly described the Anabaptist movement as the forerunner of religious and political freedom in the West. Roland Bainton, for example, states, "The Anabaptists anticipated all other religious bodies in the proclamation of the voluntary church, separation of church and state, and religious liberty."[18]

But this insight was not as clear to the members of the Anabaptist and later Mennonite traditions. Because the rejection of arbitrary religious authority was precipitated by the rejection of the clergy's right to collect the tithe and by the demand for individuals to be consciously and volitionally involved in the religious act of faith and salvation itself (expressed in adult baptism), the conflict concerning power tended to be shifted toward the theological and doctrinal nature of baptism. Freedom of belief and conscience (noncoercion in matters of faith) and nonparticipation in the military violence of the state became the salient issues, not the legitimacy of the use of power on the congregational and community level.

Yet even more important, as Bainton states, "Persecution turned the Anabaptists into the Church of the Remnant."[19] Rather than continuing to focus on the problematic relationship between power and faith, attention was directed toward survival, and a quietistic retreat from the world resulted. Anabaptism simply did not have the opportunity to incarnate its vision of the relationship between the Christian faith and human power structures. Instead, as Troeltsch and others have so cogently shown, Anabaptism became retreatist and "sectarian." The movement that started as the champion of religious liberty transmogrified the ideal into a meek and mild pacifism and nonresistance.

For most contemporary Anabaptist/Mennonite groups, scholars and laypersons alike, the central identity marker has been the ethic of love and nonresistance. Scholars assert that "in their nearly 500 years of history, peacemaking has been central to Mennonite self-understanding and public identity," noting that "the typical mode of peacemaking in . . . segregated rural settings often took the form of 'non-resistance'—an absolute rejection of the use of force that permeates all social relations within and without the community."[20] But while "the focus on 'resist not evil' led to a categorical rejection of force and coercion,"[21] it cannot be said that this has always or even most of the time been the full reality. The restricted focus on the nonresistant position has led to an evasion of full consideration of the centrality of power and its misuse in all human affairs. Anabaptism has evolved into a variety of forms and has become embroiled in a variety of structures and institutions (including highly institutionalized church congregations) that involve concentrations of power, resulting in tensions, conflicts, separations, schisms, and outright despotic abuses of power (domination).

So the paradox of Anabaptism and power remains unsolved and often unrecognized. This book attempts to put this paradox into focus and offer some insights. In the opening chapter the author presents a philosophical overview of the problem of power as it relates to the Anabaptist/Mennonite tradition. Chapter 2 surveys some of the major theories of power and their relationship to religion, providing a narrative of how thinking about power has changed over time and where the "Anabaptist Revolt" fits into this movement. Chapter 3 presents a historical analysis of the emergence of Anabaptism in the context of the Reformation and the Peasants' War, outlining where the various Anabaptist groups stood vis-à-vis the question of political and religious power. The chapter following begins by examining the issues of power and authority in the theology of Menno Simons, using the metaphor of theologizing as a "game." The discussion is then brought into the twentieth century through analysis of two prominent American Mennonite theologians, Guy F. Hershberger and John H. Yoder. Chapter 5 recounts, in often disturbing detail, the ways in which the Russian Mennonite Commonwealth compromised Menno Simons' vision of a religious people who operated without the use of worldly "force." Chapter 6 moves from the macro to the micro level by recounting a heartbreaking story of how a conservative, "plain" Anabaptist community was unable to come to terms with HIV/AIDS, resulting in the unnecessary infection of a woman and her child. Viewed within the context of the maintenance of communal norms, the story becomes one of how power can be exercised in the name of tradition and authority with disastrous results for individuals, particularly for women. In Chapter 7 the author employs the concept of "culture wars" to analyze the power differentials between various groups of Mennonites, and in Chapter 8 the authors present a wide-ranging theoretical and practical discussion of power and gender in relation to Mennonite ecclesiology. The final chapter identifies the positive implications of the Anabaptist/Mennonite movement vis-à-vis the exercise of mundane power, takes account of the movement's shortcomings, and proposes an alternative to secular views of power consonant with the original Christian message and the Anabaptist promise: "pro-humana" power.

We have aimed for a viewpoint that balances the promise with the reality. If the discussion at times seems to be more critical than hopeful, that is probably because we are still only beginning to identify the nature and parameters of the problem. But critique is rooted in hope—in the dream that things can be better than they are. This was a dream that guided the early Anabaptists, and it suggests that "recovering the Anabaptist vision" may well involve turning a sober eye to the Anabaptist tradition itself.

Power, Authority,
and the Anabaptist Tradition

CHAPTER ONE

Power

J. LAWRENCE BURKHOLDER

In this opening chapter the author presents a philosophical overview of the problem of power as it relates to the Anabaptist/Mennonite tradition. He argues that Mennonites have avoided the issue of worldly power and that "a place must be made in Mennonite ethics for power." Various ways of thinking about and examining power and its relation to justice are suggested — ways that may be of use in coming to terms with a much-neglected aspect of Anabaptist/ Mennonite life.

Any consideration of power is bound to present problems of conceptual clarity. It is not as if power were scarcely to be found. Rather, the problem is that power is too much in abundance to be brought easily under analytical control. Power is everywhere, in everything, of everything, and, in a sense, the mother of everything. As a dimension of reality, power is inescapable. Some would say (Schopenhauer, for example) that the key to ultimate reality is *Wille*, a German philosophical conception for which we would ordinarily use the word *power*. Some existentialists would attribute to power the predominance of existence over essence.

Of course, it is easy to define power in the ordinary phenomenological sense as the "ability to act" or "the capacity of agents to produce outcomes" or, as Professor Paul Lehmann of Princeton Theological Seminary used to say, "Power is what makes things happen, happen." Differences between natural power and societal power may be accounted for by the important element of intentionality. Human power is the ability to bring about "desired results." In the social realm, power is synonymous with actuated freedom. To have power is to determine outcomes. In the areas of politics, religion, and social organization, the question of authority, or the right to use power, is associated with power.

Manifestations of power are hard to classify, especially since power takes many contrasting forms. Atomic bombs and rose petals are powers; a camel and the straw that breaks the camel's back, loud voices and whispers, sunshine and moonlight, the sword and the pen, day and night, matter and spirit, God and God's creatures—all are powers. We talk about physical power, political power, economic power, intellectual power, and the power of positive thinking. In *L'être et le Neant*, Sartre dwells upon the power of a look. In some circumstances there is nothing so powerful as weakness. A well-calculated tear may evoke sympathy and demand compliance.

Can one speak reasonably about power? Not for long without focus, without objectification, without differentiation. Power is always temporal and local. It is always attached to something, somewhere, sometime. For power is nothing of itself, so far as human experience is concerned. Power is known only as it is actuated. It is analogous to electricity, which is manifest only as it is conducted. But if electricity is conducted, it produces light, heat, sound, and many other forms of energy. Power impels and repels.

On a scale of domination in relation to assent, one could plot a differential from the brute force of battering rams, through unconditional oligarchic decrees, through democratically processed laws, through rational persuasion, to uncoerced winsome compliance, with many shades and nuances in between. Power may be used against the will of people whose "power of being" is thereby destroyed, or power can be used on behalf of people whose power of being is thereby enhanced. Power may be used as with a sledge hammer to squelch resistance or as with a flower to attract free responses. Recall: "If I be lifted up, I will draw all persons to myself" (John 12:32).

Greek philosophers were the first in the Western world to speculate about power. Philosophers such as Heraclitus, having observed that all things are in motion, defined *dunamis* as the power of becoming. Henceforth, there emerged a tradition of philosophical reflection within which change, succession, evolution, and relativity became determinative. The vitalism of Schelling, the voluntarism of Schopenhauer, the cultural relativism of Nietzsche with his promotion of the "will to power" (*Wille zur macht*), the historicism of Troeltsch, and the organic pulsation of various process theologians have this in common. They think of power ontologically as the ability to act.

But alongside vitalistic interpretations has been an ancient and honored interpretation of reality for which power has been understood as the power of being itself. To be or not to be is a question of power. Essentialists' interpretations of power, at least those beginning with Pythagoras and elaborated by Plato, contended that being precedes act and not the other way around. Hence, the power of being is the presupposition of becoming. The task that Paul Tillich, an essentialist, undertakes in *Love, Power and Justice* is to provide an ontological base upon which to relate these three components of the ethical situation. It may be said that whereas most Christian theologians treat love and justice explicitly and power implicitly, Tillich, the ontologist, upholds power as an inexorable component of Christian ethics, deserving equal if not prior treatment. When conceived essentially as "power of being," power is presented conceptually as prior to the act. In other words, *being* something precedes *doing* something.

The ontological inexorability of power is paralleled by the biblical teaching that God is the ultimate source of power. The Hebrew-Christian tradition presents Yahweh as the Creator and Sustainer of all things. But the Bible is more concerned about the question of authority than about the question of might (*Macht*). Power in the Old Testament has to do fundamentally with the right of Yahweh to rule over Israel and the nations. To be sure, stories about the Exodus, the conquest of Canaan, Elijah at Carmel, and David at Mt. Zion imply that "my God is stronger than your god." But in the later stages of Israel's history and ethical development, attention is increasingly given to questions about legitimacy as prophets inject moral qualifications into the power equation. Thereupon, God's power is justified not only because of superior might but also because Israel's God is just. With the prophets, power comes under moral scrutiny—a permanent contribution of the Old Testament to Western political and ethical consciousness.

At any rate, it can be asserted theologically that God is a God of power whose authority is grounded in moral character. The Hebrew God is strong—indeed, is a ruthless God of war at times—but Yahweh is not a celestial Machiavelli. The biblical story at its best is about God's moral right to rule—a right extended to the risen Lord: "All *exousia* [power] in heaven and earth has been given to me" (Matt. 28:18).

If power is ontologically inescapable and theologically explicit, it would seem strange that Mennonites have had to wait some 450 years to raise the subject for special consideration. But neglect of the subject can be explained. Those in the Anabaptist/Mennonite tradition have simply not been where power is discussed or where power in its most obvious manifestations has been exercised. For one thing, Mennonites have almost completely neglected—indeed, have held off with deep suspicion—the philosophical tradition in which power has been discussed as an ineluctable component of reality. Almost all classical philosophers have reflected upon power ontologically and politically. But Mennonites have paid little or no attention. For whereas Aquinas read Aristotle and Scripture, Calvin read Seneca and the Old Testament, and Jonathan Edwards read Plato and the Bible, Anabaptists read only the Bible. Just recently Mennonites have begun to take philosophy half seriously, primarily because of the promptings of psychology and sociology, both empirically based and historically oriented disciplines.

Furthermore, Anabaptist/Mennonites have refused to make much of the doctrine of creation, which, when delineated as natural law or evolution, construes power as an essential element of biological and social order. To be sure, some Mennonites have acknowledged, along with Catholics and mainstream Protestants, that the civil order is somehow grounded in creation. So-called orders of creation, such as the family, the economic order, the magistracy, and the just war, are set forth descriptively and prescriptively through the language of the law of nature with the help of Stoicism.

But Anabaptists have refused to apply natural law categories to their own communities, and consequently they have failed to reflect on power as an inexorable condition of finite existence. They have resisted nature as a source of knowledge of right and wrong for the obvious reason that natural reason moves on a level lower than the "perfection of Christ," and it tends to allow, if not to make normative, an ethic of identification with the "world." Furthermore, the very idea of law itself has been resisted by some because it is thought to impinge on human freedom, the indeterminacy of the Spirit of Christ, and the independence of the church. Mennonite theol-

4

ogy is a theology of eschatological transformation, making little or no theoretical provision for lower social structures rooted in nature or the obsequies of history. Even to make use of natural law descriptively is to accept the "flesh," or so it is claimed by some.

Furthermore, since they have had little to do with juristic law and almost nothing to do with politics, Anabaptist/Mennonites have neglected power. Of course, they have acknowledged the reality and the necessity of power politics, but not as responsible participants. Even today, although politics is discussed almost ad nauseam, the actual enactment of laws and the administration of public policies have been left largely to others. Anabaptist/Mennonite experience has been mainly communal, not political. To be sure, power is a dimension of community life as well as of politics, but its reality is hidden under the deceptive cover of tradition, religious and parental authority, simple rural living, and the subtleties of unconscious coercion (see Chapter 6).

Yet the fundamental reason that Anabaptist/Mennonites have not faced head on the problem of power is hermeneutical. Anabaptist theology has exalted the weakness of the cross and the "transvaluation of values" that are implicit in the teachings of Christ. It is the meek who shall inherit the earth, not the leaders of establishments. Insofar as Christians shall exercise power, it shall be the power of the Spirit, it is claimed. After all, "not many noble, not many wise are called. God has chosen to use the foolish things of the world to shame the wise; God chose the weak things to shame the strong. He chose lowly things of this world and the despised things, and even things that are not to nullify the things that are" (1 Cor. 1:26–28). According to the Apostle Paul, the crucified Christ is the power of God and the wisdom of God. Nietzsche and the Mennonites agree in this, that Christ reverses aristocratic values of wealth, wisdom, fame, and dominion. Or, as Reinhold Niebuhr once put it, "The Christian faith is centered in one who was born in a manger and who died upon the cross. This is really the source of the Christian transvaluation of values. Hence, the ultimate success of what the world calls failure and the failure of what the world calls success."

In the New Testament power and weakness are placed in a dialectical relationship. This dialectic is implied by the incarnation. According to orthodoxy, Christ, having poured out divine prerogatives of power, took the form of a human being and even died upon a cross. That God would die is

5

the ultimate paradox. Furthermore, the paradox is compounded by the anomaly that for having accepted the cross, he is exalted above all things in heaven or earth. Recall that the disciples of Christ and the Apostle Paul looked forward to a consummation when they would reign in glory with him.

Are we to conclude then that the concept of the powerlessness of the cross is a tour de force leading to the real purpose of Christianity, which is to rule with power over all cosmic enemies, implying that, when all is said and done, absolute power is the goal of history open only to the followers of Christ? If such is the Christian interpretation of history, it would seem that there is little to be made of earthly power here and now except to renounce it for the sake of heavenly power. Obviously, the biblical story is a strange mixture of humble weakness and imperial domination: suffer now and rule later. The New Testament message about power is summed up in the promise that "the meek shall inherit the earth" and in Mary's song, "He has brought down rulers from their thrones and has lifted up the humble." Thus, the weak shall become strong, the poor shall become rich, and the have-nots shall become the haves.

We therefore must not attribute Anabaptist/Mennonite reluctance to exercise power in this world's order simply to political naiveté or to the tendency of the persecuted to rationalize their sufferings by a theology of the cross. Renunciation of worldly power here and now is a logical implication of eschatological biblical Christianity reinforced by the prophetic tradition of which Jesus Christ is the ultimate exponent. But what about Anabaptist/Mennonite experience? Clearly, Mennonite experience and theology have not been joined. With the emergence of Mennonite institutions in particular, power issues have become inescapable. After all, institutions are concentrations of power. Institutions are power structures that make claims upon, and provide benefits to, their members. Institutions are also concentrations of power in relation to other institutions. Institutions are powers organized to realize specific communal purposes. Hence, since Mennonites have founded colleges, mutual aid societies, mental hospitals, church camps, mission boards, and relief agencies, issues concerning power can no longer be avoided.

What is intriguing and arresting about the development of Mennonite institutions is that there are no New Testament precedents for institutional life. Primitive Christianity was charismatic, not institutional. Jesus and the apostles promoted at best an eschatologically oriented communal ethic, emphasizing personal relations. So biblical Mennonites are given no direct instructions or examples when it comes to formulating a theology of institutional life.

The problem faced by members of the Anabaptist/Mennonite tradition today is that while their theology makes no positive provision for the use of worldly power, they are now deeply involved in power structures, both ecclesiastical and secular—even though few have gone so far as to accept direct administrative responsibility for the political realm. As individuals they are connected with large educational and industrial establishments, and Mennonite institutions are no longer administered face to face across the back fence. Whoever runs institutions uses power, and Mennonites run institutions.

Mennonites and others like them must realize that they are a part of the world system, that they share the guilt and responsibility for corporate evil, and that their attempts to be obedient to Christ and "be" the true church must take into consideration the ambiguities of their actual situation. This realistic approach will prevent perfectionist illusions and despair.

Specifically, a place must be made in Anabaptist/Mennonite ethics for power. Traditionally Mennonites have assumed that Christians can live without the exercise of power, that is, power in the form of compulsion and force. It may be agreed that, given the ideal combination of saintliness and simplicity, a small Christian society can live with a minimum of power. But certainly business organizations, educational institutions, and even highly organized mutual aid societies cannot operate by the pure principles of the "love feast." All institutions are to a certain degree political in character even though the service motive and personal piety can mitigate the political principle.

By contrast to Anabaptist/Mennonites' suspicions of power and their reluctance to seek leverage except in rudimentary situations, the Reformed tradition has taken a positive attitude toward power through institutional and political development. It is common knowledge that Calvin, having read Roman law and the Old Testament, made a case for economic investment and political power. Calvin wanted to make a place for movers who would get things done, especially for the sake of Geneva's poor. For Calvin, personal charity was essential to social well-being, but it was not enough. Hence, he advocated the positive use of collective power, moderated, of course, by asceticism and a keen awareness of the need of checks and balances. For Calvin there was no higher calling than the magistracy; in contrast, the Anabaptists claimed at Schleitheim[1] that the magistracy lay outside the perfection of Christ and must therefore be eschewed.

What benefits could come from a denominational study of power? For one, discussion of power might lead to rational consciousness of power as a category of social analysis. To ask who has power in a social situation and who has less or no power at all is one way by which a given situation may be understood. We must discover the flow of power, its direction, its authority, and its origins. Does power flow downward or upward or horizontally, or does it flow in all directions at once? Also, one may ask, what kind of power is being used and by what authority?

In every personal and collective situation, the principal parties are related to one another consciously or unconsciously in a rank of power. The substance of power may be varied. It may include money, sex, beauty, athletic ability, age, scholarship, office, saintliness, or any merit or demerit that may make some feel superior or inferior to others. A study of power would bring to awareness a fact of social existence that may disabuse the powerful of their arrogance and strengthen the spirit of the humble.

Another value of power consciousness is its warrant against the abuse of power. If we may assume that abuse is frequently the result of unconsciously exercised power, awareness may serve to warn its agents to use power thoughtfully and respectfully and to encourage the powerless to seek redress in an effective and constructive manner. How does one disempower the powerful and empower the weak? It is obvious that Mennonite history is full of power struggles and oppression. That segment of Mennonite history that will never be fully written includes the silent suffering of women who were put down, beginning scholars who were shut up, and young preachers who were put in their place by church leaders who thought that the kingdom would be hastened by keeping people under their dominating control.

Finally, a discussion of power may help Anabaptist/Mennonites to discover positive uses of power. If power is essential to getting things done, what are the ends to which personal and corporate energies should be dedicated? In other words, whither the Mennonite Church and others like it? Shall Mennonites aspire to join the movers? If so, how and where? Or must they be weak, marginal, self-deprecating, withdrawn *Stille im Lande* (the quiet in the land) in order to be good? A consciousness of power may also bring Anabaptist/Mennonites face to face with the ambiguity of power insofar as power in nature and society stands in glaring contrast to the ethics of the cross. If one cannot agree with the Greeks, as reflected by the philosopher Jacob Burkhardt, that worldly power is inherently evil and therefore necessarily ambiguous, the inevitability of sin within the historical process can be said to make it so. The problem of Zionism in the Old Testament was that power and goodness were seldom, indeed never, satisfactorily combined in the kings of Israel. Hence, Israel looked for a messiah who would be good and powerful at the same time. But when the Messiah came, he refused to reign. His kingdom was declared to be "not of this world." His kingship took the form of a relatively nonstructured, spiritual, prophetic ministry of social criticism and miraculous healing but had nothing directly to do with such essential functions of earthly kingship such as protecting the populace, punishing the wicked, collecting taxes, and adjudicating conflicting claims.

Hence, Christendom is left with the question of whether Christians should renounce "effectiveness" for the sake of goodness or seek power for the sake of effectiveness. Furthermore, if Mennonites will speak with credibility about social ethics, they must honestly face critical issues about the relation of love to various forms of compulsion. After all, no society can exist without the use of compulsion in one form or another—even lethal force.

The relationship of love to compulsion is complex because compulsion takes many forms and love is variously defined. But given traditional definitions of Christian love as *agape*, to which classical Christianity and Schleitheim Mennonites have been committed, the relationship of love to lethal force is certainly not an easy one. While ontologists such as Paul Tillich and classical theologians such as Augustine, Luther, and Calvin look for the unity of love and force somewhere in the character of a trinitarian Godhead as manifest in nature and grace, or the law and the gospel, or the Old Testament and the New Testament, Mennonites, having rejected dialectical resolutions of that sort, are left in unabridged discontinuity or confusion. For if the Christian ethic is consistently nonresistant or even nonviolent, how can a social ethic be constructed that takes the rough needs of order seriously? How to get love and might together is an acute problem for those who, like Mennonites, try to speak about social ethics from a pacifist perspective.

Another value of a study of power is to alert us to the dangers of corruption and to distinguish between legitimate satisfaction for work well done and the lust for power. If power is the "ultimate aphrodisiac," as Henry Kissinger once claimed, how can we who are in the flesh enjoy it, yet not too much? Can we enjoy it as if we did not, recalling the Apostle Paul's admonition to the Corinthians about marriage and economics? Furthermore, since power is essential to leadership, should we encourage one another to aspire for position? Is it possible for a tradition that emphasizes humility, resignation, *Gelassenheit* (yieldedness), the small over almost anything big, feet washing, and renunciation of the pleasures of the world, to uphold power as something good? If so, how and where? What is the place of ambition in the life of "humble" Christians?

By the same token, if indeed power has the tendency to corrupt, does the conscious abnegation of power lead to another evil, namely, irresponsibility? If personal and collective egoism leads to prideful excesses prophets rise up to deplore, is it possible that those who choose not to exercise power are guilty of serious omissions? And what about the honor and credibility of abstainers who nevertheless take it upon themselves to criticize those who carry the public burden? To be sure, Anabaptist/Mennonites can be congratulated for not having done many things considered bad, like having slaves or serving as magistrates, judges, soldiers, and union leaders. Indeed, Mennonites have prided themselves in being the salt of the earth. But can salt that is set more upon preserving its savor than upon flavoring the lump claim to be innocent?

Certainly a critical examination of power is bound to examine the criteria by which power may be judged. If, indeed, we reject a Machiavellian justification of power as a law unto itself, from what principles do we draw to determine the appropriate use of power? Obviously, such a question can be fully answered only by delineating an entire system of ethics. That task is clearly beyond the scope of this chapter. But I cannot resist a few rhetorical questions that would indicate somewhat indirectly how one may approach this question.

Does not the power question lead immediately into issues concerning justice? As Paul Tillich puts it, "Justice is . . . the form in which power of being actualizes itself in the encounter of power with power." If, indeed, power is considered in relation to other powers, is not justice the principle by which the intrinsic value of other powers is acknowledged? Or could not Kant's "categorical imperative" help us to treat others always as ends and not as means only? Surely, any discussion of power, while acknowledging *agape* as the ultimate motive and judge of action, must acknowledge that in this world of complexity and sin, love must take the form of justice in order for it not to destroy the world in the process of saving it.

Of course, it must be recognized that power has its own way of defining justice. Invariably, those who have power define justice from their own perspective, and so do the powerless. That the powerful have preempted the right to determine what is just is a fact of history. Kings, emperors, industrial tycoons, and bishops invariably distort fairness in their own favor. But so do revolutionaries when they purport to represent the masses. Recall Mao and the Chinese Communist revolution, or even certain Hutterite leaders who, in the name of communal love, exploited their positions. Within institutional structures, power is never distributed equally. Power is always centered in a person or a select group. Even the most egalitarian of communities, despite claims to comradeship in Communist societies and brotherhood in Christian communities, are run by a representative group, if not a power elite. So it is not enough for churches to be committed to love and justice while ignoring power. Tillich is right. The ethical equation must consist of love, power, and justice, all three dynamically and dialectically related to one another.

We shall have to consider the *modes* of power, from physical force to the pressures of tradition and parental direction. We must consider whether physical force is ever justified. If so, by what authority and for what purposes? Is coercion implicit in organized life? If so, how can it be used in a positive manner? How can power be used to empower, that is, to add to the power of another's being rather than to take it away? How can power be used to build up rather than put down? How can power be used to reinforce power in the other person?

Is there a structural design that could be said to characterize truly Christian institutions? If we were to acknowledge that all institutions must be organized vertically, what are the legitimate claims of egalitarianism within institutional structures? Is there an administrative style that is Christian? Is there an essential difference between how power flows at a Mennonite institution as compared to the flow of power at Blue Cross and Blue Shield, or at a Christian college as compared with a state university?

What assumptions about the place and propriety of power are implicit within the social system at large that need to be acknowledged and in some instances corrected? I refer to the excessive power of certain corporate structures, economic institutions, and male-dominated organizations in relation to human rights and environmental concerns.

What makes it right, if it is right, for some people to have power and authority over other people? In other words, how is hierarchy justified in principle? Why may it be right for parents to have authority over children, teachers to have authority over students, employers to have power over employees, and administrators to have power over practicing professionals such as doctors in hospitals, teachers in colleges, and novitiates in the churches? Can the principle of lordship, which pertains to deity, be extended into the human realm at any point? May it be said by any human being to another, "This power that I wield is justified by God himself, herself, itself?" If so, where is the point of conveyance between God and the powerful? Are chapters 16 and 18 of Matthew such points of a conveyance? Or is the power principle to be interpreted entirely in conventional terms as are most modern theories of law?

Do powerful people who try to serve their neighbors through the exercise of their power have accessible to them a special measure of forgiving grace that the powerless do not need? Should provision be made in the doctrine of justification by grace for people in decision-making positions who are caught up in moral conflict? And how shall we respond to Nietzsche's interpretation of Christianity, outlined in Chapter 2, as "resentment" against aristocratic power? Shall we concede that the Judeo-Christian tendency to subvert power only to gain power is at least of sufficient credibility to warn us against the dangers of hypocritical envy?

What are the implications of vocation for power? For if indeed power may be said to be not good or evil in itself but dependent upon its use, may the power question be decided in some such sense as marriage? Marriage is good but not for everyone. Some may be called to be eunuchs for the kingdom's sake and others to marry and perpetuate the species and culture. And if the uses of power are so diverse that the application of a universal principle by which to judge its use is difficult to determine, should not power be subordinated to vocational choice?

Such is the case with most ordinary, day-to-day uses of power. Problems arise, however, with certain applications of power, particularly with respect to political decisions related to military power and to lethal struggles.

Mennonites and other pacifist groups have discerned that callings to the military are contrary to the will of God. But Mennonites find illegitimacy difficult to apply as a universal Christian principle. While most Mennonites would not encourage their own members to run for the office of president or vice president of the United States, they would hesitate to suggest that Bill Clinton and Al Gore, both Bible-carrying Baptists, should become nonviolent Anabaptists. For if Mennonites were to claim that under no circumstances should Christians say or do anything in support of physical force, they would appear to undercut public order. At the same time, if they make a vocational case for certain Christians to be involved with the military, they have, in effect, undercut pacifism in principle. And so goes the dilemma of power in its most dramatic form.

Finally, the ramifications of power are inestimable. Discussion of power moves on many levels. Any profound discussion of power would take the shape of a theology of power. But a theology of power is not easy since it would be necessary to move beyond biblical conceptions if it were to speak to the modern mind. At issue would be the question of how to understand the connection between God as the noncontingent source of all power and the contingent power of nature and society. Were we to attempt to go beyond finite power, we would be limited to the metaphysics of analogy, which by definition is "speculative" rather than real. At any rate, a theology of power lies beyond these preparatory pages.

CHAPTER TWO

Power and Religion in the Western Intellectual Tradition

BENJAMIN W. REDEKOP

Because Anabaptists have tended to ignore the larger tradition of thinking about power, it seems useful to step back and survey the intellectual landscape, paying particular attention to some of the formative thinkers in the Western intellectual tradition. Besides surveying some of the major theories of power and its relationship to religion, this chapter provides a narrative of how thinking about power has changed over time and where the "Anabaptist Revolt" fits into the larger transformation.

If J. Lawrence Burkholder is correct in saying that Anabaptists "have al-most completely neglected—indeed, held off with deep suspicion—the philosophical tradition," and hence have missed out on important thinking about power, then it seems worthwhile to place the present discussion into a broader intellectual context. In this chapter I provide an analysis of classic and contemporary theories of power and the place occupied by religious and priestly power in those theories.

Besides providing a view of some of the main conceptual categories and problems as they have emerged over time, the following overview points to a broad historical pattern: a movement from notions of power as some-thing suffused in a larger, divinely ordered world system, to views of power as a more or less independent entity that can promise great benefits but needs to be structured by reason or experience or tradition, to contemporary understandings of power as a productive, ubiquitous, and inescapable feature of human knowledge and experience. Throughout, the relation between power and justice remains a central problem. In the course of this pattern of development, metaphysical and religious, priestly power becomes separated off into a category of its own, becoming one of the primary negative foils for the development of modern theories of power.

Viewed within the sweep of history, the "Anabaptist Revolt" and its aftermath were part of the emerging modern critique of abusive priestly and religious power as well as the increasing secularization of power. Mennonites may have more to do with Machiavelli than they think. Yet their treatment of secular power consisted mainly in banishing it to the margins of their own communities, or so they thought. There is an increasing recognition that this was an illusion and perhaps even a painful mistake. And with the decline of closed, separated communities, few can pretend anymore to live outside of immanent structures of power, authority, and domination.[1] Identifying power's presence within the gates requires taking stock of its manifestations in time and the thinking that has gone along with it.

Plato and Aristotle

For thinkers like Plato and Aristotle, power over other human beings was placed in a larger framework, that of the just society in which individual members were in harmony with themselves and with the natural order of things. In their social and political theories, both Plato and Aristotle raise the question of whether "might makes right" only to reject it, using it as a foil for their own notions of justice and the attainment of the good life and human happiness (*eudaimonia*). Thus, early in Plato's *Republic* the sophist Thrasymachus introduces what looks to be an unanswerable definition of justice: "What I say is that 'just' or 'right' means nothing but what is to the interest of the stronger party." Laws are made by the ruling party in its own interest.[2] *The Republic* can be read as an attempt to provide a satisfying rebuttal to this assertion that justice is simply an expression of power.

Instead of searching for the roots of justice in existing earthly arrangements, Plato appeals to an ideal notion of the "Good," which rational human beings may glimpse from the confusion of the material world, where sheer power can be confused with justice. Once philosophers gain a vision of the Good and hence of "the cause of whatever is right and good" (226), they are enabled to institute a just society in which the essential order and nature of things is made manifest. The just society is one in which raw power evaporates into an ideally structured polity. Knowledge of the Good obviates misbegotten struggles for power over appearances; to know the Good is to do it. Might dissolves into right.[3]

Aristotle retains the idea that power is not an end in itself but rather a means to the end of the attainment of human excellence (*arete*) and happiness (*eudaimonia*). In Book 7 of the *Politics*, he too raises the question of whether might makes right, dismissing the notion as irrational and a contradiction in terms: "To a reflecting mind it must appear very strange that the statesman should be always considering how he can dominate and tyrannize over others . . . How can that which is not even lawful be the business of the statesman or legislator?" Might is might, and right is right, and it is simply a logical mistake to confuse the two. The mighty are suited to command if they are born to it, that is, if they are fitted by nature to rule; but then they rule by right rather than coercion. "Hence we see very plainly that warlike pursuits, although generally to be deemed honourable, are not the supreme end of all things, but only means. And the good lawgiver should inquire how states and races of men and communities may participate in a good life, and in the happiness which is attainable by them."[4]

For Aristotle there is a natural order of things, each in its place striving to realize its final end (*telos*) of development. The highest end of action for human beings is to achieve the best life of which they are naturally capable. To become fully human is to live the good life and to be happy, not in a trivial sense, but in the sense of being complete and lacking nothing of value. In his ethical and political writings, Aristotle aims to determine the nature of this good life and happiness for human beings, and how to achieve it.[5]

The good life consists in the pursuit and arrangement of human goods into a coherent and properly balanced whole. Aristotle divides the goods available to human beings into three classes: external goods, goods of the body, and goods of the soul. Most people agree that the happy person has all three, but there is disagreement as to their proper proportions. Some feel that a moderate amount of excellence—goods of the soul—is enough, but set no limit to their desires for wealth, property, power, reputation, and the like. "To them we shall reply by an appeal to facts, which easily prove that mankind does not acquire or preserve the excellences by the help of external goods, and that happiness . . . is more often found with those who are most highly cultivated in their mind and in their character, and have only a moderate share of external goods, than among those who possess external goods to a useless extent but are deficient in higher qualities" (166–67). It is for the sake of the soul that external goods and goods of the body are desirable, not the other way around.

The exercise of political power is viewed within this framework: power is an external good that, exercised for its own sake, detracts from the attainment of excellence and hence the good life. It is due to those who are in a natural position to exercise it over those who naturally are fit to bear it, all in the name of serving the common good. The political community is the structure in which the good life can best be attained, and "it is evident that the form of government is best in which every man . . . can act best and live happily" (168). Power is neither to be wholly renounced nor to be embraced as a good in itself, "for there is nothing noble in having the use of a slave, in so far as he is a slave; or in issuing commands about necessary things" (170). But Aristotle goes on to assert that although power is not a good in itself, that does not mean that there is not a proper place for its exercise.

The legitimate exercise of power is dependent on natural merit. Merit is determined by excellence, which, as we have seen, is a good of the soul and draws upon external goods—including raw power—only as helps and not as ends in themselves. If one is excellent, power is exercised appropriately in monarchical rule; if a few are excellent, the best form of government is aristocratic; and if excellence is spread through the polity in a warlike multitude, a constitutional government is best. Dissension occurs when natural equals are put at odds with each other or when those who are equal seek superiority over each other (71, 90, 122).

Thus for both Plato and Aristotle, the just exercise of power occurs within the context of the proper relations between the formal qualities of natural beings. They are not theorists of power per se, but of justice and the "good life." The exercise of power is simply a means to an end, the realization of potential; and those who know what is good for them will avoid seeking it as a good in itself.[6] While there is no inherent contradiction between such a view and what became the normative Anabaptist/ Mennonite view on the exercise of power, theologies that built on the classical philosophical tradition became the basis for a system of intermingled secular and religious power that Anabaptists were to reject.

Augustine and Aquinas

Subsequent Christian thinkers tended to deploy classical ideas and perspectives in a Christian framework. St. Augustine of Hippo and St. Thomas Aquinas are only two of the more well-known Christian thinkers who drew upon the classical heritage in building a viable Christian theology. And as one might expect, the notion of power becomes even more suffused within the world system, viewed both as an emanation of the divine power and an unfortunate result of fallen human nature. Power exercised by human beings over each other is a means to the end of living out one's life in the earthly city but is never to be confused with the ultimate power of God. A will turned toward God has little need of constraint by earthly powers.

In *The City of God* Augustine notes of justice and power that "'the just lives by faith,' for we do not as yet see our good, and must therefore live by faith; neither have we in ourselves power to live rightly, but can do so only if He who has given us faith to believe in His help do help us when we believe and pray."[7] Yet a human being has a rational soul with which he might "regulate his actions ... that he may thus enjoy the well-ordered harmony of knowledge and action which constitutes ... the peace of the rational soul" (589). The exercise of the intellect, however, requires a master so as not to go off the rails into error.

Endowed with an intellect disciplined by faith, the Christian experiences earthly power as a divine emanation in which he at most participates as a cautious instrument. I say "he" here because Augustine, like Aristotle—and indeed most ancient writers—advanced a gendered conception of power at its most fundamental level, that of the "household." Augustine's ruminations on power exercised in this intimate sphere indicate both the gendered roots of power and Christian uneasiness with any exercise of power: "This is the origin of domestic peace, or the well-ordered concord of those in the family who rule and those who obey. For they who care for the rest rule—the husband the wife, the parents the children, the masters the servants; and they who are cared for obey—the women their husbands, the children their parents, the servants their masters. But in the family of the just man who lives by faith and is as yet a pilgrim journeying on to the celestial city, even those who rule serve those whom they seem to command; for they rule not from a love of power, but from a sense of the duty they owe to others—not because they are proud of authority, but because they love mercy."[8]

Augustine goes on to say that God did not intend for his rational creatures, who are made in his image, to have dominion over anything but the irrational creation: "not man over man, but man over the beasts." Dominion of men over men (and women)—what Augustine calls "slavery"—is the result of sin: without the violation of natural law "there would have been nothing to restrain by penal servitude." Therefore, "the apostle admonishes slaves to be subject to their masters heartily and with goodwill, so that, if they cannot be freed by their masters, they may themselves make their slavery in some sort free, by serving not in crafty fear, but in faithful love, until all unrighteousness pass away, and all principality and every human power be brought to nothing, and God be all in all" (590). If the exercise of earthly power over one's equals is the result of sin, then the rejection of sin, the turning of the will toward the good—God—and away from "things of the lowest order,"[9] puts one more nail in the coffin of fallen human power.

In *On Christian Doctrine* Augustine again equates the exercise of dominion over men with sin.[10] Yet the earthly and heavenly cities must coexist, which means that the heavenly city must be subjected to earthly powers as far as possible without renouncing its heavenly citizenship:

> The things necessary for this mortal life are used by both kinds of men and families alike, but each has its own peculiar and widely different aim in using them. The earthly city, which does not live by faith, seeks an earthly peace, and the end it proposes, in the well-ordered concord of civic obedience and rule, is the combination of men's wills to attain the things which are helpful to this life. The heavenly city . . . makes use of this peace only because it must, until this mortal condition which necessitates it shall pass away. Consequently, so long as it lives like a captive and a stranger in the earthly city, though it has already received the promise of redemption, and the gift of the Spirit as the earnest of it, it makes no scruple to obey the laws of the earthly city.[11]

Yet when it comes to religion, Augustine points to what was to become an enduring problem in social and political theory: "It has come to pass that the two cities could not have common laws of religion, and that the heav-

enly city has been compelled in this matter to dissent, and to become ob-
noxious to those who think differently."[12]

The medieval synthesis as exemplified in the work of St. Thomas Aquinas, while retaining strong Augustinian elements, further blurred the lines
between heavenly and earthly cities, and hence between divine and human power. In fact, in the *Summa Theologica* Aquinas blends Aristotle, Augustine, Scripture, and the church fathers so completely that it would be
difficult to read a coherent secular notion of power out of it. Aquinas treats
of both God's power and human power, but the latter is clearly subordinated and entwined in the former in the same way that human beings are
bound up in a great chain of being stretching from God to the lowest orders of creation. Responding to the question of "whether all things are
subject to the divine government," Aquinas writes, "God [is] the ruler of
things for the same reason as He is their cause, because the same being
gives existence as gives perfection, and this belongs to government. Now
God is the cause not indeed of some particular kind of being, but of the
whole universal being . . . Therefore, as there can be nothing which is not
created by God, so there can be nothing which is not subject to His government . . . Foolish therefore was the opinion of those who said that the
corruptible lower world, or individual things, or that even human affairs,
were not subject to the Divine government."[13]

Aquinas immediately goes on to address the question of "whether all
things are immediately governed by God," which he answers, "God governs all things immediately, but as to its execution, He governs some things
by means of others" (532). All things are part of a divinely ordained, providential natural order, which can be considered in two ways: "in general,
according as it proceeds from the governing cause of all; and in particular,
according as it proceeds from some particular cause which executes the
order of divine government" (534). Clearly, human government is in the
latter category. Human beings, as rational creatures, can partake of eternal
law both by way of knowledge, which can discern the divine order directly,
as well as by the particular cause, shared by irrational animals, of an "inward moving principle," a "natural inclination to that which is in harmony
with the eternal law," a kind of instinct for the good. Both ways of achieving
harmony with divine law are imperfect, however, "and to a certain extent
destroyed, in the wicked, because in them the natural inclination to virtue
is corrupted by vicious habits, and, moreover, the natural knowledge of

good is darkened by passions and habits of sin." The good, however, are bolstered by knowledge born of faith—wisdom—and the added interior motives of grace and virtue.[14]

Consequently, when it comes to the actual exercise of human rule by law, people may be subject to that law in two ways: as a matter of coercive force (for sinners), or as a matter of already being subject to a higher law, which obviates the need for coercion to the lower set of laws. "Thus the subject of a proconsul should be ruled by his command, but not in those matters in which the subject receives his orders from the emperor . . . In this way the virtuous and the just are not subject to the law, but only the wicked. Because coercion and violence are contrary to the will; but the will of the good is in harmony with the law, while the will of the wicked is discordant from it" (234). When it comes to actually talking about forms of government, Aquinas adopts a typical stance, following Aristotle in the light of Scripture (in this case the Old Testament): "For this is the best form of polity, being partly kingdom, since there is one at the head of all; partly aristocracy, in so far as a number of persons are set in authority; partly democracy, that is, government by the people, in so far as the rulers can be chosen from the people, and the people have the right to choose their rulers" (308). Power is more than ever suffused in a divinely structured, harmonious chain of being. While some clearly have less need of coercion by human law, all are subject to government to the degree that its end is goodness—Aristotle's "the good life" translated into Christian terms. Human government is an executive form of divine government, and in both together the eternal law prescribed by God is enacted in the lives of all things in heaven and earth, or so it seemed. In reality, things were much different, and by the early modern period such a system seemed problematic, not only to religious reformers like Luther, Zwingli, and especially the Anabaptists, but also to decidedly secular thinkers like Machiavelli, Bacon, and Hobbes.

Machiavelli, Bacon, and Hobbes

Niccolò Machiavelli, writing in the context of the intrigues and power struggles of Renaissance Italy, broke decisively with classical and Christian ways of thinking about princely power. Earlier princely advice books counseled princes to act morally for the good of their souls and taught that it is in fact rational to be moral. "Honesty is the best policy" became proverbial by the time of the Renaissance.[15] In *The Prince*, Machiavelli effectively de-coupled statecraft from traditional moralities, concentrating on how to acquire and maintain power as a good in itself. In so doing, he signaled a decisively "modern" turn toward conceiving of power as independent of the larger world system, a sublunary quality that operates according to its own rules and as such is worthy of study on its own. Power is of men, and hence in Machiavelli's work princes are advised to act as if they were gods.

"The chief foundations of all states, new as well as old or composite, are good laws and good arms; and as there cannot be good laws where the state is not well armed, it follows that where they are well armed they have good laws."[16] Good laws are not the result of understanding and placing oneself in a cosmic order, rather they result from sheer force of arms. But the ma-jor point Machiavelli wants to make in this regard is that to be well armed, one should not rely on mercenaries, a common practice in Renaissance Italy (111–12). Machiavelli is clear about what a prince who wants to re-main a prince, or become a greater one, must do: study, think, eat, and sleep the art of war and its rules of discipline (115–16). Larger moral ques-tions are not of much use: "A man who wishes to act entirely up to his professions of virtue soon meets with what destroys him among so much that is evil. Hence it is necessary for a prince wishing to hold his own to know how to do wrong, and to make use of it or not according to necessity" (121–22). Princes must *appear* to have good qualities, "but with a mind so framed that should you require not to be so, you may be able and know how to change to the opposite" (143). And such changes must occur in concert with the times, with the vagaries of Fortune, "arbiter of one half our actions," leaving us to direct the other half, "or a little less" (203). A fundamental point made by Machiavelli in *The Prince* is this necessity to be in step with the times, to read the winds of circumstance and respond accordingly. And men must do so actively, "because fortune is a woman, and if you wish to keep her under it is necessary to beat and ill-use her; and it is seen that she allows herself to be mastered by the adventurous rather than by those who go to work more coldly" (206–7). Invoking the Boethian figure of female Fortuna spinning her wheel, Machiavelli inserts a gendered image of power at the very heart of his political theory.

The virile prince must occasionally act contrary to received moralities, swiftly and decisively as circumstances dictate. "Severities" such as slaying leading citizens and senators in order to assume power, for example, are best applied once and for good, rather than continuing with time (72). Good is not to be prosecuted for its own sake, or evil for evil's, but both toward the end of maintaining and increasing one's (earthly) power. Divine power, however, is simply left out of the picture. Living at a time when popes were a military force to contend with, Machiavelli had plenty of reasons to suspect that divinity was but a particularly powerful support for earthly dominion: ecclesiastical principalities, he wrote, "are sustained by the ancient ordinances of religion, which are so all-powerful, and of such a character that the principalities may be held no matter how their princes behave and live . . . But being upheld by powers, to which the human mind cannot reach, I shall speak no more of them, because, being exalted and maintained by God, it would be the act of a presumptuous and rash man to discuss them" (92). This is Machiavelli at his most cheeky and ambiguous. But what is certain is that Machiavelli is concerned to disentangle, in his hugely influential little treatise, earthly power relations from the divinely rational world order in which they traditionally had been embedded.

Rejection of traditional authorities was an emerging theme in the early modern period. Francis Bacon became one of the enduring symbols of this rejection, and indeed his writings, like Machiavelli's, enact a fairly dramatic rupture with the past despite his own rather scholastic proclivities. Bacon did not invent modern science, but he advanced a vision of natural philosophy that did portend of things to come. And he did so in the name of increasing the power and dominion of human beings over the natural world. "Knowledge and human power are synonymous, since ignorance of the cause frustrates the effect; for nature is only subdued by submission."[17] For Bacon there is "almost an identity between the ways of human power and human knowledge" (137), yet reliance on traditional intellectual authorities, along with the corruptions and habits of the human mind, had resulted in a sterile and fruitless system of knowledge. "Only let mankind regain their rights over nature, assigned to them by the gift of God, and obtain that power, whose exercise will be governed by right reason and true religion" (135). Natural philosophy, in Bacon's view, should be seen as religion's "most faithful attendant," for while the Word of God exhibits God's will, inquiries into nature demonstrate his power (124).

There can be little doubt, however, that divine power was to become human power. Bacon divides human ambition into three parts: "First, that of men who are anxious to enlarge their own power in their country, which is a vulgar and degenerate kind; next, that of men who strive to enlarge the power and empire of their country over mankind, which is more dignified but not less covetous; but if one were to endeavor to renew and enlarge the power and empire of mankind in general over the universe, such ambition (if it may be so termed) is both more sound and more noble than the other two. Now the empire of man over things is founded on the arts and sciences alone, for nature is only to be commanded by obeying her" (107). While Machiavelli had been led to develop a theory of power devoted to princely power (an ambition that Bacon finds vulgar), Bacon asserts the sovereignty of human power over the whole universe. Machiavelli usually suffers under the opprobrium of having spoken candidly about the workings of power in politics, but such talk seems rather paltry in comparison to Bacon's cosmic ambitions.

Like Machiavelli, Bacon presented a gendered discourse of power. Female nature, like Fortuna, must be followed and obeyed as well as tormented in order to be commanded. Early in the *Novum Organum*, Bacon states that if any individual really wishes to go beyond received (and erroneous) understandings, "and not to overcome his adversaries in disputes, but nature by labor, not in short to give elegant and specious opinions, but to know to a certainty and a demonstration, let him, as a true son of science . . . join with us; that when he has left the antechambers of nature trodden by the multitude, an entrance may at last be discovered to her inner apartments" (106). However, it would appear that once Bacon's "man of mature age" has followed nature into her inner chambers, then "the secrets of nature betray themselves more readily when tormented by art than when left to their own course." That is to say that the "many excellent and useful matters [that] are yet treasured up in the bosom of nature" will be yielded up by our experimental "interrogations." Men who engage in subtle scholastic disputes "otherwise catch and grasp at nature, but never seize or detain her; and we may well apply to nature that which has been said of opportunity or fortune, that she wears a lock in front, but is bald behind."[18] The Machiavellian prince and the Baconian scientist are each given remarkably similar—and gendered—advice about how to gain real power over their "subjects."[19]

Thomas Hobbes, onetime secretary to Bacon, incorporated emerging perspectives of the new science into a coherent and exceedingly influential political theory, a theory of the state and sovereignty that put severe limitations on religious authority and asserted the ubiquity of power and the need to control it in human life. A number of streams fed into Hobbes's masterpiece, *Leviathan*. He wrote during a period of extreme instability and dissension in European life. The wars of religion and the English civil war threatened the very foundations of social and political order. Skepticism was growing among intellectuals disgusted and dismayed by a world increasingly torn by religious dogmatism and fruitless debate. At the same time, new philosophies of order were beginning to emerge, not least among them the natural law theory of Hugo Grotius, and the mathematical and mechanistic natural philosophies of Galileo and Descartes. Hobbes combined these and other elements into a comprehensive and profoundly materialistic social and political vision, a vision so challenging to received understandings that his name became a byword for atheism and licentiousness.

Following Galileo, Hobbes assumed that motion is the natural state of things, including human beings. Humans are never at rest, always striving after those things that secure their own continued well-being, power being at the top of the list. Power is what secures for us our future comfort and survival, so power is what most people strive for.[20] Power, in the sense of a mechanical force, is what drives the Hobbesian universe, and consequently the notion of power is ascribed an independent existence with a number of aspects: "The Power of *Man*, (to take it Universally,) is his present means, to obtain some future apparent Good." There is *"Naturall Power"*; *"Instrumental"* powers; the power of riches, reputation, good success, affability (of men already in power); the power of a reputation for prudence; the power of nobility, science, and "arts of publique use, as Fortification . . . and other Instruments of War"; and so on (150–51).

Human beings, when left to themselves in a state of nature, tend naturally to scramble for power and in the process come into conflict with each other. Hobbes made the cessation of conflict, or what he called "peace," into a foundational principle of his political philosophy: politics should secure peace and allow human beings to live with some measure of security. Natural law theorists were beginning to assert that self-preservation is a fundamental principle that can and should structure social and political relations. Such a view accorded well with the emerging foundationalism of the new science and allowed the exclusion of traditional (and troublesome) forms of power and authority, most notably that of religion. Rather than sanctioning government as a component of divine order, Hobbes argues from the perspective of isolated human beings who have certain basic desires and wants and who tend to lord it over each other when left to themselves. The problem is how to transform this situation into a peaceable one from the ground up, how to harness the chaotic powers of the natural world into a self-sustaining rather than a self-destroying system.

The type of political system that can accomplish this features an all-powerful sovereign or "Leviathan," whom Hobbes also calls a *"Mortall God"* (227). Divine power has truly come down to earth. Such a sovereign is a purely artificial person authorized by each citizen in a compact amongst themselves to represent "the Person of them all" (217ff., 228). Hobbes maintained that the actual type of government did not matter so much as that it was given unlimited power in order to keep peace. "And though of so unlimited a Power, men may fancy many evil consequences, yet the consequences of the want of it, which is perpetuall warre of every man against his neighbor, are much worse." Liberty, in this system, just as in the case of external bodies in motion, consists in "the absence of opposition" (260–61). "In cases where the Soveraign has prescribed no rule, there the Subject hath the liberty to do, or forbeare, according to his own discretion" (271).

An all-powerful sovereign is required to sanction rules of *"Meum* and *Tuum,"* of *"Good, Evill, Lawfull,* and *Unlawfull,"* otherwise "to every man remaineth, from the naturall and necessary appetite of his own conservation, the right of protecting himselfe by his private strength, which is the condition of Warre; and contrary to the end for which every Commonwealth is instituted" (234). While Hobbes derives notions of right from natural laws, there is a strong conventionalist flavor to his work: the proper use of language depends on settled definitions of words agreed upon by all, just as geometry proceeds by settled axioms. Similarly, a just society can operate only if the rules of mine and thine are universally agreed upon. Such a state of agreement was only possible in a commonwealth with the backing of the sword. Might, informed by natural law, makes right.

Hobbes felt that language, and particularly religious and metaphysical language, was too easily manipulated by men seeking dominion over others (609ff., 689ff.). He argued that the abuse of religion and religious language had led to many of the wars and disputes of his age, and that religion was a product of human beings' ignorance of natural causes and fear of the unknown and invisible (168ff.). But Hobbes did not simply dismiss religion; rather, he devoted a large part of *Leviathan* to critiquing and attempting to limit the role of religious and other sorts of metaphysical power in social and political life. Thus, he did not argue for a separation of church and state so much as a subordination of the church to the state; any other arrangement inevitably leads to divided loyalties and hence to civil war:

> *Temporall* and *Spirituall* Government, are but two words brought into the world, to make men see double, and mistake their *Lawfull Soveraign*. It is true, that the bodies of the faithfull, after the Resurrection, shall be not onely Spirituall, but Eternall: but in this life they are grosse, and corruptible. There is therefore no other Government in this life, neither of State, nor of Religion, but Temporall; nor teaching of any doctrine, lawfull to any Subject, which the Governour both of the State, and of the Religion, forbiddeth to be taught: And that Governor must be one; or else there must needs follow Faction, and Civil war in the Common-wealth, between the *Church* and the *State*; between *Spiritualists*, and *Temporalists*; between the *Sword of Justice*, and the *Shield of Faith*; and (which is more) in every Christian mans own brest, between the *Christian*, and the *Man*.

To avoid this situation, there must be "one chief Pastor" who, "according to the law of Nature . . . is the Civill Soveraign" (498–99).

Hobbes spills a great deal of ink in the later sections of *Leviathan*, arguing, in essence, that Augustine was wrong. The two cities cannot coexist on earth, rather they must be one, presided over by one supreme and chief pastor, the civil sovereign. Any other arrangement allows false prophets to arise who "seek reputation with the people, by phantasticall and false Doctrines; and by such reputation (as is the nature of Ambition,) to govern them for their private benefit" (609–10). The result is a commonwealth divided into factions and civil war. As part of Hobbes's limitation of this sort of abuse of language, he proposes that there are just two essential "Vertues" necessary to salvation: "*Faith in Christ,* and *Obedience to Laws*" (610). In the end, *Leviathan* is a very big book designed to produce, by stripping away the accretions of centuries, some very fundamental and thereby useful truths.

Although they are repugnant to religious sensibilities, the theories of Machiavelli, Bacon, and Hobbes laid the foundations of modern, secularized, and immanent theories of power. The worldly powers that Anabaptists had by now banished to the margins of their faith communities were coming to be theorized in their own right. Both developments were based, in a certain sense, on a growing recognition of independent, secular, and decisively *human* powers with their own logic and possibilities. Whereas Anabaptists responded by attempting to expunge earthly powers from their midst, others began seeking to structure and control the unruly powers of human beings and nature in what they believed to be a useful fashion.

Locke, Rousseau, and Burke

Subsequent contract theorists like John Locke and Jean-Jacques Rousseau followed the Hobbesian premise that power is something possessed by individuals in a state of nature that is then transferred to the political body, which is designed to structure human relations and the exercise of power in a fair and secure manner. The origin and justification of political institutions became a central intellectual problem during the period of the Enlightenment, and modern Western democracies still operate on principles developed during this period. While Hobbes was undoubtedly the "greatest of all contract theorists,"[21] Locke and Rousseau followed in his footsteps, each developing his own distinctive theory of government based on contractarian premises.

Locke, for his part, reasserted the traditional role of contractarian theories, stretching back to the eleventh century, as a justification of resistance to princely tyranny. Locke posits all human beings in an original state of equality and "perfect freedom to order their actions and dispose of their possessions and persons as they think fit, within the bounds of the law of nature." The law of nature, accessible by human reason, teaches that "no one ought to harm another in his life, health, liberty or possessions." In the state of nature everyone has the "power to execute that law, and thereby preserve the innocent and restrain offenders." Those who attempt to put another into their "absolute power" by harming them thereby put themselves into a state of war with them. "To avoid this state of war . . . is one great reason of men's putting themselves into society and quitting the state of nature. For where there is an authority, a power on earth, from which relief can be had by appeal, that the continuance of the state of war is excluded, and the controversy decided by that power."[22]

Whereas natural liberty is to be "free from any superior power on earth," "the liberty of man in society is to be under no other legislative power but that established by consent in the commonwealth." The freedom of men under government "is to have a standing rule to live by . . . made by the legislative power erected in it," as well as a "liberty to follow my own will in all things, where the rule prescribes not" (89–90). This notion of freedom, already present in Hobbes, was to become a foundation stone of modern democratic liberalism: state power is necessary only up to a point, beyond which individuals are free to follow their own inclinations. There may be a need to empower a common "umpire" (95) to decide breaches of natural law, but when acting in accordance with the law of nature as embodied in civil laws, individuals are free to do as they wish (102).

Thus, the legislative power dare not extend arbitrary rule over the lives and fortunes of the people. Since each member can only give up as much power to the state as each possesses in the state of nature, and since that power was devoted to self-preservation, the state power can never be more than the sum of individual powers and can extend no further than preserving life and limb. Obligation to the law of nature does not cease in society, "but only in many cases are [natural laws] drawn closer, and have by human laws known penalties annexed to them to enforce their observation." Thus "the people" retain a "supreme power to remove or alter the legislature, when they find the legislative act contrary to the trust reposed in them; for all power given with trust for the attaining an end being limited by that end, whenever that end is manifestly neglected or opposed, the trust must necessarily be forfeited, and the power devolve into the hands of those who gave it, who may place it anew where they shall think best for their safety and security" (103–4). And thus the power of government is returned to its original source, equal individuals concerned with their own self-preservation in a natural state.

The contractarian theory of Jean-Jacques Rousseau retained many elements found in Hobbes and Locke but with its own distinctive twist. Indeed, while sharing certain basic suppositions and perspectives that I have outlined, contract theorists differed on numerous points both of principle and in the ways in which the theory was elaborated and embodied in political institutions. Rousseau's famous *Social Contract* is in fact a subtle blend of natural jurisprudential and classical republican discourses, so if he cites Hobbes and Grotius, he also has in view the examples of ancient republics in which the practice of civic virtue and public spirit were fundamental components of social and political life. That is to say that if he affirmed the nascent liberal principles of natural law theory, he also envisioned a polity that was more than a necessary way of structuring chaotic natural powers but also a locus of positive freedom, an expression of will that emanated from and returned to individual citizens within the quasi-mystical union of the sovereign.

The problem of the social contract, according to Rousseau, "is to find a form of association which will defend and protect with the whole common force the person and goods of each associate, and in which each, while uniting himself with all, may still obey himself alone, and remain as free as before."[23] The essence of the social compact, then, reduces itself to the following terms: "Each of us puts his person and all his power in common under the supreme direction of the general will, and, in our corporate capacity, we receive each member as an indivisible part of the whole" (191). Rousseau is concerned to advance a notion of sovereignty and government in which each individual will is transformed into an indivisible part of the general will, so that in obeying laws laid down by the sovereign, individuals are really only obeying themselves. Public interest and private interest are to be the same. While this notion had always been a part of contract theory, Rousseau raises it to a central problem to be addressed by his theory. Whereas the Hobbesian Leviathan was like a balloon that, once blown up by the individual members, was left free to float on its own, Rousseau's sovereign is and remains a creature of its citizens, and much of his treatise is devoted to exploring how an interacting part-whole relationship is to be structured and maintained.

Yet like Hobbes, although from a slightly different angle, Rousseau sets a firm limit to religious power, transforming Christian observances into civil religion. Although Rousseau's sovereign differs in important respects from Hobbes's Leviathan, Rousseau too fears the divisive consequences religion can have upon political sovereignty. In his view, "Hobbes alone has seen the evil and how to remedy it, and has dared to propose the reunion of the two heads of the eagle, and the restoration throughout of political unity, without which no State or government will ever be rightly constituted. But he must have seen that the masterful spirit of Christianity was incompatible with his system, and that the priestly interest would always be stronger than that of the State" (298). Thus, if, on the one hand, priestly interest threatens the power of the state, on the other hand, "Christianity as a religion is entirely spiritual, occupied solely with heavenly things; the country of the Christian is not of this world. He does his duty, indeed, but does it with profound indifference to the good or ill success of his cares . . . If the State is prosperous, he hardly dares to share in the public happiness, for fear he may grow proud of his country's glory; if the State is languishing, he blesses the hand of God that is hard upon His people" (301). Christianity, in other words, is not a religion that inspires civic feeling or public spirit, detracting from the intense part-whole relationship that Rousseau is keen to delineate. How can individual citizens feel their wills to be ineluctably bound up (and hence free) in the workings of the state, if their ultimate loyalties are elsewhere?

Rousseau's solution is similar to that of Hobbes. Outward forms of religious expression must be harnessed by the state in a civil religion; in fact, religion must be turned to the service of the state as it was among the ancients. So while otherworldly beliefs that have no bearing on public life are not subject to control by the sovereign, those beliefs and practices that bear on the life of the community are subject to its mandate.

> There is therefore a purely civil profession of faith of which the Sovereign should fix the articles, not exactly as religious dogmas, but as social sentiments without which a man cannot be a good citizen or a faithful subject. While it can compel no one to believe them, it can banish from the State whoever does not believe them . . . The dogmas of civil religion ought to be few, simple, and exactly worded, without explanation or commentary. The existence of a mighty, intelligent, and beneficent Divinity, possessed of foresight and providence, the life to come, the happiness of the just, the punishment of the wicked, the sanctity of the social contract and the laws; these are its positive dogmas. Its negative dogmas I confine to one, intolerance, which is a part of the cults we have rejected. (303–4)

Civil and theological tolerance are inseparable, and hence theological intolerance will have a divisive civil effect: "The Sovereign is no longer Sovereign even in the temporal sphere: thenceforth priests are the real masters, and kings only their ministers" (304).

Thus, throughout the classical period of contract theory, the limitation of religious power remained a central concern. If the chaotic powers of nature needed to be harnessed, structured, or restrained in a sovereign power or by scientific mastery, the competing force of religious belief and priestly power had also to be constrained, when not eliminated entirely. It seems less than surprising that while such views were gaining currency, Anabaptist/Mennonites continued either to separate themselves from, or accommodate themselves to, prevailing sociopolitical systems. For if religious toleration was on the rise, it occurred within the context of religion's banishment from the sphere of politics.

During the course of the eighteenth century, the notion that a state could not only find sanction outside of orthodox religion but that it also might subordinate such troublesome powers to the commonwealth itself in a civil religion was clearly gaining wider currency. And by 1789 such notions sprang forth in full political blossom with the revolution in France. The Bastille was stormed in July 1789, and on August 4 of that year the newly formed National Constituent Assembly abolished feudal privileges. In 1790 the French Catholic Church was reorganized in what was called the Civil Constitution of the Clergy, whereby the clergy was put under state control. The pope remained a spiritual leader, but clergymen were to be appointed by, and answer to, the state. Religious orders were abolished. The property of the clergy had already been confiscated in 1789 and became the basis for the new fiscal system of the Constituent Assembly, serving to underwrite the issuing of *assignats*, which became the currency of the new regime. The Catholic Church in France became in effect a national church, the Catholic faith a civil religion.

Edmund Burke was famously incensed by these events and more importantly by the positive reception they were being given by certain radical Britons. The result was a masterpiece of conservative polemic, *Reflections on the Revolution in France*. In this book, Burke employed his vast rhetorical skills in attacking the legitimacy of the French Revolution and indeed many of the presuppositions and methods of early modern social and political theory. A fundamental, threatening image underlying the treatise is that of power stripped of all its supports and constraints, not least among them religion. Rather than seeing religious belief as a divisive force, Burke argued that without it, as without other forms of deference and traditional usage, the atavistic powers of human nature would simply run amuck and devastate the subtle civilizing work of time and custom.

The unbounded power of the National Assembly was an important locus of Burke's discontent: "That assembly, since the destruction of the [feudal] orders, has no fundamental law, no strict convention, no respected usage to restrain it. Instead of finding themselves obliged to conform to a fixed constitution, they have a power to make a constitution which shall conform to their designs. Nothing in heaven or upon earth can serve as a control on them . . . In such a state of unbounded power, for undefined and undefinable purposes, the evil of a moral and almost physical inaptitude of the man to the function, must be the greatest we can conceive to happen in the management of human affairs."[24] The securing of natural rights whose "abstract perfection is their practical defect" is not the end of government and only makes men think they have a right to everything. Government is rather to provide for human wants and restrain human passions. "Society requires not only that the passions of individuals should be subjected, but that even in the mass and body . . . the inclinations of men should frequently be thwarted, their will controlled, and their passions brought into subjection. This can only be done *by a power out of themselves;* and not, in the exercise of its function, subject to that will and to those passions which it is its office to bridle and subdue. In this sense the restraints on men, as well as their liberties, are to be reckoned among their rights" (65).

The "due distribution of [governmental] powers" is "a matter of the most delicate and complicated skill," not to be taught a priori by professors of metaphysics. "The nature of man is intricate; the subjects of society are of the greatest possible complexity: and therefore no simple disposition or direction of power can be suitable either to man's nature, or to the quality of his affairs" (66–67). Burke called for a return to a notion of society as a providentially ordered chain of being, using (and subverting) the modern language of contracts:

> Society is indeed a contract . . . but the state ought not to be considered nothing better than a partnership agreement in a trade of pepper and coffee, calico or tobacco, or some other such low concern, to be . . . dissolved by the fancy of the parties. It is to be looked upon with other reverence . . . it is a partnership in all science; a partnership in all art; a partnership in every virtue, and in all perfection . . . it becomes a partnership not only between those who are living, but between those who are living, those who are dead, and those to be born. Each contract of each particular state is but a clause in the great primeval contract of eternal society, linking the lower with the

higher natures, connecting the visible and invisible world, according to a fixed compact sanctioned by the inviolable oath which holds all physical and moral natures, each in their appointed place. (105–6)

Burke's extended defense of traditional organized religion—a national religion, to be sure—is therefore unsurprising. Religion is both an ideological power outside of human control that serves to order earthly affairs and relationships, and a profound institutional support of the social order from within, clearly in tune with the aims of (British) government. The "sense of mankind" purveyed by the Christian church "hath built up the august fabric of states," helping to "preserve the structure from profanation and ruin," consecrating the commonwealth and its officials. Men of government are made to undertake their position as that of a holy office, and free citizens are put into a necessary awe of government by this consecration "because, in order to secure their freedom, they must enjoy some determinate portion of power." Religion tempers the power of those in government and those whom they serve. "All persons possessing any portion of power ought to be strongly and awfully impressed with the idea that they act in trust; and that they are to account for their conduct in that trust to the one great Master, Author and Founder of society" (100–102).

The maintenance of religion in a democracy is doubly necessary because, in Burke's view, "a perfect democracy is the most shameless thing in the world." The actions of the mass of people go unchecked in a way that government by a few, whose individual honor is at stake, cannot. It is only when "the people have emptied themselves of all the lust of selfish will, which without religion it is utterly impossible they ever should," that they will be careful into whose hands they place power, "which to be legitimate must be according to that eternal, immutable law, in which will and reason are the same" (102–3). With the demise of traditional bases of social structure and restraint, power "will survive the shock in which manners and opinions perish; and it will find other and worse means for its support ... plots and assassinations will be anticipated by preventive murder and preventive confiscation, and that long roll of grim and bloody maxims, which form the political code of all power not standing on its own honour, and the honour of those who obey it. Kings will be tyrants from policy, when subjects are rebels from principle" (85). The prescience and eloquence of statements like these has assured Burke, despite his reactionary excesses, an enduring place in social and political theory. Clearly, Burke's trenchant attack on the events and principles of the French Revolution was underwritten by a critique of the emerging modern constitution of power, signaling the emergence of a self-conscious appeal to a worldview long since in decline.

There was no going back, however, and a problem for subsequent theorists became how to reconstitute human power and dignity as somehow transcendent, when the mass of people no longer accept such power and dignity to be based upon their own subjection. Once a world of entrenched—and accepted—rank and hierarchy has been lost, how can human dignity be restored? And without the support of traditional religion, how can power be employed in the service of life rather than the chaos of the multitude—of individual powers wantonly employed—which can only result in spiritual if not physical death?

By the early nineteenth century many of the main lines of modern political theorizing had been drawn and were being put into practice in modern constitutional states. Despite Burke's fears, atavistic human powers were at least provisionally tamed by emerging bureaucracies, armies, and a host of other public institutions that grew up with capitalism and modern nation-states. Subsequent theories of power that have had valence for late moderns have focused on the liberation of human beings—and the self—from social and political constraints that were imposed in the name of liberty and humanity but have proven to be troublesome in new and myriad ways. Critique of the effects of modernity on human life has consequently become the norm among late modern theorists of power, as the project of liberation has been coupled with a reassertion of human dignity.

Nietzsche and Foucault

There are many figures one could cite in this movement, but Friedrich Nietzsche, a thinker who has had an enormous impact on twentieth-century thinking on power, is undoubtedly the most important. Nietzsche emphatically rejected first principles drawn from transcendent external sources, seeking to carve out a new picture of "man" from immanent naturalistic principles, from the will, desire, human energies and powers, and the experience of the self. Nietzsche, as much as anyone, heralded the end of traditional metaphysics. He was a destroyer of what he felt to be a now-decadent Western intellectual and moral tradition and a builder of something new—not a system, but an outlook, a sensibility, an attitude of striving toward an ideal of human existence drawn from within the very resources of human beings living in the world.[25]

Like others before him, Nietzsche's notion of power was based in part on a rejection of Christian priestly power. Nietzsche defined his own significance in terms of his opposition to Christianity. His attack on Christianity included not only the Christian religion and the Protestant church of his day but also the whole Western philosophical and religious tradition of positing a transcendent order that exists in nature and the universe, that can be accessed by our rational faculties or our intuitive faith, and that gives meaning to our existence here on earth. Nietzsche sought to find meaning without having to appeal to a higher power or external order of things.

The "will to power" (*Wille zur Macht*) became one of Nietzsche's central and most important concepts in this quest. It became the key to understanding human motivation and activity, both healthy and unhealthy. "What is good?—All that heightens the feeling of power, the will to power, power itself in man. What is bad?—All that proceeds from weakness. What is happiness?—The feeling that power *increases*—that a resistance is overcome."[26] Nietzsche came to see the will to power as the driving, vital force of human life and of nature, which can be expressed in two basic ways. The healthy/active will to power is affirmative of the self; it is invigorated with life, creative, ascendant, willful, and overflowing. The diseased/reactive will to power denies the self; it displays a weariness with life and resentment toward the attainments of others.

The will to power is an acknowledged explanatory principle emerging out of human experience and history; it crosses the boundaries between reason and feeling, expressing the strivings of both. It is the basic drive of all human efforts: political and cultural achievements, religion, art, and philosophy are thus to be explained in terms of the will to power. Power is no longer a means but an end. As Walter Kaufmann put it, "To Bacon, knowledge meant power over nature, and truth could thus be utilized as a means to new comforts. For Hobbes, too, power was essentially a tool, an instrument, a means for security. Nietzsche, on the other hand, values power not as a means but as a state of being that man desires for its own sake as his own ultimate end."[27]

Nietzsche thus framed the problem of human identity and culture in terms of the ways in which the will to power was expressed. He sought to point toward what he considered to be healthy, life-affirming expressions of the will to power; too often the will to power has been turned against life, against natural, human forces and drives as a way of realizing itself. The "ascetic" was an important figure in this regard—someone who achieves power over the self by complete *denial* of the natural self; all passions are to be extirpated as a way of overcoming our animal nature. The ascetic priest is a *"life-inimical* species . . . here rules a *ressentiment* without equal, that of an insatiable instinct and power-will that wants to become master not over something in life but over life itself, over its most profound, powerful, and basic conditions."[28]

Nietzsche advocated a form of self-overcoming that he felt to be more affirmative toward the natural self. We have this need to overcome, to raise ourselves up higher, but the way to do it is not by self-denial. It is rather by a kind of sublimation of the lower drives and instincts into a higher form: this was the healthy way in which to express the will to power. Thus he did not advocate simply satisfying one's drives and desires one after the other in their lowest forms; rather, they need to be brought to a higher form of expression. Great art and other such forms of self-expression were the result of a creative grappling with human drives and their sublimation into higher forms. Christian asceticism, on the other hand, was for Nietzsche less a form of sublimation than of denial.

Nietzsche's theory of the will to power and its expression presaged important currents in twentieth-century psychological thinking: there are forces within us, of which we are not fully conscious, that require expression but that can become perverted by being turned against us. This, Nietzsche felt, was a fundamental fault of Christianity and other forms of metaphysical thinking: they were based on the assumption that the only way to rise above ourselves was by denying ourselves in all our physicality. "The church combats the passions with excision in every sense of the word: its practice, its 'cure' is *castration*. It never asks, 'How can one spiritualize, beautify, deify a desire?'—it has at all times laid the emphasis of its discipline on extirpation (of sensuality, of pride, of lust for power, of avarice, of revengefulness). But to attack the passions at their roots means to attack life at its roots: the practice of the church is *hostile to life*."[29]

In the *Genealogy of Morals*, Nietzsche distinguished between "master" and "slave" moralities, arguing that the latter had become dominant in the modern world: a herd-animal morality, suited to the mediocre but stultifying and detrimental to the development of the full range of human potencies. The figure of the ascetic priest emerges as the historical leader of this herd movement. "We must count the ascetic priest as the predestined saviour, shepherd, and advocate of the sick herd: only thus can we understand his tremendous historical mission. *Dominion over the suffering* is his kingdom, that is where his instinct directs him, here he possesses his distinctive art, his mastery, his kind of happiness."[30] Such a person becomes defender of the "herd" against the strong, the superior, the "healthy." The priest also defends his herd against its own baseness and resentment, altering its direction: "For every sufferer instinctively seeks a cause for his suffering; more exactly, an agent; still more specifically, a *guilty* agent who is susceptible to suffering—in short, some living thing upon which he can, on some pretext or other, rent his affects." The shepherd tells his sheep that they are to blame for their suffering—as a result of sin—and in this way their resentment is directed back onto themselves, "to *exploit* the bad instincts of all sufferers for the purpose of self-discipline, self-surveillance, and self-overcoming" (127–28). Guilt, rather than sublimation, is produced as a method of self-overcoming for the weak and sickly.

The will to power is somewhat more positively served by injunctions to love one's neighbor—an indirect way to achieve superiority over others. "By prescribing 'love of the neighbor,' the ascetic priest prescribes fundamentally an excitement of the strongest, most life-affirming drive, even if in the most cautious doses—namely, of the *will to power*. The happiness of 'slight superiority,' involved in all doing good, being useful, helping, and rewarding, is the most effective means of consolation for the physiologically inhibited, and widely employed by them when they are well advised: otherwise they hurt one another, obedient, of course, to the same basic instinct." Mutual aid is interpreted in much the same light, as a cautious expression of the will to power (135–36). The question that might be asked at this point is Does this view have any valence at all for Christians, particularly those like Anabaptist/Mennonites who have tended to stress mutual aid and love of neighbor? Would partial acceptance of Nietzsche's viewpoint necessarily be a scandal, or might it not aid in understanding some of the sources and dynamics of such behavior?

Nietzsche does not advocate trampling on others as a healthy way of exercising the will to power; rather, he consistently values, in his writings, behaviors like self-discipline, honesty, courage, generosity, intellectual integrity, and so forth. But the root of such behaviors must not come from guilt and resentment; rather, they must be an overflowing of the creative and life-affirming powers of the strong individual. If someone gets hurt, it is more by accident than by design, a byproduct of their superiority; if an elephant hurts me by stepping on my foot, it does not do so on purpose.

This is a ruggedly individualistic and masculinist ideal. Indeed, much of Nietzsche's writings are marred by a misogyny that has tended to be ignored or explained away by his interpreters. But even if one ignores such statements (or finds them merely pathetic and laughable, the outbursts of a profoundly unsuccessful lover), they are underwritten by a decidedly ancient view of women as existing under the dominion of men, as property. For example, marriage, in Nietzsche's view, is not established on the basis of love, but rather "one establishes it on the basis of the sexual drive, the drive to own property (wife and child considered as property), the *drive to dominate* which continually organizes the smallest type of domain, the family, which *needs* children and heirs so as to retain, in a physiological sense as well, an achieved measure of power, influence, wealth."[31] While it may be a mistake to read such diagnostic statements as prescriptive, when they are coupled with his obvious distaste for feminine qualities, they nevertheless point to a fundamentally gendered notion of power.

Broadly speaking, for Nietzsche the Judeo-Christian religious and philosophical tradition had resulted in a world ruled by herd mentality and *ressentiment*, a perverted will to power that stifles human dignity and the freedom to fully realize the potencies of the self. The original metaphysical impetus for this world was in decline, and its destroyer, modern science, did not offer values that could again ennoble the human spirit. For subsequent theorists working in the Nietzschean tradition, the nemesis of Christianity is replaced by humanistic social, political, and scientific structures of control and domination, but the basic suspicion of insidious forms of self-surveillance and social control, underwritten by a universalist metaphysics, remains in place. Nietzsche himself attacked those "moderns" who have refined the Christian ascetic ideal into a "faith in truth," an "unconditional will to truth"—that is, the ideal of modern science.[32] And for Nietzsche Christianity had also underwritten the leveling force of modern democracies: "The poison of the doctrine of '*equal* rights for all'—this has been more thoroughly sowed by Christianity than by anything else . . .

Christianity has waged a war to the death against every feeling of reverence and distance between man and man, against, that is, the *precondition* of every elevation, every increase in culture."[33]

Thus, encased in Nietzsche's harsh judgment of Christianity was a more general critique of modernity, a critique that has been expanded and applied in various ways during the twentieth century. All roads do not necessarily lead back to Nietzsche, but he as much as anyone must be credited with articulating a perspective that has proved to be highly resilient and fruitful for subsequent social and political theorists, literary critics, and philosophers. And this perspective is at root suspicious of universalist and essentialist doctrines of which Christianity has been the most important exponent in the West. Clearly, Christianity has been a central negative foil for modern theories of power, and in many places the ongoing abuse of Christian priestly power, for example, remains an enduring image of power to be rejected. Many Christians, including utopian groups like the Anabaptist/Mennonites, have failed to recognize and confront this fact (and the grounds for it), and it is only the growing marginalization of Christianity during the past century or so that has muted the ongoing critique.

Late modern critiques of power doubt the contractarian scenario that each individual has a measure of power that added together produces government. Power produced in various social and institutional structures may in fact operate against individual liberty in a process of disempowerment. The bureaucratic capitalist state is not the collection of individual powers but a locus of power that can itself dominate its members.

Michel Foucault took this perspective a few steps further. For Foucault, there is an important relationship between power and knowledge: each is productive of the other, and together they have operated in a variety of modern disciplinary and normalizing contexts—in schools, prisons, hospitals, asylums, armies, and a range of therapeutic practices. Foucault argued that the modern world, with all of its "humanizing" innovations in areas like medicine, social welfare, criminology, and psychiatry, has become a world of constraint and social discipline; that relations of power have migrated right into the human soul, have in fact produced the soul in its modern form, and have come to exercise control over the body in ways unheard of in previous eras. The rise of the human sciences and their application to the body politic has produced an inherently disciplinary society ruled by a "physics" of power that has penetrated to the very pores of its human subjects.

In *Discipline and Punish: The Birth of the Prison*, Foucault laid out his basic narrative of modern power: "Beneath the increasing leniency of punishment . . . one may map a displacement of its point of application; and through this displacement, a whole field of recent objects, a whole new system of truth and a mass of roles hitherto unknown in the exercise of criminal justice. A corpus of knowledge, techniques, 'scientific' discourses is formed and becomes entangled with the practice of the power to punish."[34] The human sciences began overlapping with penal law, producing a "political technology of the body" (24), a modern sort of tyranny based on the application of "scientific" forms of knowledge to the abnormal and the criminal, and the direction of the anatomizing "gaze" of the master/scientist onto the bodies of his "subjects." Penal leniency became a "technique of power" as the individual soul—and its reformation—became an object of penal intervention. "Man" becomes a distinct object of scientific knowledge in the modern period, and power is produced in the increasing scrutiny and analysis of his parts: "What the apparatuses and institutions operate is, in a sense, a micro-physics of power" (26). Instead of visiting miscreants with catastrophic punishments once and for all, in the modern world they are housed in various institutional settings—most importantly prisons—in which they are subjected to a disciplinary surveillance that keeps its subjects suspended in a network of power relations, investing them with disciplinary power and producing forms of self-surveillance and psychic as well as physical control.

The general movement is "from a schema of exceptional discipline to one of generalized surveillance," which "rests on a historical transformation: the gradual extension of the mechanisms of discipline throughout the seventeenth and eighteenth centuries, their spread throughout the whole social body, the formation of what might be called the disciplinary society" (209). The human sciences took their rise from this modern movement of "discipline and normalization."[35] By "discipline" Foucault means "a type of power, a modality for its exercise, comprising a whole set of instruments, techniques, procedures, levels of application, targets; it is a 'physics' or an 'anatomy' of power, a technology." And such a physics of power "may be taken over either by 'specialized' institutions (the penitentiaries or 'houses of correction' of the nineteenth century), or by institutions that use it as an essential instrument for a particular end (schools, hospitals), or by pre-existing authorities that find in it a means of reinforcing or reorganizing their internal mechanisms of power . . . [such as the family] . . . or by appa-ratuses that have made discipline their principle of internal functioning (the disciplinarization of the administrative apparatus from the Napoleonic period), or finally by state apparatuses whose major, if not exclusive, func-tion is to assure that discipline reigns over society as a whole (the police)."[36]

While Foucault's work ranged over the fields of criminality, medicine, psychiatry, and sexuality, it was underpinned by the notion that an intimate relationship between power and knowledge exists in the modern world. Far more intimate and insidious than previously suspected, it is clearly tied to the rise of modern science (including the human sciences) and technol-ogy, the spread of bureaucracies, the growth of capitalism, and the need to control unruly yet expanding populations. Foucault was less concerned with traditional analyses of "the regulated and legitimate forms of power in their central locations"—that is, of governments, sovereignty, and obe-dience—than with "power at its extremities, in its ultimate destinations, with those points where it becomes capillary"—that is, where power "be-comes embodied in techniques, and equips itself with instruments."[37] The French word *savoir* conveys the close relationship between knowledge and ability or power that Foucault was concerned to delineate in his works. To know is to be able, and vice versa, in a never-ending circulation of power and knowledge between and through human subjects. "The exercise of power perpetually creates knowledge and, conversely, knowledge con-stantly induces effects of power" (52). Power "is never localised here or there, never in anybody's hands, never appropriated as a commodity or piece of wealth. Power is employed and exercised through a net-like organ-isation. And not only do individuals circulate between the threads; they are always in the position of simultaneously undergoing and exercising this power . . . In other words, individuals are the vehicles of power, not its points of application" (98).

Here one can see quite clearly the all-pervasive Nietzschean will to power permeating and structuring the world in an endless play of forces. Foucault openly acknowledged the Nietzschean character of his work (53), and he effectively extended the Nietzschean analysis of power, initially fo-cused on a critique of Christianity and Western metaphysics, into an all-embracing critique of modernity, its "experts" and its social institutions. The growth of scientific knowledge and the spread of information assumes a sinister hue in Foucault's thought. These are not benign forces; rather, knowledge and what both Nietzsche and Foucault called the "will to truth" are insidious agents of domination and subjection that are both constitutive of power and constituted by it. The linear Baconian notion of knowledge as power via control over nature is made circular and expansive: power radiates from all points, passing through fine channels and constituting new ones, egged on by its carriers who "act as the vehicle for transmitting a wider power." Power is all, antedating even individual identity: "It is my hypothesis that the individual is not a pre-given entity which is seized on by the exercise of power. The individual, with his identity and characteristics, is the product of a relation of power exercised over bodies, multiplicities, movements, desires, forces" (72–74).

There is a dark sort of reenchantment of the world going on here, and indeed Foucault has sometimes been cast by his critics as a kind of medieval sorcerer. Nevertheless, his general viewpoint and insights have been tremendously influential in a number of disciplines, becoming appropriated very often for liberatory uses and helping keep the issue of the use and abuse of power at the top of the intellectual agenda. While traditional Anabaptist/Mennonite views on Christian love, nonresistance, and the regenerated self may seem naive in light of the theories of Nietzsche and Foucault, and while Christians of whatever stripe may for their part want nothing to do with such counterintuitive and deeply disturbing notions, they do provide an account of power that helps to confront the reality of power and domination in Christian contexts. Once we acknowledge the ubiquity of power and the myriad ways in which it can operate, it becomes more difficult to pretend we can somehow live beyond its reach in communities of pure love, and hence it also becomes more difficult to overlook and allow abuses of power within the faith community.

Postmodernism and Feminism

While postmodernism and feminism are highly heterogeneous movements, they share a critical stance toward inherited systems of power and domination and the various technologies, languages, and knowledges that have upheld those systems. Strategies vary, however, in how to address asymmetries of power; and while the work of seminal poststructuralist thinkers working in the Nietzschean tradition, like Foucault and Jacques Derrida, stand behind many aspects of contemporary postmodernism and feminism, there has also been resistance to what are perceived to be *disempowering* aspects of poststructuralism.

Hans Bertens identifies two varieties of postmodernism: a textual and linguistic movement that attacked foundationalist representation, whose leading exponents are Jacques Derrida and Roland Barthes, and a movement led by Foucault and Jacques Lacan that focused on power and the constitution of human subjects. Although the latter movement

> does not necessarily follow Foucault in his extreme epistemological skepticism, which virtually equates knowledge with power and thus reduces it to the effect of a social relation or structure, it fully accepts that knowledge, and language *tout court*, have become inseparable from power. This postmodernism interrogates the power that is inherent in the discourses that surround us—and that is continually reproduced by them—and interrogates the institutions which support those discourses and are, in turn, supported by them. It attempts to expose the politics that are at work in representations and to undo institutionalized hierarchies, and it works against the hegemony of any single discursive system—which would inevitably victimize other discourses—in its advocacy of difference, pluriformity, and multiplicity. Especially important are its interest in those who from the point of view of the liberal humanist subject (white, male, heterosexual, and rational) constitute the "other"—the collective of those excluded from the privileges accorded by that subject to itself (women, people of color, non-heterosexuals, children)—and its interest in the role of representations in the constitution of "otherness."[38]

Bertens concludes that it is this kind of postmodernism that has "enabled the close links with feminism and multiculturalism that is now generally equated with postmodernism" (8). While this is not the whole of postmodernism by any means (and indeed the term has become inflated to mean just about anything), postmodernism as it is generally understood is underwritten by a larger common denominator, "that of a crisis in representation: a deeply felt loss of faith in our ability to represent the real, in the widest sense" (11).

While postmodernist theory is in fact fairly heterogeneous and does not focus exclusively on power, feminist thinkers have concentrated on a thoroughgoing critique of power—male power—which has been informed to some degree by the kind of postmodernist perspectives outlined above. And whatever its intellectual provenance, feminism has undoubtedly been the single most salient arena for reflections on power in the West during the last few decades. While there is evidence that the movement has given rise to its own forms of power and domination, by and large it has addressed a real problem present in almost all human societies. As we have seen, some of the more important theorists of power in the Western tradition advanced gendered theories of power that reflected—and reinforced—asymmetrical power relationships between the sexes. Thus, feminist critiques of power are often aimed not only at empowering women within the present social and political arrangements but also, in their more radical forms, at asserting the need to fundamentally rethink the whole Western social and intellectual tradition from the ground up. Chapter 8 in the present collection argues for just such a wholesale rethinking of Christian ecclesiology. While some find this debate troubling, it is also possible to see it as a moment of intense creative possibility.

The historian Gerda Lerner has been a pioneer in exploring the historical roots of patriarchy and patriarchal power. Toward the end of the first volume of *The Creation of Patriarchy*, she states in summary:

> We have seen how men appropriated and then transformed the major symbols of female power: the power of the Mother-Goddess and the fertility-goddesses. We have seen how men constructed theologies based on the counterfactual metaphor of male procreativity and redefined female existence in a narrow and sexually dependent way. We have seen, finally, how the very metaphors for gender have expressed the male as norm and the female as deviant; the male as whole and powerful, the female as unfinished, mutilated, and lacking in autonomy. On the basis of such symbolic constructs, embedded in Greek philosophy, Judeo-Christian theologies, and the legal tradition on which western civilization was built, men have explained the world in their own terms and defined the important questions so as to make themselves the center of discourse.[39]

As it has throughout the modern period, Christianity comes under fire for abuse of power, this time over women as a group. In fact, the notion that religion in general is a fundamental source of female subjection has become a truism of feminism, leading many to ask the question posed as the topic of a divinity forum at the University of Cambridge: "Is Religion

Good for Women?" The conference brochure states: "The critics say that religions are human-centred (or even man-centred) ideologies of dominance, with no concern for the rest of plant and animal life, in which male dominance over female is the 'God-given' norm. Yet against this analysis must count the fact that most of the world's peoples are religious, many of whom are women. Surely these women are not all ideological dupes?"[40] Herein lies one of the most important challenges to religious consciousness and practice today.

Feminist analysis of Anabaptist groups has begun to take place within this larger feminist critique of religion. In a recent study of dress among Holdeman Mennonite women, Linda Boynton Arthur concludes: "The constraints on Mennonite women seem overwhelming . . . Clothing is a major source of conflict between men and women. It is the site of struggle—a struggle between the patriarchal social system and collective agency of the women's age set-groups . . . Dress is a metaphor; it is interpreted as a visual symbol for the suppression of the self to the demands of the community. In this conflict, the physical body becomes a symbol for the social body . . . While men exercise both private and public power over the female body, women help keep each other in line and overlook some deviations from normative behaviour."[41] Like an increasing number of contemporary feminist theorists, Arthur seeks to strike a balance between viewing women as victims of imposed power structures and recognizing their agency and resistance to those structural forms of domination.

One might thus identify two basic positions for feminist critique of male power, which need not be mutually exclusive. On the one hand are broad-scale analyses of historical and systemic forms of oppression in which male domination is emphasized and female resistance and agency receives less emphasis. Lerner's work on patriarchy and Nancy Hartsock's quest for a "feminist historical materialism"[42] might be used as examples of this approach. Such analyses tend to assume that there is a category "women," which stays more or less the same throughout history, and that those belonging to it have been systematically dominated by men. On the other hand, there is a growing body of work that incorporates postmodernist perspectives and tends to focus more on the workings of power at its extremities and the resistance that women make to hegemonic male power. This approach asserts that there are no essential categories of "men" and "women"; rather, gender is a construct that has taken on different forms and is hence malleable. Whereas the former approach tends to point to a radical restructuring of society from top to bottom, the latter approach, while certainly productive of radical critique, is also amenable to smaller scale, incremental adjustments. Fisher and Davis put the matter this way: "As long as women's subordination is viewed as the result of systemic forms of repression, that is, capitalism and patriarchy, the only solution is a massive collective movement and a total overhaul of those systems. If this political project seems overwhelming, the more modest course of political action suggested by the postmodern focus on knowledge and power—on how power is discursively constructed and how politics are about contestations over meaning—seems appealing."[43]

Yet some find this latter course too modest and ineffective. Nancy Hartsock argues that "domination is not part of . . . [the postmodernist] image; rather, the image of a network in which we all participate carries implications of equality and agency rather than the systematic domination of the many by the few."[44] In this view, postmodern/anti-Enlightenment theories of power hinder rather than help feminism, obscuring the macrostructures of domination and over-emphasizing female agency and access to power. But there is a growing sense that unless female agency is acknowledged, the active/passive dichotomy between men and women will simply be replicated. To portray women as being passive victims of forces utterly beyond their control does not empower them. Secondly, acknowledging women's agency and power effectively answers those critics of feminism who have questioned whether it is even historically accurate to say that half the human population has ever been entirely excluded from all important operations of power.

The problem, then, becomes one of balancing systemic analysis and critique with a recognition of women's agency and the shifting sands of power and meaning in human interaction. But this is a difficult problem, and there has been a tendency, as Fisher and Davis point out, to focus either on structure or on agency, each to the exclusion of the other.[45] Consequently, new and more all-encompassing syntheses have begun to appear, like Ben Agger's attempt to formulate a "feminist postmodern critical theory," a blend of Marxism, feminism, Frankfurt school critical theory, and postmodernism. Essentially, Agger seeks to use the insights of postmodern feminism to transform older theories of alienation and domination: "Whereas Marx theorized the alienation of labor and the Frankfurt theorists theorized domination, I theorize *productivism* — a logic involving but going beyond alienation and domination that produces the fateful hierarchies of men over women, capital over labour, white over coloured, straight over gay."[46] Using insights drawn from contemporary feminism, Agger argues that the valuation of production over reproduction (child-rearing, household work, etc.) is "the underlying source of economic exploitation, domination, and male supremacy" (5). For Agger, "Reproduction is secret production that production requires for its dominance of reproduction . . . This is a liberating insight because it shows that 'merely' reproductive activities are productive in their own right and should be valorized, claiming their share of social and economic power" (95). Here activities traditionally assigned to women are seen as important sources of social and economic power that have been turned into instruments of their own oppression. Women have always held power, but it has been employed in a classic master/slave dialectic: the master requires the service and recognition—and hence power—of the slave to guarantee his dominance. Once this relationship is recognized and disassembled, new and more egalitarian power relations become possible.

Conclusion

This overview of theories of power throughout the course of Western history reveals an identifiable trend in the way power has been understood to operate and how it has been employed. Speaking very broadly, ancient, classical theories like those of Plato and Aristotle infuse power into a larger world system as a function of a reality that structures human experience and understanding. Once the underlying order of things is recognized, the exercise of power takes its place as a means to a higher end: achievement of *eudaimonia* (happiness, or the good life). Augustine and Aquinas employed classical conceptions in a Christian framework, and despite the differences between them, the notion of power becomes even more suffused within the world system, viewed both as an emanation of the divine power and an unfortunate result of fallen human nature. One of the salient revolutions of the early modern period is a conscious break with this understanding of power. Machiavelli, Bacon, and Hobbes each play a part in the secularization of power, abstracting it from the great chain of being and reformulating it as an entirely natural, human quality that can and should be manipulated and structured so as to serve human needs. Modern political theory becomes in many ways a discussion (often an argument) about how best to structure human power in government so that its individual constituents—property-holding males—are able to achieve self-determination without dominating others. By the late nineteenth century and into the twentieth, theorists like Nietzsche and Foucault detach power from a transcendent, rational human subject that constitutes and controls it, arguing instead that power is a productive force ineluctably bound up with knowledge, the modern bureaucratic/scientific establishment, that can at best be sublimated or resisted rather than obliquely controlled and directed. The feminist critique of male power takes a place in this "postmodern" development.

There is indeed a great deal of continuity between early modern, modern, and late modern theories of power. Critique of the abuse of religious, priestly power has been a defining feature of modern theories of power, and the Protestant Reformation (with its radical Anabaptist wing) was undoubtedly the first crucial battle in a long struggle to separate and contain this elemental force in human experience. Priestly power—or perhaps "pastorly power"—is a very real force that has been present throughout history and is not likely to disappear in the near future.

Anabaptist/Mennonites have not been immune from the depredations of abusive religious power, as some of the chapters in this collection demonstrate, despite the fact that the movement itself coalesced around a strict rejection of corrupt priestly/worldly power and an attempt to live purely by an ethic of love and mutual submission. By ignoring and hence demoralizing power, sectarian groups like the Mennonites have allowed it to creep back into life in a number of guises and without restraint. Thus, if the tradition continues to hold great promise as a radical critique of religion compromised by worldly attachments and powers, the only way it can truly live up to its potential is by confronting and in a sense re-moralizing the exercise of power by its members.

CHAPTER THREE

The Anabaptist Revolt and Political and Religious Power

JAMES STAYER

In this chapter the author provides a historical analysis of the emergence of the Anabaptist movement in the context of the Reformation and Peasants' War, outlining just where the various Anabaptist groups stood on the question of political and religious power. The story is by no means a uniform and simple one, as groups and individuals differed over the proper role of the "sword" in political and religious life. Yet there were commonalities, and by the later 1530s, in the aftermath of the Münster debacle, a common, if increasingly quietistic, stance had begun to emerge.

Anabaptism was a product of the German Reformation in its earliest, most spontaneous and popular phase. The German Reformation was, above all, a radical lay revolt against the priestly, sacramental character of the old Latin Christian church headed by the pope in Rome.[1] Martin Luther, whose break with Rome was the opening gun of the Reformation, provided slogans for this revolt—all Christian believers were priests; the Bible was the only authority for Christians; faith alone, not the practices prescribed by the church, opened the way to heaven. But the popular appeal of the Reformation lay in its destruction of an old order that had lost its authority. Only later was a new order constructed and its theological justification in-

50

culcated among the laity, beginning with catechisms for children. Anabaptism was a phenomenon of the period between the breakdown of the old church and the rise of the new churches.

There is always something mysterious about the collapse of a long-accepted order of authority and privilege. We are still very close in time to the collapse of the authority structure of the former Soviet bloc. We have a vast amount of detailed knowledge about that event, but very few of us think that we understand it. We understand the revulsion against the old church, its priests, and its practices even more imperfectly. It is not clear that Rome's control of appointment to high offices in the church worsened the quality of ecclesiastical office holders. Theology and biblical studies were not in a state of degeneration; on the contrary, they seem to have been flourishing. If many parish priests kept concubines, there is no evidence that their congregations (or their superiors) seriously disapproved. Celibacy, like holiness, appears to have been regarded as an admirable goal, beyond the reach of most sinful human beings. Pilgrimages, masses for the dead, all the externalities of popular religion seem to have been on the increase just before the Reformation.[2] Although there was much corruption, venality, and worldliness in the Latin church on the eve of the Reformation, it is by no means clear that it was a declining institution or that these factors can be regarded as "causes" of the Reformation.

The Reformation and Peasants' War

The epoch-making German Reformation began with the scholars. In a sense, Erasmus's new Latin translation of the New Testament (1516), very influential for the vernacular translations of the Reformation era, began the Reformation. But since this work was dedicated to the pope, Leo X, it was clearly not intended as an attack on the structure of the Roman church. Erasmus hoped for a reformation in the older, medieval sense, one that would be validated and consolidated by papal endorsement. When the Roman court stumbled into condemning Luther in 1520, many of the younger generation of German-speaking theologians and biblical scholars turned against it. Certainly there were elements here of German cultural rebellion against the Latinate clerical caste that had dominated northern Europe throughout the Middle Ages. From the jaundiced standpoint of Erasmus, the reform of the church was botched when it passed from the hands of careful humanist biblical scholars to quarrelsome dogmatic theologians. It was ruined, he continued, when the theologians lost control of it and it became the affair of the uneducated masses.[3] Now the revolt of German against Latin merged with a revolt of the commoners against the clergy and aristocracy. Such a revolt was climaxed in wide areas of South Germany by the German Peasants' War of 1525–26. This so-called war united the unprivileged in towns and rural districts, and it was the high-water mark of the Reformation as a spontaneous popular movement.[4]

It was not coincidental that the beginning of Anabaptism in Zurich in January 1525 occurred at about the same time as the outbreak of the Peasants' War and that Anabaptism and the Peasants' War touched most of the same regions of Switzerland and South Germany. Both the Peasants' War and Anabaptism were affected by the flood of around five thousand pamphlets that were so influential in creating a Reformation public opinion in the 1520s. Demands of the pamphlets that congregations be empowered to choose and dismiss their pastors and that clerical tithes be wrested from the control of monasteries and cathedral chapters and put back into the power of the donors not only appeared as articles 1 and 2 of the "Twelve Articles of the German Peasantry," but they were also basic ideas of the group centering on Conrad Grebel that initiated Zurich Anabaptism.[5]

Despite the bad reputation that Martin Luther gave "the murdering, robbing hordes of peasants," the movement began, not as a war or revolution, but as an economic boycott of landlords, especially monastic landlords, who treated their peasants in what was perceived as an exploitative manner, contrary to the law of the Bible, newly recovered by the Reformation. Christoph Schappeler, coauthor of the "Twelve Articles," wrote in the preamble that "the gospel does not cause rebellions and uproars, because it tells of Christ, the promised Messiah, whose words and life teach nothing but love, peace, patience and unity." Since this peaceful gospel was "the basis of all the articles of the peasants," the rebellion was really caused by boycotted "antichrists," who denied the justice of the gospel to their subjects.[6] The violent end of the Peasants' War, however, convinced Schappeler that his cause was unjust: he and his fellows had "embraced the gospel and doctrine of salvation impatiently and clumsily," interpreting it in terms of their own needs.[7] The voices of the last stages of the Peasants' War were less peaceful. "To the Assembly of Common Peasantry" tried to straddle Schappeler's disinclination to aggression with a call for the commoners to lock their horns together in a just resistance, just as the Swiss had earlier done against predatory Austrian aristocrats.[8] And Thomas Müntzer convinced himself that this was the apocalyptic moment: "Forward, forward, strike while the fire is hot! Don't let your sword become cold or blunt! Smite, cling, clang on Nimrod's anvil; cast their towers to the ground!"[9]

The Anabaptist Movement

A similar variety of voices marked the early Anabaptist movement, which, after all, spread in northeastern Switzerland in 1525 because of the breakdown of authority resulting from the Peasants' War, and then appealed to Peasants' War veterans in Franconia, Thuringia, and the south Tyrol.[10] On the eve of the Peasants' War in September 1524, Conrad Grebel wrote to Müntzer, admiring his theology but at the same time rejecting his calls to advance the gospel "with the fist." The famous words that have been seen as the first statement of Mennonite nonresistance read: "True Christian believers are sheep among wolves, sheep for the slaughter; they must be baptized in anguish and affliction, tribulation, persecution, suffering and death; they must be tried with fire, and must reach the land of eternal rest, not by killing their bodily, but by mortifying their spiritual, enemies. Neither do they use worldly sword or war, since all killing has ceased with them."[11] However, as in the Peasants' War, sometimes peaceful words stood in contradiction to militant actions. Balthasar Hubmaier, pastor of Waldshut, in Austrian territory just across the Rhine from Switzerland, agreed with Grebel on the baptism of adult believers and wrote some very effective treatises opposing Zwingli on that subject. But to defend his Anabaptist congregation, Hubmaier allied himself with the Black Forest band in the Peasants' War. Moreover, Heini Aberli, one of the cosigners of Grebel's pacifist letter to Müntzer, was probably involved in recruiting Zurich citizens to help defend Waldshut.[12]

In initiating believers' baptism, the Grebel group caused a schism in the Zurich Reformation. They defied not only Zwingli but also the government that had, with the Reformation, made itself the guardian and custodian of the Zurich church. Anabaptism began in defiance of ecclesiastical and civil authority. Although the government of Zurich was in reality an oligarchic republic ruled by a few hundred urban males over a population of about 55,000, in its own eyes it was a government empowered by the whole community, ruling for the "common good," and moreover one that had put itself at considerable risk for "the rebirth of the gospel." Therefore, it was capable of draconic intolerance against individuals who resisted its power. In 1526 it introduced the death penalty by drowning for rebaptism.[13]

The Zurich Anabaptists, for their part, thought of themselves as restorers of the New Testament church described in the first chapters of the Acts of the Apostles. They were a further extension of the laicist impulse of the Reformation movement. Although the traditional Anabaptist/Mennonite view that Zwingli betrayed his principles in establishing a church backed by the Zurich government is wrong in assuming that that was not his intention from the beginning, in more subtle ways the Grebel group had a just complaint that Zwingli first led them on and then abandoned them. At first he encouraged laymen to interpret the Bible for themselves on the basis of the vernacular translation. Later, he insisted on interpretations based on the original Greek and Hebrew texts and informed by the authority of Greek and Latin church fathers. Persons who could read only German should defer to those who knew the three languages of humanist biblical scholarship.[14] At first, like Erasmus, Zwingli emphasized the authority of the New Testament. Later he stressed that the Old Testament was the holy scripture of Jesus and the apostles, and that God's covenant with Abraham was the same as his covenant with the Pentecostal church.[15]

So for Zwingli, Zurich became God's Israel, with all the militant connotations of that ideal. The first Anabaptists saw themselves as New Testament Christians choosing to obey God rather than man. Their preference for the New Testament was no doubt partly because during the height of their controversy with the Zurich church the New Testament was available in a Swiss German translation, while the work on the Old Testament was only completed in 1531.[16] Felix Mantz, the first Anabaptist leader in Zurich to suffer martyrdom as a religious dissenter, was also the first to spell out clearly the meaning of the New Testament ideal taken from Acts. He taught the newly baptized adults to practice "love, unity, and community of all things, like the apostles in Acts 2." His was also the first clear statement that "no Christian should be a government official, nor judge with the sword, nor kill or punish anyone."[17]

The Peasants' War, however, provided the opportunity for Anabaptism to spread from Zurich. In the midst of social upheaval the apostolic ideal was sometimes difficult to practice. In Grüningen, when peasant rebellion and Anabaptism blended into each other, the Anabaptist Uli Seiler shot pigeons in the church tower while the Zwinglian minister was trying to preach.[18] In the village of Hallau, where nearly everyone was an Anabaptist, the villagers defended the Anabaptist preacher, Wilhelm Reublin, recently exiled from Zurich, against constables seeking to arrest him.[19] Further afield, one of Thomas Müntzer's closest followers, Hans Hut, after escaping the slaughters that concluded the Peasants' War, was excited to hear of the new people of the covenant practicing believers' baptism in the New Testament manner. He too was baptized in Augsburg on the day of Pentecost, 1526. He became the first highly successful Anabaptist missionary, spreading the new baptism from his Franconian homeland through the Austrian lands to Moravia. Hut, however, continued to read the Bible in the apocalyptic, prophetic manner of Thomas Müntzer. Together with adult baptism, he brought a message of the tribulations of the last days, of a Turkish invasion. He told his converts, some of them Peasants' War veterans, to return their swords to their scabbards for the time being. The Lord would come again in 1528, and then the covenanted elect could join in the punishment of their wicked persecutors.[20]

The early Anabaptists' manner of winning converts among the semiliterate and illiterate was to use concordances of biblical texts that supported their fundamental beliefs.[21] One very important concordance devoted to faith and baptism, probably originating with Conrad Grebel himself, was seized from an Anabaptist leader in the St. Gall region.[22] The concordance carried by Hans Hut at the time of his arrest focused on apocalyptic judgment.[23] There seems to have been no comparable inculcation of ideas of peace and nonresistance by means of a concordance. This lack was partially remedied by the wide dissemination among Swiss Anabaptists of the Seven Articles of Schleitheim, following February 1527.

Schleitheim was a village in the rural territories of Schaffhausen, where early Anabaptism and peasant rebellion were closely connected. In form the Seven Articles remind one of similar collections of articles from the commoners' movement of 1525, but in content they put a great distance between Anabaptism and the Peasants' War.[24] The group behind the Schleitheim Articles was led by the former monk Michael Sattler, but it almost certainly included Wilhelm Reublin, who in the same region had been protected from arrest by armed peasants.

The dominant theme of the Schleitheim Articles[25] is struck by article 4 on separation from the world. The mood is one of eschatological urgency, confirmed in Sattler's other writings, "to go out from Babylon and from the earthly Egypt, that we may not be partakers in their torment and suffering, which the Lord will bring upon them." Specifically, this meant boycotting all ceremonies and practices of the churches, whether the pope's church or those of the new popes of the Reformation. Likewise, true Christians should shun "the diabolical weapons of violence—such as swords, armor, and the like, and all their use to protect friends or against enemies," with reference to Matthew 5:39. The longest article, number 6, elaborates that the sword is "an ordering of God outside the perfection of Christ," established by the Old Testament law to punish the wicked and protect the good but superseded by the nonviolent ban in the New Testament order. That Christ left the severity of the law behind is demonstrated by his unwillingness to command the stoning of the woman taken in adultery (John 8:11). His removal from worldly disputes is illustrated by his unwillingness to adjudicate two brothers' quarrel over their inheritance (Luke 12:13). That Christians should not be rulers, even if chosen, could likewise be inferred from the example and command of Christ. He fled when people wanted to make him king (John 6:15), and he told his followers not to lord it over each other like the princes of this world (Matt. 20:25). Like the churches, rulers belonged to this world: "The rule of the government is according to the flesh, that of Christians according to the spirit."[26] The last of the Seven Articles reinforced the separation of Anabaptists from life in the world through the prohibition of oath-swearing, an essential glue in early modern civic affairs. The powers of church and government were to be avoided: "We have no fellowship with them and do not run with them in the confusion of their abominations."

The Schleitheim Articles' attempt at a total boycott of the authorities of the world was an expression of end-time expectancy. At the same time, it was the voice of the persecuted, totally rejecting their persecutors. Michael Sattler's martyr testimony lent special credibility to the Articles only three months later. Its mood comes out in questioning about Sattler's views on fighting the Turks. Some Anabaptists, after all, seem to have been hoping for the Turks to come, since this would mark the beginning of the tribulations of the last days. Sattler opposed resisting the Turks because of the command: Thou shalt not kill. But, he added, he would rather fight his persecutors than the Turks, if war were allowed. The Turk was an ignorant heathen, but the persecutors who claimed to be Christians were "Turks according to the spirit."

There is documentary evidence of the execution of 679 Anabaptists in Switzerland and the South German regions from 1527 through 1533. This accounts for 80 percent of the authenticated Anabaptist martyrs in the Swiss–South German area from 1525 to the Thirty Years' War.[27] One is inclined to ask, Why the initial wave of persecution? And what accounts for its rapid abatement? After all, the notoriety of Münster Anabaptism, which showed that under some circumstances Anabaptism could be dangerous to civil authority, would lead one to expect that the mid to late 1530s would be the time of most cruel persecution of Anabaptists. Outside of the Münster region and the neighboring Netherlands, this was not the case. The large majority of Anabaptist martyrs suffered, like Michael Sattler, under Catholic rulers, in the Habsburg lands and Bavaria, as part of a systematic and brutal attempt to stamp out heresy of all kinds. Yet Protestant rulers, like Catholics, joined in issuing the Imperial Mandate of Speyer (1529), which prescribed the death penalty for Anabaptism.[28]

After the fright of the Peasants' War, which helped to convince them that unsupervised religion could make their lands ungovernable, Protestant rulers applied themselves to organizing evangelical territorial churches. Since the Anabaptists refused to fit into these territorial churches, they seemed to threaten to continue the religious disorder of the Peasants' War. Their aspirations for a Christianity modeled on the community of goods of Acts 2 and 4 seemed, if anything, more radical than the peasant programs.[29] Some Anabaptists were former followers of Thomas Müntzer and continued his ideas. Motivated by the desire to avenge "his father, Thomas Müntzer," the apocalyptic Anabaptist Hans Römer was apparently intending to seize control of Erfurt on New Year's Day 1528.[30] So the idea held by some rulers that the Anabaptists threatened a renewal of the Peasants' War had a degree of plausibility even though it overestimated the Anabaptists' strength and, on the whole, misunderstood their intentions.

There was absolute rejection and repudiation, mutual damning between the Anabaptists and the established churches and states of the German-speaking lands. Given this intense hostility and the great preponderance

of power of the established churches, it seems remarkable that a movement
of a few thousand Anabaptists survived at all in the Swiss–South German
regions. One factor was that the Anabaptists became adept at seeking out
the nooks and crannies of the political and ecclesiastical landscape. After
they were driven out of Zurich, their center became Basel, where the government, until 1529, tried to stay above the quarrels of the several religious
parties.[31] The outlying rural regions of Bern in the west and St. Gall and
Appenzell in the east, where governmental authority was weak, became
main areas of concentration for Swiss Anabaptists. In the German lands
some Imperial cities, especially Strasbourg, were relatively tolerant. Philip
of Hesse made a point of refusing demands for the execution of Anabaptists by the Wittenberg theologians and his political ally, the elector of
Saxony. Although there were exceptions on both sides, Protestant rulers
were more reluctant to shed Anabaptist blood than Protestant theologians.
It cannot have completely escaped the latter, however, that in their actions
against the Anabaptists they were forging possible legal precedents for
their own suppression by a resurgent Catholicism.

Above all, however, Swiss–South German Anabaptism preserved itself
by the first major emigration of the Reformation era, down the Danube to
the tolerant land of Moravia. In Moravia a strong non-Catholic aristocracy, left over from the inconclusive Hussite wars of the previous century,
had considerable practical local independence from its sovereign, the
Habsburg monarch in Vienna. These nobles were ready to lease their lands
to peaceful, economically productive religious dissidents.[32] Anabaptists
brought to Moravia the records of their early history—the account of the
first believers' baptisms of January 1525 in Zurich, their first congregational ordinance,[33] and the Seven Articles of Schleitheim.

The Tyrol, which had had a bitter experience of the Peasants' War and
regarded its Habsburg rulers and Catholic prelates as foreign occupiers,
had the strongest Anabaptist movement in South Germany. With great
effort and much bloodshed, and despite much passive resistance from the
population, the Vienna government suppressed Anabaptism there, but the
outcome was a large-scale secret migration to Moravia.[34] Although the Ty-
rolians were the most prominent group of Anabaptist migrants to Moravia,
they were joined by Swiss, Rhinelanders, Swabians, Hessians, and Sile-
sians. Moravia became a melting pot for early Swiss–South German Anabaptism. There the controversies about community of goods, the authority

of the Bible and the freedom of the Spirit, and government and nonresistance, were battled to a provisional resolution.

Anabaptism and the "Sword"

Before the Anabaptist emigration to Moravia, despite apparent differences on the Christian's approach to temporal power ("the sword" in the language of the day), there is no evidence of major inter-Anabaptist quarrels on the subject, and no pamphlets were devoted to it. There was dissent in the Waldshut congregation against Hubmaier's endorsement of military resistance against the Austrians. One Waldshuter, Jacob Gross, refused to participate and was punished with exile and confiscation of his property, after which he led a wandering life as an Anabaptist leader in Switzerland, Strasbourg, and Augsburg.[35] Hubmaier himself wrote the first Anabaptist pamphlet "On the Sword."[36] Arriving in the first wave of Anabaptist refugees to Moravia in the summer of 1526, he won over the small lordship of Nikolsburg to Anabaptism, including its pastors and its noble ruler. Seeking patronage and protection from the non-Catholic aristocracy of Moravia, he was unwilling to take the antigovernmental positions either of Thomas Müntzer or Conrad Grebel. "On the Sword" tried to use the New Testament to justify nonresistant, peaceful behavior of subjects, combined with deference to their Christian rulers. Romans 13, argued Hubmaier, could be observed much better with Christian than non-Christian rulers. Christ could say "my kingdom is not of this world," but Christians were entangled in the world and should not presume to separate themselves from its needs, one of which was government.

After the horrific experience of worldly power that the Anabaptist refugees to Moravia had behind them, it is not surprising that most rejected Hubmaier's legitimist ideas. When Müntzer's former follower Hans Hut visited Nikolsburg, he and Hubmaier got into Anabaptism's first memorable internal quarrel. Hubmaier had Hut temporarily jailed, accusing him of "stirring up conspiracy and rebellion under the appearance of the baptism and communion of Christ." Clearly Hubmaier rejected Hut's apocalyptic message, and Hut rejected Hubmaier's deference to temporal power. More confusing is the fact that in his interrogation in Augsburg a few months later in 1527, Hut also appeared to denounce the Schleitheim Articles, which he described as a regulation drawn up in Switzerland "that

Christians should not bear weapons."[37] In these hearings Hut often seemed more interested in misleading his captors than in laying down a testimony to his faith, but some of Hut's followers in Esslingen made the same points: "The government should be obeyed, oaths sworn, weapons carried."[38]

Whatever the precise nature of Hut's anti-Hubmaier position, he played a role in the background of the split in the Nikolsburg congregation in 1528. Most of the Moravian host community remained *Schwertler* (sword-carriers) in Hubmaier's manner, later becoming Sabbatarians as their leaders taught that Saturday was the biblical Lord's Day. But most of the Anabaptist immigrants to Moravia became *Stäbler* (staff-carriers), consolidating the Swiss ideas about rejection of weapons and government and combining this New Testament ideal with community of goods as outlined in Acts 2 and 4. The Stäbler tradition produced the first writings about Anabaptist nonresistance.[39]

In 1529 the Silesian Anabaptist Clemens Adler produced the earliest nonresistant treatise, "The Judgement concerning the Sword." Adler was probably a member of the Gabrielite community in Moravia composed of refugees from Silesia. His pamphlet outlined a series of successive divine covenants, first with Adam, then with Abraham and his physical descendants, and finally with Christians, the spiritual descendants of Abraham. The rich and powerful had perverted the original covenant, and the Jews had kings only due to their wickedness and rebellion, so there was no place for coercion and killing in the spiritual kingdom of Christ: "He who attempts to rule by force in this kingdom attempts to drive Christ out of his kingdom."[40]

One of the issues among the early Stäbler groups was whether or not to pay taxes specially earmarked for defense of Moravia against the Turks. Wilhelm Reublin, Peasants' War survivor and probable coauthor of the Schleitheim Articles, on arriving in Moravia agitated against paying this "blood money."[41] Soon explicit refusal of war taxes became a general part of the Moravian Anabaptist standpoint. The next nonresistant tract, "The Uncovering of the Babylonian Whore,"[42] appeared in the early 1530s and engaged in polemic against the Lutheran princes who had recently organized the Schmalkaldic League (1531) to defend themselves against the German Emperor, should he try to suppress the Reformation. Given Martin Luther's many protestations against persons like Thomas Müntzer who resorted to violence to defend their versions of the Reformation and thus showed that they were led not by God but by the devil, here was an obvious opportunity to reveal the hypocrisy of the Protestant established powers. The author appealed to the early church with the idea of a "Constantinian fall": "Christians did not use physical force or the sword from the time of the apostles until that of the Emperor Constantine." The anonymous pamphlet was published in Strasbourg by the same printer as a number of Pilgram Marpeck's writings of 1531, and there is a growing consensus that Marpeck was its author.[43] At the time, Marpeck was commissioned to baptize by the preeminent Stäbler community in Moravia, that of Austerlitz. The "Uncovering" advocated community of goods and attributed the existence of temporal government to people's anti-Christian desire to defend their private property: "Among the wicked there properly belong the sword of the wicked and wicked rulers according to their wicked, fleshly nature. Out of selfishness they preserve physical peace among one another for the sake of property."[44]

Like much else in early Anabaptism, nonresistance seems to have been a series of ideas without a general consensus behind it in its Swiss origins, but it became a major focus of the movement in the Moravian emigration before 1535. The quarrel between the sword-carriers and the staff-carriers, and the broad acceptance of the ideas of the latter, established the Schleitheim tradition among the southern German Anabaptist groups. The Hutterites, who established their sectarian identity in an acrimonious Moravian Anabaptist schism in 1533, accepted nonresistance together with community of goods. What distinguished them from the other Anabaptist groups was their tenacious persistence in Moravia in the persecution of 1535–37, when the other exile communities were driven back to their Silesian and South German homelands.[45]

The Hutterites maintained the early Anabaptist ideal of replicating the early New Testament church more tenaciously than their sectarian competitors, the Swiss Brethren and the Marpeck brotherhood. In a fitting paradox, however, because of these formal similarities to early, desperate, persecuted Anabaptism, the Hutterites achieved the greatest worldly success of all sixteenth-century Anabaptists and created a nonviolent, nonmilitary Anabaptist republic in southeastern Moravia. By maintaining themselves in Moravia when the other groups were driven out, the Hutterites absorbed fragments of other Moravian Anabaptist groups committed to community of goods, and after the late 1530s they became virtually the sole beneficiaries of continuing Swiss and South German Anabaptist emigration to Moravia. The Austrian government in Vienna was only able to organize sporadic persecutions of Moravian Anabaptism, in 1535–37, and again in 1547 at the time of the Schmalkaldic War, the Habsburgs' ultimately unsuccessful effort to suppress German Protestantism. Until mid-century the Vienna government was in constant conflict with the Moravian nobility, which profited greatly from the prosperous Anabaptist settlements. After the accession of the tolerant Emperor Maximillian II in 1564, the Vienna court abandoned all efforts to eradicate the Hutterites for a period lasting until the Thirty Years' War began in 1618.

Jesuit observers of late-sixteenth-century Hutterite life like the polemical writer Christoph Fischer were appalled by the secure, established position these heretics had assumed in the life of Moravia. At the end of the sixteenth century, 20,000 to 30,000 Hutterites lived in seventy tightly organized communities of 500, prospering from a high level of craftsmanship. Unlike their communitarian predecessors of the 1530s, they abandoned single-family households as the focus of life and work, constructing large multi-family dwellings. Their communities were led by "servants of the word" (preachers) and "servants of temporal needs" (economic managers). The Hutterites were dominated by a male leadership that tended to be of Tyrolian origin and artisan rather than peasant in occupation and that enforced its claim to preferential treatment ("double honor") within a system of community of goods. In another sense, however, they had created a Peasants' War utopia in which the functions of political leadership, religious ministry, and economic direction were no longer the possessions of hereditary estates but were dissolved into the community. The leading settlement at Neumühl was the Hutterite capital, presided over by the successor of Jakob Hutter. The Jesuit Fischer wrote scornfully of "Klaus Braidl, the shoemaker king."[46]

Of all Anabaptist groups, the Hutterites wrote most extensively on nonresistance—first in Peter Riedemann's "Account of Our Religion, Doctrine and Faith," and then with a more extensive mustering of biblical evidence in the "Five Articles" (1547) and Peter Walpot's "Great Articlebook" (ca. 1577).[47] They were concerned to work out the practical implications of nonresistance, which led them not only to refuse taxes for military purposes but also to ban the manufacture of weapons. In Riedemann's words: "The power of the sword has passed to the heathen, that they may punish their evildoers with it. But that is no concern of ours . . . Thus no Christian can rule over the world." Originally written in a Hessian prison, Riedemann's account denounced Münster Anabaptism, and its primary purpose seems to have been to convince Philip of Hesse that the Hutterites eschewed politics and could safely be tolerated.[48] Although they elaborated Michael Sattler's ideas into a "sectarian distinctive," the Hutterite attitude to the Moravian nobility was very different from his. The Jesuits complained about the Hutterites' friendly relations with their aristocratic protectors and how they familiarly referred to the Hussite governor of Moravia, Friedrich von Zerotin, as "our Fritz."[49] In the Hutterite "Golden Age" the original hostility to authority of the Schleitheim Articles was subtly eroded on the Anabaptist side, and on the side of the feudal ruling class, Anabaptist nonviolence became accepted as the peculiar religious practice of tolerated nonconformists.

Recent research has widened our conception of the "Swiss Brethren" as an Anabaptist grouping. The term came into use around 1540 in connection with many Anabaptists' abandonment of their original goal of reconstituting the church of the apostles that practiced community of goods in the manner of Acts 2 and 4. The Hutterites referred to Moravian Anabaptists, who persisted in single-family living and refused to accept their strict discipline, as "Swiss Brethren." The Philipite community, which returned from Moravia to South Germany in the major persecution of 1535–37, contributed the basic collection of songs in the Swiss Brethren hymnal.[50]

Anabaptists who maintained themselves in Switzerland, the Upper Rhine region, and Swabia accepted the label of Swiss Brethren. Their ideal became that of the early New Testament church after its dispersion from Jerusalem, and they accepted private property, provided that their members share it in a spirit of generous mutual aid. This group was exposed to attacks on many fronts. Hutterite missionaries criticized their abandonment of community of goods and recruited their members for the journey to Moravia. A small Anabaptist brotherhood led by Pilgram Marpeck attacked their legalism and their fractiousness. They were formally still subject to the death penalty in most jurisdictions of South Germany and Switzerland, and although it was carried out less frequently, they were constantly harassed. Also the Imperial edict against Anabaptism caused numbers of their intellectual leaders to defect. At any rate, it cannot have been a complete coincidence that immediately after the Diet of Speyer (1529), a number of Anabaptist leaders began to reconsider whether it was possible, or even desirable, to return to the practices of the New Testament church. The church of Christ, these "Spiritualists" held, was an invisible church of the spirit, scattered among all lands and peoples.[51] In these conditions, persistence in the early Swiss belief in the paramount authority of the New Testament over the Old and in the Schleitheim Articles' positions on the sword and the oath marked the Swiss Brethren attitude. Swiss Brethren treatises stressed separation from the established Reformed churches, and in religious disputations forced upon them by the Bern government and church in Zoffingen (1532) and Bern (1538), their spokesmen doggedly maintained the traditions of Grebel and Sattler.[52] These nonresistant Anabaptist survivors in Bern, Alsace, and the Palatinate became the ancestors of the "Pennsylvania German" Mennonite migrants to America in the seventeenth century.

Melchior Hoffman and Münster

Melchior Hoffman, the furrier from Schwäbisch-Hall, was the sect leader who brought Anabaptism from the southern to the northern part of the German-speaking world, to the territories bordering the North Sea and the Baltic. Hoffman had been a radical lay preacher in the Baltic and Scandinavian lands from 1522 to 1529, sometimes winning official protection for his proclamation (for example, from the King of Denmark for his activity in Holstein in 1527). His message had been apocalyptic from the start. Already in 1526 he published a tract on Daniel 12, setting 1533 as the date for the end of the world. Expelled from Lutheran North Germany for denying the real presence in the Lord's Supper, he turned up in Strasbourg in 1529 and quickly made contact with the numerous religious dissenters there. Among the Anabaptists in Strasbourg were prophets, both men and women, who assigned revelatory significance to their dreams and visions. Some of them were former adherents of Hans Hut's apocalyptic message. Hoffman, like Hut, was preoccupied with Revelations 11 and the appearance of Elijah and Enoch, the two apocalyptic witnesses. While Hut had thought that Thomas Müntzer and Heinrich Pfeiffer were the apostolic witnesses, the Strasbourg prophets convinced Hoffman that *he* was the promised Elijah, and that Strasbourg was the New Jerusalem.

Traveling from Strasbourg to East Frisia on the border of the Netherlands in 1530, Hoffman began to baptize adults in the Anabaptist manner. However, the apocalyptic message had priority over baptism for Hoffman. When some of his newly baptized followers were executed by Habsburg officials in the Netherlands in 1531, a shocked Hoffman suspended baptism until 1533, when he expected the second coming of Christ.[53]

Hoffman's message was not nonresistant in the southern Anabaptist manner. Although his booklet "On the Sword" is lost, we know his views from other writings of the early 1530s. He was respectful to rulers and did not view them as unchristian. He predicted an apocalyptic siege of Strasbourg by the emperor, intent on reimposing the papalist religion. The godly rulers of the New Jerusalem were expected to resist with arms. On the other hand, the sword had no place in the church, and his followers would not fight but would proclaim God's word. So there was a sort of vocational division of labor between godly rulers who had their appointed role in the events of the last days, and Hoffman's sect, the Melchiorites, who would proclaim the message of grace throughout the world. Hoffman and his followers would not take the sword into their own hands. When 1533 came, Hoffman, now in Strasbourg again, courted imprisonment, believing his imprisonment to be another sign of the end of the world. Once in jail, he smuggled out a tract, "On the Pure Fear of God," in which he prophesied cooperation between a second King Solomon, representing temporal power, and a second prophet Jonah, embodying spiritual power. Together, the invincible king and the infallible prophet would prepare the ground for Christ's return.[54]

The Melchiorite sect of apocalyptic Anabaptists would no doubt have waned and perhaps disappeared with the passing of 1533 had the Reformation of the episcopal city of Münster not connected them with the realities of power.[55] The combination of Anabaptism with the struggle of Münster's ruling class for independence from its prince bishop had consequences that were to be extremely detrimental to the historical reputation of Anabaptism. The Treaty of Dülmen of February 1533 confirmed Münster's adherence to the Reformation, under the protection of the Lutheran Schmalkaldic League. However, the leading reformer of Münster, Bernhard Rothmann, was a rebellious figure, unwilling to accept Lutheran theological formulas and church ordinances. Rothmann welcomed into Münster some preachers from Wassenberg in Jülich led by Heinrich Roll, a radical non-Lutheran theologian who was likely a Melchiorite.[56] By summer 1533

Rothmann was preaching against infant baptism, and Münster became a magnet for Anabaptists from the Netherlands like Jan Beukelsz, the future Anabaptist king, who visited briefly at that time. In fall 1533 the Haarlem baker Jan Matthijs proclaimed himself the Enoch of Revelations 11, reinstituted the adult baptisms previously suspended by Hoffman, and set Easter 1534 as the date of the end of the world.

In Münster the town oligarchy split more or less evenly between persons horrified by the dangers of Anabaptism (a capital offense since 1529), and persons convinced that expelling the Anabaptists would lead inexorably to the collapse of the Münster Reformation and the surrender of the town's newly won independence to the prince bishop. The crisis came to a head in three days of riots from February 9 to 11, 1534, during which the pro-Lutheran council failed to expel the Anabaptists. The Anabaptists abandoned the Melchiorite injunction not to use weapons now that their prophets told them to defend themselves. They claimed that they saw miraculous signs in the sky, and they regarded the agreement that permitted them to remain in the town at the end of the riots as a miraculous rescue by God. A new council elected in late February brought into power Anabaptists and Anabaptist supporters, led by the patrician burgomaster Bernhard Knipperdolling.[57] At the same time, the prophet Jan Matthijs and some of his followers from the Netherlands arrived in Münster. Jan Matthijs' charismatic power overshadowed the council completely.

Anabaptist Münster began with an exchange of populations, Lutherans and Catholics either fleeing the prospect of Anabaptist rule or expelled shortly after it began, and Anabaptists from the Netherlands fleeing to the safety of Münster until officials in the Netherlands and the besieging army around Münster blocked their entrance. The prince bishop of Münster began a siege at the same time the Anabaptists took power. He received financial and military support from both Catholic and Lutheran princes in accordance with Imperial laws passed in 1526 to prevent the reoccurrence of a rebellion of subjects like the Peasants' War.[58]

If the Hutterite settlements in Moravia were a sort of Peasants' War utopia, the history of Münster under siege from February 1534 to June 1535 was an Anabaptist dystopia. To begin with, Anabaptist Münster's authority in the Netherlands was short-lived. At first, to be sure, Münster had a great impact in neighboring lands. The spectacle of the Anabaptists' coming to power in Münster galvanized the Dutch response to years of war, pestilence, and unemployment into an apocalyptic mass movement. The political miracle in Münster gave credibility to the Münster prophets' declaration that Münster, not Strasbourg, was the New Jerusalem, and that it would be the only place of safety when the world ended in April 1534. Thousands of people tried to get to Münster, mostly by ship across the Zuider Zee. But when Easter 1534 came and Jan Matthijs was killed in battle in a desperate attack on the besiegers, most of his credibility perished with him. Whatever remaining authority Münster had was lost with the failure of King Jan of Leiden's prophecy that the world would end, now a year later, on Easter 1535. This, not the peaceful character of Dutch Anabaptism, accounts for the pathetic failure of Münsterite efforts to organize uprisings in the Netherlands, at Oldeklooster and Amsterdam.[59]

Community of goods, begun with great enthusiasm by Rothmann and Jan Matthijs, lost its momentum following the prophet's death. The resistance of the Münster notables to an exchange of houses was too strong to overcome. Under Jan of Leiden, government in Münster became a careful power-sharing arrangement between native Münster oligarchs and Dutch immigrants. The lavish royal court created in September 1534 cemented the great inequality between rich and poor that hid behind the facade of apostolic community of goods.[60] Polygamy undoubtedly had much to do with the sexual appetites and imagination of Jan of Leiden. Its introduction provoked an internal uprising that came very close to success. The reality of polygamy occurred in the context of exaggerated slogans of male supremacy and a great preponderance of women over men in the Anabaptist kingdom (ca. 5,000 to 2,000). Divorce had to be allowed as a remedy for the worst cases of abuse of women and girls in this system.[61]

The power of the Anabaptist government in Münster was above all devoted to an ingenious and tenacious military resistance extending over sixteen months of siege, a resistance that included the defeat of two assaults on the city walls and that could hardly have been so successful without the full cooperation of the female majority. The defenders of Münster hoped for an apocalyptic deliverance, knowing that no mercy awaited them if they were to be "trampled under the foot of the beast." At the same time, however, Münster's government engaged in playacting at world domination by copying imperial regalia. King Jan insisted, "We shall yet march around the world."

Under the kingship of Jan of Leiden, Rothmann wrote and circulated three tracts, "Restitution," "On Vengeance," and "On the Mystery of Scripture," that justified Münster's claims in the most expansive terms. Scripture, he argued, contained several dispensations. In the New Testament order, the apostles exemplified humility and suffering; but in the age of the Reformation, which was a sign of the imminent second coming of Christ, glorious vengeance was the task of Christians. Indeed, Christ, the peaceful Solomon, could only return after a promised predecessor, a king David, had humbled all his enemies: "The throne of David must be reestablished, the kingdom prepared and armed, and all the enemies of Christ humbled by David. Then the peaceful Solomon, the eternal king and anointed God, Christ, will enter." Rothmann complained that the Anabaptists outside Münster "have advanced only a little way beyond the knowledge of suffering in Christ."[62]

The inglorious fall of Anabaptist Münster in June 1535 threw the Melchiorite sects of the Netherlands and Westphalia into turmoil. A group of unrepentant Münster escapees established a headquarters in the Oldenburg area; and another, even more violent group, the Covenanters of the Sword, sometimes named for their leader, the bastard nobleman Jan van Batenburg, repudiated the Münster leadership for their failed prophecies but dedicated themselves to a campaign of surreptitious vengeance against the established church and state and against Anabaptist defectors.[63] Other Melchiorites, meeting at an assemblage of leaders at Bocholt in Westphalia in August 1536, moved toward abandoning the distinctive practices of Münster Anabaptism: polygamy and a physical kingdom. Their spokesman, David Joris, however, spiritualized many of the themes of Rothmann's writings. He continued to place his own prophecies on a par with Scripture and claimed for himself the spiritual role of the messianic David, a humbler, lesser successor of Christ. Throughout the late 1530s David Joris, still a radical apocalyptic leader, dominated the remnants of Netherlands Anabaptism. He permitted his followers to be Nicodemites, to outwardly conform to Catholic practice in order to escape persecution. In 1539, after a desperate, hunted career, Joris took asylum with wealthy supporters in Antwerp and turned to spreading his ideas by pamphlet and letter. More and more of a spiritualist, he abandoned adult baptism and expectation of a literal second coming.[64] A vivid end-time mood continued in the Anabaptist-Mennonite-Hutterite tradition, but after the 1530s it had subsided to the extent that it no longer distorted Anabaptists' reading of the Bible.[65]

The rejection of the militant Anabaptism of Münster did not signify adoption of the nonresistance of the Schleitheim Articles in the Netherlands and North Germany. Until the translation of the Seven Articles into Dutch in 1560, together with an account of the martyrdom of Michael Sattler, the characteristic Schleitheim ideas about the incompatibility of rulership and Christianity seem to have been unknown in the region. Not only David Joris but also Menno Simons, the leading peaceful Anabaptist leader in the north during the 1540s and 1550s, took Christian rulership for granted and conceded rulers a certain role in the reform of the church. Menno was against war and renounced Münster with its practices of community of goods and polygamy in the most decisive terms. In his eyes, David Joris, who had tried to spiritualize some of the beliefs and practices of the Münster Anabaptists, had created a corrupt sect. The Bible should be read literally. There was no promised David except Christ, and Christ as described in the New Testament remained a valid model for Christians. In his later years, Menno Simons also spoke out against capital punishment.[66]

One of the ironies of Mennonite experience is that rules against assuming governmental office became firm at about the same time that the state assumed a friendlier face. About one thousand Mennonite martyrs perished at the hands of the Spanish Habsburg rulers of the Netherlands. Their peaceful testimonies graced *Het Offer des Heeren*, the predecessor of the *Martyrs' Mirror*.[67] When the aristocratic and Calvinist-led resistance to Spain began the Dutch War of Independence, it was impossible for the Mennonites to be entirely neutral. Waterlander congregations helped Prince William of Orange financially with a free gift "for the advancement of the common cause."[68] The prince, in his turn, decreed toleration for the Mennonites in the 1570s. The United Netherlands of the late sixteenth century was, like Moravia, a religiously pluralistic land.[69] Although the Calvinists had civil and economic advantages, they were only about 10 percent of the population,[70] frequently outnumbered by Catholics, or, in Frisia, by Mennonites.

The 100,000 baptized Anabaptists in hundreds of congregations throughout the Netherlands[71] splintered into native Waterlanders and Frisians as well as refugee Flemings. Despite the recurrent ill will of Calvinist pastors who dished up warmed-over memories of Münster, the Mennonites settled into the peaceful life of tolerated nonconformity that was to be typical of future generations. Ideas of separation that came into being in an atmosphere of revolutionary and apocalyptic excitement in the 1520s and 1530s lent themselves very well to the quietism of the end of the sixteenth century.

Conclusion

The sixteenth-century Anabaptists began by attacking the authority of established power structures in church and rulership. Although some Anabaptist leaders originated in the clergy (Menno Simons, Balthasar Hubmaier, Melchior Rinck, Michael Sattler) or the patriciate (Conrad Grebel, Bernhard Knipperdolling, Pilgram Marpeck), they abandoned the prerogatives of estate that set them above commoners. These members of the higher estates joined commoners like Hans Hut, Melchior Hoffman, Jan Matthijs, Jakob Hutter, or David Joris in subjecting themselves to the authority of the vernacular Bible and the Holy Spirit. When the apocalyptic vision of the end days did not intoxicate them, the standard of authority for sixteenth-century Anabaptists was the early church as described in the Acts of the Apostles, whether before or after the dispersion from Jerusalem. In relation to believers' baptism, the most distinctive practice of the Anabaptists, again New Testament authority was decisive. Felix Mantz wrote: "It is no small matter to practice the only two ceremonies left to us by Christ otherwise than as Christ commanded."[72] Mantz also declared that "no Christian should be a government official, nor judge with the sword, nor kill or punish anyone,"[73] presumably because the Christians described in the New Testament did not do such things. The statements in the Seven Articles of Schleitheim that Christians were entirely separated from the old and new churches of the Reformation era and all temporal power, and that the latter was an ordinance of God outside "the perfection of Christ," arose quite naturally from the early Anabaptists' modeling themselves on the New Testament.

But from the beginning, occasions arose when Anabaptists wanted to exercise power in a way the New Testament Christians could not be shown to have done. The first Anabaptists emerged in 1525, the year of the German Peasants' War, which seemed for an intoxicating moment to shake the entrenched power of church and government. So some of them could defend Waldshut, an Anabaptist town, or protect Anabaptist preachers from officials coming to arrest them. When a far greater temptation arose in Münster in February 1534, it was quite impossible for Melchiorite Anabaptists simply to surrender themselves like sheep for the slaughter, since they had the means to defend themselves. The Münster Anabaptists elaborated an idea already current from the time of Thomas Müntzer and Hans Hut—that in the last days of the world, God's elect people could progress beyond the suffering of the New Testament apostles to smite the empire of evil, to bang on Nimrod's anvil.

After the 1530s the anger of the Anabaptists' attack on the powers that they labeled "the world" diminished in its intensity—even though, particularly in Moravia, the teaching of nonresistance to worldly powers became more elaborate and formal. The eschatological mood was no longer so intense that, as had been the case earlier, prophetic liberties were taken in interpretation of the Bible and specific dates set for the coming of the Lord.[74] Nor was the explicit dualism of Michael Sattler's suggestion that formal Christians were "Turks according to the Spirit" when they slaughtered the true sheep of Christ so likely to be heard. Sattler's was a martyr testimony, and martyrdoms became rare after the 1530s in South Germany and Switzerland and after the 1560s in the Netherlands.

Among the Hutterites formal separation from the world went together with such excellent relations with the religiously diverse Moravian nobility that in the eyes of visiting Jesuits it was not the Anabaptists but ordinary Catholics who were disadvantaged and oppressed. Menno Simons denounced war, but he never denied that rulers could be Christian. And the Waterlanders, at least, became noncombatant supporters of the revolt of the Netherlands against the persecuting Spaniards. True to the tradition of Melchior Hoffman, the post-Münster Anabaptists of the north eschewed arms for themselves but supported Christian governments with their prayers. By the time toleration was granted to the Dutch Anabaptists in the 1570s, the foundation was laid for the acceptance of the Mennonites as one element in a Protestant-dominated religious mosaic.

That Mennonites did not carry arms or swear oaths was no longer construed by either the Mennonites or the tolerant secular rulers as a challenge to the legitimacy of the United Netherlands. Toward the end of the sixteenth century, whether in Moravia or the Netherlands, Anabaptist non-resistance was a nonconformist practice, not an attack on the wickedness of the world. In Switzerland the persecution of Anabaptists by the Reformed governments occasionally flared up with a bit of the ferocity of the 1520s and 1530s. There Anabaptist nonresistance maintained some of its original meaning as a symbol of the absolute mutual rejection of the Anabaptists and the world.[75] But Switzerland was the source of emigration of Anabaptists to the relative toleration of the Palatinate and the absolute tolerance of Pennsylvania. It was hard for the Pennsylvania German Mennonites to be sure that their hosts, the Penns, the Lord Proprietors of Pennsylvania, were "outside the perfection of Christ." What they *were* certain about was that they, the Mennonites, were a separate people who did not bear arms or swear oaths.

CHAPTER FOUR

Power and Authority in Mennonite Theological Development

LYDIA HARDER

Taking up where Chapter 3 left off, the author begins by examining the issues of power and authority in the theology of Menno Simons. The discussion is then brought into the twentieth century through analysis of two prominent American Mennonite theologians, Guy F. Hershberger and John H. Yoder. The author notes how the "rules of the game" of theology have been adapted and adjusted over time and delineates the "boundaries" of the game as they have been established in various settings. The chapter concludes with suggestions as to ways in which the evolving "game" may be played in the future.

The metaphor of theology as a game provides a useful framework for describing power and authority in Mennonite theological development. A game, whether soccer or cards, usually includes a variety of players, diverse strategies, shifting interpretations of rules, and an often elusive goal. Using this metaphor to describe Mennonite theologizing suggests that there is a complexity and plurality in Mennonite theology that contributes to making the game a dynamic and ever-changing reality.[1] But games also have underlying rules that establish the basic framework distinguishing one game from another. So too there are "family resemblances" and regulatory principles that help distinguish Mennonite theologies from other similar Christian theologies.[2] In this chapter I concentrate on illuminating the basic rules of the game by describing the strategies and moves made by individual players in a variety of circumstances.

I have chosen the writings of Menno Simons, the sixteenth-century reformer from whom Mennonites received their name, to illustrate the rules that defined the game during a crucial period of its conception. The definitions of power and authority that began to be assumed by this group of Anabaptists created basic strategies for a game played during a time of social unrest and upheaval. The second part of this analysis moves into the twentieth century. The focus on a different time and setting allows us to evaluate the degree to which the basic rules were still intact several hundred years later, and the degree to which subtle changes and adjustments were made to fit new circumstances. The writings of two influential theologians will demonstrate some of the adjustments made to suit a new time. The conclusion will suggest that the definitive word has not yet been spoken in Mennonite theologizing—new players are continually being invited to join the game. These bring ambiguities and tensions to the surface, but they also introduce new vitality and energy into play. The future shape of the game is thus open, awaiting involvement by many players as the rules are debated, adapted, and reapplied.

Menno Simons

Menno Simons' theological approach to issues of power and authority grew out of a long personal struggle, as a member of the Catholic clergy, to live a life of integrity and to speak an authentic word of truth. This latter task was not easy during a time when a unified tradition based on the political stability of Christendom and the religious mediation of the sacraments by the church could no longer be assumed. The gradual breaking apart of this unity created space for various dualistic worldviews to emerge and thrive. Thus, divisions between the spiritual world and the material world can be recognized in the various debates among Reformers around polarities such as spirit/letter, invisible/visible, gospel/law, or the inner/outer word.[3]

These were not only theoretical debates for the Reformers; rather, the struggles between various theologies were also political struggles between religious leaders seeking to reestablish authority on a firm basis. A focus on the authority of the Word of God did not do away with a merging of the power of the state with a newly reformed church. Paramount leaders such as Luther and Zwingli did not hesitate to use the power of the state to enforce the authority of the Word. However, the use of the "sword of righteousness" was not limited to these Reformers. As we have seen in Chapter 3, figures associated with Anabaptism led the seizure of the city of Münster, proclaiming it to be the New Jerusalem of the last days. Those who resisted were executed or expelled. The failure of this vision, based on a wedding of spiritualism and apocalypticism, led not only to a time of disillusionment but also to persecution for the Anabaptists in the Netherlands.

In this volatile and dangerous context, Menno Simons found a point of integration that allowed him to proclaim a new kind of kingdom with Jesus Christ as its authoritative foundation. Though there were many shifts and changes in Menno's thinking, the notion of radical regeneration was fundamental.[4] In his view, baptism signified a transformation of human nature in the individual, a dying to the old life of sin and a rising with Christ to a new life in anticipation of the heavenly Jerusalem. The Lord's Supper celebrated the coming together of the new people of God as the body of Christ. The church proclaimed a new way of truth as it sought to be light and salt in the world.

The anticipation of God's kingdom in the *Fundamentboek*, Menno's most complete attempt at theological writing, is, according to Helmut Isaak, "universalist and holistic."[5] The time of God's grace includes all people and all nations, and it affects all areas of life. Thus Christians can already be citizens of the New Jerusalem in anticipation of the kingdom coming in its fullness because Christ is already Lord and King over heaven and earth.

This holistic worldview, based on God's grace in Jesus, did not do away with all dualisms. In fact, the dualisms that are found sprinkled throughout Menno's writings reflect the notion of the "new" breaking into the "old" and creating a radical division between people. Thus Menno insists that

> there are two opposing princes and two opposing kingdoms; The one is the Prince of peace; the other the prince of strife. Each of these princes has his particular kingdom and as the prince is so is also the kingdom. The Prince of peace is Christ Jesus; His kingdom is the kingdom of peace, which is His

church; His messengers are the messengers of peace . . . ; His body is the body of peace . . . our weapons are not swords and spears, but patience, silence, and hope, and the Word of God. With these we must maintain our heavy warfare and fight our battle . . . with these we intend and desire to storm the kingdom of the devil . . . the other prince is the prince of darkness, Antichrist and Satan. This prince is a prince of all tumult and blood. Raging and murder is his proper nature and policy. His commandments and teachings and his kingdom, body, and church are of the same nature.[6]

Though these divisions are starkly stated, they do not coincide neatly with the dichotomy between spirit and matter. Rather, Menno understands both the spiritual kingdom of God and the fleshly kingdom of the devil as embodied realities. Both include an inner and an outer nature. Both include a visible church, a concrete message, weapons to defend themselves, and methods to pass this message on to others. Both are games, although played by a different set of rules.

As we read Menno's writings in more detail, we may be surprised at their polemical and argumentive tone. His descriptions of the kingdom of God are almost always set against the backdrop of false teachers, representing false Christs and false churches who offer faltering foundations on which to build the kingdom. For Menno is not concerned primarily with speculative theology, nor is he only striving for logical consistency. Rather, he is seeking to empower and encourage those struggling to live in peace in a world in which the church, whether Catholic, Reformed, or Anabaptist, could be the initiator of violence and bloodshed. His suspicion rests on the experience of persecution and violence, which he cannot name as the fruit of the Spirit.

The concern that spiritual reality be of one piece from eternity to eternity permeates Menno's writings. It is often expressed by the hermeneutical principle that "the same brings forth the same" or "every tree beareth fruit after its own kind."[7] This implies that only the Spirit of God is able to establish a spiritual kingdom here on earth. Because Menno rejected the mediation provided by the sacramental system of the Catholic Church in which the material sacraments literally became Christ's body on earth, he had to enter the more theoretical discussions about the nature of God and of human beings, and the mediation between them. For him, the incarnate Christ became the vital clue to a kingdom that was spiritual but visible on earth.

Menno interpreted John 1:14 to mean that Jesus embodied the Word of God in his very being, a being in which the inner life and the outer visible reality were unified in one spiritual body.[8] Thus, Jesus was not a sinful human born of Adam's seed but rather a new creation, a new Adam, the Word of God made flesh. He was the perfect Lamb, able to atone for all sin, but he was also the one who initiated a new way of being human in this world. Menno thus insists, "The regenerate . . . have received a new heart and spirit. Once they were earthly-minded, now heavenly; once they were carnal, now spiritual; once they were unrighteous, now righteous; once they were evil, now good, and they live no longer after the old corrupted nature of the first earthly Adam, but after the new upright nature of the new and heavenly Adam, Christ Jesus."[9] In this optimistic view of regenerated human nature, the church, the bride of Christ, literally becomes "flesh of his flesh and bone of his bone."[10] The church became a kind of sacrament, the literal body of Christ in this world, charged with the mission of representing God's grace.[11]

This theology of incarnation allowed Menno to connect God's authority and power to human authority and power when it was exercised within the true church. The Bible as Word of God and the church as body of Christ received their essential nature from God through Jesus Christ. Thus the power of God's revelatory Word in the Bible and the authority of a church that would incarnate in a visible way the mind and spirit of Christ were placed under the grace of God active in the world. This intimate connection resulted in "heavenly" power, which makes the regenerated active, confident, and joyful, able to bring forth good fruit. No longer are Christians "bound by any person, power, wisdom, or times but we must be governed by the plainly expressed commands of Christ and the pure doctrines and practices of His holy apostles."[12] Christ's life of love, service, suffering, and death becomes the measure of any embodiment within history that is empowered by the Spirit.

For Menno these convictions grew out of a personal experience of conversion and transformation. Before he could teach and preach to the scattered flock eagerly waiting for a word of truth, he had to give up all his own ambitions and dreams of financial security and power, and become instead a man slandered and persecuted, accused of being a heretic and false prophet. But these convictions also contributed to a new notion of the visible community named "church." A leveling of social hierarchies under God greatly limited the power of the educated, the aristocrats, and the clergy over the "common people." Thus, Menno can say, "Before Him, the great and the commoner are alike, the rich and the poor, the strong and the weak, the learned and the unlearned, the wise and the foolish. With him is no respect of persons; all who do not fear Him, do not conform to His counsel, doctrine, spirit, and example, whether emperor, king, doctor, or licentiate, he must bear His punishment eternally and be subject to His judgment and wrath."[13] Menno Simons' motto, "No other foundation can anyone lay than that which is laid, which is Jesus Christ" proved to be a "provocation for all who based their religiosity on human resources, whether tradition and human convention, learned understanding or worldly power. It smashed the foundations of the powerful and laid bare the one foundation that could sustain a Christian existence."[14]

The effects of this understanding of power and authority soon became evident within a number of the early Anabaptist communities. Nonordained persons such as women began to gain a new authority through prophetic gifts, members in need received aid through sharing within community, and the power of official leaders was limited by empowering all to be involved in biblical interpretation.[15] The hierarchies, which had been assumed to be God-given or in the nature of divine order and creation, and the offices, which gave authority to certain people, were challenged when measured by the standard of Christ. But not all issues of power and authority in Anabaptist communities were solved through this radical theology of the kingdom of God and the incarnation of Jesus in history.

In the World, but Not of the World

Within the Anabaptist community the dynamic associated with equality before God and the understanding of nonviolence as the way of discipleship created a shift in patterns of power and authority. The only power that members of the church were to have over each other was that of "fraternal admonition." Physical violence should not be used to discipline those who go astray. Balthasar Hubmaier, one of the most articulate theologians of the Anabaptists, states this rather clearly in his "baptismal order." In baptism new members of the church voluntarily submitted themselves to the church in order to learn to live according to the law of Christ.[16] Through the use of the ban (excommunication) and shunning (social avoidance of those walking in sin), members were encouraged to repent and renew their covenant with God. This process of "binding and loosing," based on Matthew 18 and John 20, was seen as necessary to maintain the moral integrity and unitary authority of the church.

It did not take long before the need for leadership and oversight emerged as small congregations struggled for unity. However, Anabaptists insisted that sacramental ordination, apostolic succession, or education were not adequate legitimations for leadership.[17] They generally agreed that only an upright person who lived a pure Christian life and who was taught by the Holy Spirit could be considered a true shepherd of the sheep. The measure of the spirituality of leaders was to be the congruence of their life with the Word of God.

This appeal to the Word of God did not solve the disagreements about authoritative biblical interpretation and the designation of leaders. Should authority be vested in illumined "apostles," ordained preachers, biblically learned teachers, or everyone in a congregation? There were those such as Conrad Grebel and Michael Sattler who emphasized letter over spirit, those such as Hans Denck who emphasized the priority of spirit over letter, and those such as the Melchiorites and the prophetesses Ursula Jost and Barbara Rebstock who focused on both prophetic spirit and prophetic letter.[18]

As churches began to focus more and more on their own purity, leaders were chosen who demonstrated the external, legislated marks of spirituality, marks more easily discerned than the inner, experiential side of Christian faith. Menno Simons' optimistic anthropology and his growing insistence on obedience to the literal word of God in order to ensure a church "without spot or wrinkle" greatly contributed to a tendency toward a harsh, legalistic approach to church discipline. The weight of leadership began to fall more and more on officially designated leaders; charismatic and prophetic leadership within the church became difficult. Boundaries thus became important as the church moved from emphasizing the gracious empowerment by God through the work of the Spirit, to judging the moral integrity of members of the community who were to embody God's holiness. Differences could not be tolerated when unity and conformity within the community were the signs of obedience to God. Offending members were thus "sent out of the church, God's kingdom, into the world, the kingdom of Satan."[19]

The issue of power and authority as related to governance in the larger society was complicated during a time when the legitimacy of the Anabaptist churches themselves was being contested. In the early years it was not yet clear how the established church would respond to the small communities of Anabaptists, whose advocacy of various shifts in social and religious patterns of relationships threatened to disturb the stability of church and society. Menno appealed to the magistrates to become true Christian rulers and admonished them to use their powers for the good in words such as the following: "Your task is to do justice between a man and his neighbour, to deliver the oppressed out of the hand of the oppressor; also to restrain by reasonable means, that is, without tyranny and bloodshed, manifest deceivers who so miserably lead poor helpless sons by hundreds of thousands into destruction."[20] Menno did not consider these powerful rulers to be outside of the perfection of Christ simply by virtue of their office, the external sign of power. He suggests that the "calling" of the magistrates was to "enlarge, help and protect the kingdom of God." He calls them to rule wisely and to exercise justice and accountability for the stewardship of their resources. At the same time, he accuses rulers of seeking "fat salaries and a lazy life," wanting to be called "doctors, lords, or masters" and thus abusing their authority. As one of the oppressed and persecuted, Menno calls for the conversion of rulers, to be expressed as toleration and protection of the Anabaptists in the name of Christ and the gospel. Integrity for Christian magistrates implied that the weapons used must be related to the kind of kingdom that was being established. This meant that the Christian's weapons were not to be "weapons with which cities and countries may be destroyed, walls and gates broken down, and human blood shed in torrents like water."[21]

Menno soon admitted that he could find only a few who demonstrated that they truly feared and loved God in the way they used their worldly power. The key marks of Christian faith identified by Anabaptists did not fit well with the political reality of the times. Anabaptists soon found themselves on the margins of society. As the clash between differing views of power and authority became stronger, choices had to be made by both the magistrates and the Anabaptists. Would they accommodate to each other's views by moderating their positions, or would there need to be a strict separation between them? Snyder suggests that there were, in fact, five different political arrangements that occurred during the sixteenth century.[22] These ranged from Anabaptism as the official religion, to toleration of Anabaptists, to outright enmity between Anabaptists and the governing power in a region.

Separation increasingly came to be seen as the best option, especially when the rejection of the sword and the oath became normative in Anabaptism. The Schleitheim Confession (1527)[23] already states this unambiguously: "It does not befit a Christian to be a magistrate: The rule of the government is according to the flesh, that of the Christians according to the Spirit . . . The weapons of their battle and warfare are carnal and only against the flesh, but the weapons of Christians are spiritual, against the fortification of the devil."[24] This implied that a commitment to the kingdom of God made visible in Christ's body could easily be distinguished from the visible manifestations of a commitment to a false kingdom. Authority and power in society became disconnected from God and began to be considered outside of the "perfection of Christ." Therefore, Anabaptists did not consider positions of authority in the broader society to be proper for their members. They became more and more suspicious of anyone holding an office in the government or the established church. The position of the church on the margins of society became the normal one for a faithful community.

The conviction that the eschatological kingdom of God was already becoming a reality on earth became the basis on which both the goal of the game and the criteria for legitimate moves was based. There were two opposing teams or sides, only one of which could be identified with God's coming kingdom. For the early Anabaptists the goal of the game was to participate in this kingdom (now and in the hereafter), but how to know who were the true players? Identification with God's kingdom could not center on the uniform of the players (the outer ceremonies or the words spoken), since some of the false prophets were also "baptized with one and the same baptism, and were one with us in appearance."[25] Instead, the congruence between the inner and the outer, between the uniform and the play, became the primary criterion. This created a visible church with definite marks identifying it as God's church, but the marks were taken as outward expressions of an inner reality. In this game Mennonites had to wrestle with questions of power and authority by seeking to incarnate the unity of inner and outer in their play. The measure was Jesus, the Word becoming flesh, who embodied true authority in his very being. The use of power became valid—authoritative—if it moved the church toward the goal of embodying the Word of God.

However, over time standardized uniforms and a sharper delineation of the boundaries of the playing field became primary marks of membership on the team. Different interpretations of the game created new suspicions, separations, and competition among team members. Disunity, domination by a few, and new hierarchies began to threaten a game whose goal was to embody the rule of God on earth. The tension within the game centered on how to participate in God's transforming power in the world without using the false strategies of the world, which created worldly power plays and domination. The answer seemed to be a game in which players united in small enclaves on the margins of the larger society, determined to at least bring together word and deed on their own team and within the boundaries of their own communities. Obedience to the norms established by the community became the signs that identified these teams as faithful representatives of the kingdom.

Twentieth-Century Approaches

Over the next few centuries, Mennonite confessions of faith revolved around ecclesiology and mission, with the focus on the inner life of church membership and the outer life of Christian discipleship.[26] A keen sense of boundaries, together with a long history of deprivation in a world that was often hostile, created a faith community with a strong sense of separation from the surrounding culture. However, as societies changed and Mennonites began to depend on friendly governments to protect their traditional beliefs and practices, a crisis in Mennonite identity developed. Hans-Jürgen Goertz suggests that in the twentieth century "a way of life patterned on gestures of resistance against a past age" produced a crisis of historical depth and increasing intensity. The outward markers of membership in the Mennonite side began to be eroded as hostilities with the outside world were replaced by often close collaboration. Mennonites found it increasingly difficult to tell one side from the other as boundaries between sides became permeable. The Mennonite "cognitive center" had dissolved, creating a vacuum that needed to be filled if Mennonites were to continue to play in the same game.[27] It was time for a restatement of the rules.

Harold Bender, a historian and churchman, sensed this need. His 1943 presidential address to the American Society of Church History, entitled "The Anabaptist Vision," was only in part an effort to convince other Christians that Anabaptism was a valid part of the Reformation.[28] His voice was also directed to the church and its need to be revitalized. In Bender's eyes, Anabaptism had taken the Reformation to its proper conclusion by emphasizing the practice-oriented nature of the Christian faith. Disciple-ship, the church as a brotherhood, and the ethic of love and nonresistance were identified as the common core of beliefs that were characteristic of "evangelical and constructive Anabaptism." Bender summarized the es-sence of Anabaptism in this way: "The whole life was to be brought liter-ally under the lordship of Christ in a covenant of discipleship, a covenant which the Anabaptist writers delighted to emphasize. The focus of the Christian life was to be not so much the inward experience of the grace of God, as it was for Luther, but the outward application of that grace to all human conduct and the consequent Christianization of all human relation-ships."[29] Bender hoped that the institutional Mennonite Church would re-gain its vigor while finding its own place in the larger context of denomina-tional Christianity.

According to John D. Roth, the renewal of the "Anabaptist Vision" sparked by this speech served as a symbolic theological anchor, a source of identity and renewal within the Mennonite Church during the era follow-ing World War II, "as Mennonites became increasingly acculturated into the mainstream culture of North America."[30] Two theologians influenced by this vision significantly shaped Mennonite understandings of power and authority in the next half-century. Their way of intertwining the rules into an integrated approach of their own created some shifts and adjustments. However, the influence of the basic rules as set out by Menno Simons can easily be discerned in their theological approach to power and authority.

Guy Franklin Hershberger

Guy F. Hershberger's *War, Peace, and Nonresistance*, first published in 1944, was based both on the historical consensus that had arisen in Anabaptist-Mennonite experience over the centuries and on biblical interpretation focused on the teachings of Jesus in the Sermon on the Mount.[31] The im-petus for his writings came from the experiences and challenges facing

American Mennonites during the first half of the twentieth century. Interestingly enough, Hershberger did not see the greatest temptation for Mennonites at this time coming from the opponents of the way of peace as it was defined by Mennonites. Rather, he saw the greater challenge coming from the subtle temptation to compromise with a society that had begun to tolerate Mennonites and their convictions.[32] The boundaries between Mennonites and the rest of society were becoming blurred; therefore, issues of identity and authority were coming to the fore. The need, as Hershberger saw it, was to focus on the visible difference between the kingdom of God and the kingdoms of this world. This difference could best be stated in the clear principle of "nonresistance."

Hershberger begins his book with a definition of war as "social conflict in which one party endeavors with the use of force, to compel the submission of the other."[33] Because he recognizes that physical and armed force are not the only kinds of coercive power, he speaks about conflict not only between nations but also between races, political parties, social classes, and even families and individuals. His notion of nonresistance, the strategy that he connects with the kingdom of God, excludes all kinds of force. "Force" includes the nonviolent resistance of Gandhi and the tactics of organized labor and organized agriculture as well as the oppressive methods of the employer class, organized capital, or big business. Pressure groups that operate for selfish ends use methods that become vicious in their attempt to impose justice, violating the greater ethic of love and nonresistance found in the Bible.

Therefore, Hershberger makes a clear distinction between "doing justice" and "demanding justice."[34] Christians seek to obey the principle of love, not to compel the enemy to comply with their wishes against his will. Social changes that are brought about for personal, class, or national advantage are not primarily motivated by obedience to the divine will. They are therefore not rooted in the experience of regeneration through the atoning work of Christ.

For Hershberger the church is to be a "colony of heaven" that is neither a human institution nor a mystical phenomenon but a society of regenerate Christians, a Christian brotherhood that belongs to the true kingdom of God.[35] Christians who really follow Christ will live a nonconformed life, a life on a "different level" than those of non-Christians. This is so because through the coming of the Holy Spirit they have access to a source of greater power, the power of love. Because of Jesus, who gives freedom from the passions of "natural man," Christians live in a new covenant relationship that allows them to become "the salt and light of the earth."

The New Testament is "entirely unpolitical" for Hershberger because it has nothing to say about how the affairs of state should be conducted.[36] Rulers may be agents of God to maintain order in society, but this only allows the "law of cause and effect" to be administered in society. While Christians must be subordinate to the state's purposes (unless it requires disobedience to the higher law of love), they do not need to be involved in administrating this lower law. Therefore, they should not feel obligated to fill the office of policeman or magistracy. Others who live on a "sub-Christian" level can aspire to those roles. Christians should aim for the higher place that only they can fill.

Hershberger moderates this radical separation between the two realms when he stresses that Christians must be creatively engaged in witness and service to society by offering alternatives to conventional political activity. They will provide leadership for a "curative" not a "political" mission, which can bring healing to human society and prevent further decay through consistent witness to the truth.[37] Hershberger spells out some of these implications in a discussion of practical service such as relief work and creative initiatives in mental health services. But he insists that ideals such as freedom of religion and loving community are best modeled by the faith community. Thus Hershberger includes a chapter on personal relationships in his subsequent book, *The Way of the Cross in Human Relations* (1958). In this world of family and friends, the spirit of cooperation and love should permeate all relationships. There is no room for attitudes of superiority, but all must think of themselves as "brethren in the faith, not as high or low, leaders or followers, rulers or subjects."[38] Only with this kind of humility can relationships function according to the will of God. Cooperation and community come about through "mutual forbearance, and love, and the doing of justice; not by means of self-assertion and the demand for justice."[39]

Though Hershberger is usually thought of as a clear spokesperson for a two-kingdom theology, he bases this division on an integrated ethical principle derived from Christ's teaching in the Sermon on the Mount. History has taught him that it is difficult to live out this principle of love in a world that operates by coercive power. He is suspicious of the blurring of principles that will happen as Mennonites become more fully integrated into society. Therefore, he emphasizes not only the distinction between church and world but also the different levels of morality by which people can choose to live. In doing so, he creates a theology in which new dualisms threaten to divide people from each other, hierarchies are created in which Christians can easily assume their own superiority, and God's presence is removed from whole spheres of life.

Hershberger's theological perspective continued to stress that living according to God's criteria will create separate teams. However, Hershberger goes further, emphasizing that separate playing fields are necessary in order to remain a team faithful to the kingdom. In order to strengthen the team, Hershberger emphasizes the unique and higher mission of God's team while admitting that the other team has its own, though inferior, place in God's overall plan. This allows the tensions between the Mennonite community and the rest of society to be alleviated somewhat, because each participates in its own variety of the power game without interference. At the same time, suspicion of the other team's strategies is nourished in order to encourage nonconformist strategies faithful to the standards demonstrated by Jesus.

The overall goal of the game is not forgotten by Hershberger. In fact, the principle of love and nonresistance stresses the need to bring the inner and outer, word and deed, together. This encourages the players of the Mennonite team to work at this integration within their own community while occasionally moving "to the other playing field" in order to visibly model and witness to Jesus' self-giving way of the cross. This approach is based on confidence in God, who will use this witness to move the game in the right direction.

John Howard Yoder

In the context of a Mennonite identity that seemed increasingly shaped by establishment culture and indiscriminate borrowing from mainstream Protestantism, John H. Yoder sought to find a theology that met two primary goals. He hoped that his theology would bring about repentance and renewal within the church, while at the same time leading to a greater witness by the church to the larger society. He therefore insisted in his writings that the mainline Protestant labeling of Anabaptist theology as inherently separatist (as demonstrating a "Christ against culture" stance as classified by H. Richard Niebuhr)[40] is inadequate and misleading. Instead, he pointed to the transformational dynamic of the embodied nature of the church *in* culture, patterned after Christ's incarnational presence in history.

In his popular book *The Politics of Jesus*, first published in 1972, Yoder spells out the relevance of Jesus to social ethics and therefore to the broader society.[41] In the chapter entitled "Christ and Power," he concentrates on "power structures" or "patterns" that transcend or precede or condition the individual capacity to make things happen.[42] In line with Hendrikus Berkhof, he suggests that the "principalities and powers" spoken of in the New Testament refer to somewhat the same phenomena that we call religious, intellectual, moral, and social institutions or structures. He suggests, therefore, that the biblical narrative points to the sinfulness of these structures as well as to the continuing providential control that orders them according to the divine will. He thus describes human sin as obedience to these rebellious powers of the fallen world.

The Bible testifies that Jesus has broken the sovereignty of these powers by living a restored and genuinely free human existence, "not the slave of any power, of any law or custom, community or institution, value or theory."[43] That Christ is Lord is "a social, political, structural fact which constitutes a challenge to the Powers . . . It is a declaration about the nature of the cosmos and the significance of history, within which both our conscientious participation and our conscientious objection find their authority and their promise."[44] Thus, Jesus has brought about a radical shift in the human relationship to power by liberating Christians from "the way things are" and creating the possibility of a radical new kind of social order.

Yoder does not focus primarily on the liberation or transformation of the individual person or deal directly with the inner psychological or spiritual factors that have created a loss of autonomy or sense of powerlessness in a person. Instead, he focuses on helping Christians understand external structures and institutions so that they will not be seduced by them. His analysis concentrates on identifying a particular sociopolitical pattern that he names the "Constantinianization" of the church in which a fusion happens between the authority of the church and the power of structures of governance. These create a "framework of normalcy" in which particular power relationships are evaluated on the basis of reason, the orders of nature, common sense, or generalizations arising out of observations of social processes, instead of by the will of God as revealed in Jesus Christ.[45] He insists that when these secondary authorities are fused with the authority of divine providence, the church is not able to see the radical challenge of the gospel of Jesus Christ.

Yoder suggests that Anabaptism, in its attempt to break with this fusion, demonstrated a model of the church as a "messianic community" of reconciliation and agape love under the exclusive lordship of Christ. Because Anabaptism broke with the "fallen powers," creating a visible alternative, it had a revolutionary impact on society. However, the present church has not been suspicious enough of these powers. It has readily accepted the definitional categories of the "world." Therefore, judgment and renewal, rather than gradual reform and nurture, are most necessary.

This revolutionary impulse in Yoder's writings is softened by notions of subordination and obedience. Even though the church knows that the final victory has been won and that Jesus is now the new Lord, it must not impose this new order upon the larger social order violently. It cannot use unworthy means even for worthy ends. Instead, it is "revolutionary subordination" as demonstrated in Jesus' own life, in the early church's attitude to the state, and in the household codes that characterizes the biblical response to domineering power.[46]

This subordination is characterized by servanthood, a radical giving up of the need to control the direction in which society is moving. For those in superordinate positions, this implies a giving up of all domineering uses of their status. For those in subordinate positions, this implies an acceptance of life within a given status without resentment. Following the way of the cross means accepting the cost of social nonconformity, living the life of servanthood, self-giving, and even "self-abasement" in order to demonstrate the reality of the confession that Christ is Lord.[47] Thus Christians can participate "in the character of God's victorious patience with the rebellious powers of his creation."[48]

Yoder's efforts to disentangle the authority structures that determine how we live often focus on the language we use to talk about power. He suggests that there are three different kinds of language built on differing assumptions of authority.[49] When the church speaks in "marketplace semantics," it must use the ordinary definitions set by the establishment. Thus it will use the terms of sociology and politics to describe the governing structures of society. When the church speaks constructively and critically to the governing power in society, it can make use of the self-justifying language of the rulers to call them to accountability. Then it will speak of responsibility and integrity. But when speaking within the church, Yoder wants to use the covenant language of ministry and service, which claims "the authority of incarnation for the content of messianic servanthood."[50] Instead of the language of power and authority, the church will therefore speak about the gifts of the Spirit, about servant leadership, and about love for the enemy.

In the use of these different languages, Yoder is most concerned about the substantial difference between the language of legitimation, by which power is justified, and the language of prescription, which authorizes the way of discipleship, since both are based on claims of truth. He is concerned that the absolute claim of revelation by which the church is to live should not be polluted by norms drawn from other sources. At the same time, he does not believe that the church should coercively try to control society with its prescriptive language. Instead, the church can demonstrate an alternative social order, thus producing changes within the larger social structure.

In Yoder's theology the notion of two playing fields is rejected. The two kingdoms are not understood to be on two separate levels that therefore cannot clash directly; instead, Yoder understands the time of the church as a period of "the overlapping of two aeons" that exist simultaneously in time. "They differ . . . in nature or in direction; one points backward to human history outside of (before) Christ; the other points forward to the fullness of the kingdom of God, of which it is a foretaste. Each aeon has a social manifestation: the former in the 'world,' the latter in the church or the body of Christ. The new aeon came into history in a decisive way with the incarnation . . . the new aeon involves a radical break with the old."[51] The different goal toward which each team is moving can be seen most clearly if one examines the strategy used by the church. Those identifying with the reign of God will accept the place given them on the margins of society, confident that their leader will win the game in the end. They will insist that power or control not be used to move the game in the direction of the goal as they see it. Instead, they will concentrate on proclaiming their leader's power, identifying false authority, and attempting to bring conformity to the team by stressing the proper strategy. This strategy, based on obedience to Christ's lordship, is expressed in the language of servanthood and the way of the cross as modeled by their leader. Yoder assumes that this strategy will not result in social withdrawal, but rather will encourage a unified move toward the proper goal by a team united by a common strategy.

Seeking God's Kingdom Incarnate

The writings of Menno Simons, Guy F. Hershberger, and John H. Yoder illustrate both the variety of ways in which the Mennonite theological game can be played and the boundaries of the game as they have been established through time. They also illustrate that the goal and basic strategy of the game continue to be debated as the players change and the game shifts to various parts of the playing field.[52] Anyone entering the game in the early days of this new millennium quickly realizes that the game is already well under way. However, the basic challenge continues to be discerning the direction the game should go to reach the goal while reinterpreting the criteria that characterize the strategies used by God's team.

Howard Loewen has suggested that there are two primary directions that are being debated in the Mennonite theological game.[53] The first, arising out of the heart of Mennonite theology, is a "strong sense of the incarnational reality of the Gospel in culture." This creates a "transformational grammar" strongly linked to the "paradigmatic way of Israel, Jesus and the early Church." This seems to be in accordance with the rules of the game captured by Menno Simons' understanding of the newness of the kingdom of God and the importance of regeneration. It is also caught by Hershberger's emphasis on the noncoercive power of love in a church that creatively seeks alternatives to the normal power games that are a part of most social institutions. And it continues to be expressed in the freedom that comes with the knowledge that dominating powers are already under the authority of Christ as stressed by Yoder. All of these point to the empowerment of individuals and the church through God's grace, and they name the goal of the theological game as a transformation of the team into God's people.

This emphasis leads to a game in which the team is constantly changing as new members are invited into the game and existing members confess their need for transformation. The focus is not on competition between players, but rather on the transformation of strategies that destroy and damage into strategies that heal and transform. Thus, any truth claim that is made is tied to the empowerment and freedom gained through Christ by the power of the Holy Spirit. In this model of the game, God is seen as the ultimate source of power and authority. Human power that moves toward the goal is always power that is in the midst of being transformed. God's revelation becomes embodied in salvation. Thus, the church "is the world being transformed."[54] Though this may result in nonconformity to the strategies of society, it also allows cooperation with society when it moves in the direction of healing and salvation.

Loewen also points to the other direction that the game can go by admitting that sectarianism and separatism have been a part of the Mennonite ethos during much of their history. He suggests that this direction came about because the transformationist center was overshadowed "internally by the social reality of physical separation from culture and moral deterioration in the community, and externally by the theological definition given to this separatism by mainstream religion."[55] The problem, as Loewen sees it, was that the transformationist ethos at the heart of Mennonite life was not applied to the broader spheres of surrounding culture and not lived out in the moral community itself.

While the external definitions during the early time of persecution as well as in more recent times did support unwanted separations, and Mennonites did not always live up to their best moral understandings, this brief overview of power and authority in Mennonite theologizing suggests that the impulse for separation was present in the theological articulations themselves. Menno Simons' understanding of the church "without spot or wrinkle" already contained the seeds of a dualistic theology that polarized people, thus creating domination and oppression. This perfectionist impulse expressed itself in strict criteria that could easily be used to judge other persons and institutions as unworthy of being the church. Thus the Schleitheim Confession could draw a boundary suggesting that being a magistrate was already outside of the perfection of Christ because the rule of government is by nature "fleshly." So too, Hershberger could draw another boundary placing resistance to injustice outside of the church's mandate because any resistance is by nature selfish and therefore not motivated by love. Yoder's boundaries are more subtle. However, his insistence on a particular language and institutional form to express the lordship of Christ allows him to put strict boundaries between the faithful church and the unfaithful church, between prophets and other Christians. A church that is not Anabaptist according to his definitions is suspect of Constantinianism and therefore of being unfaithful.[56]

Separation is rooted in suspicion and obedience, two hermeneutical approaches or strategies that at first glance seem opposite to each other. They are, however, similar in that both are responses to authority and exhibit themselves in a community in both word and deed. Suspicion of the "world" and its idolatry has been basic to Mennonite theology since the time of Menno. This suspicion has created an important and necessary understanding of nonconformity that has encouraged the church to question society's norms and to work creatively at discernment in its involvement in the larger culture. However, it has also separated Christians from each other and contributed to a division between the secular and religious exercise of power. Banning ideas and people who do not conform to the accepted norms of the church to the sphere of the "world" has therefore been justified theologically.

Suspicion of the "other," the one different from the self, continues to permeate much of Mennonite theological literature even when the issues of the separation of church and state are not central. This separation is not expressed so much by overt articulation as by the absence of a variety of voices present in the churches. It is still difficult to find theology written by women or by persons from non-European ethnic and cultural backgrounds. Though the voices of these persons may not have been deliberately silenced, they have heard the subtle message that names them outsiders to the theological game. This silencing has correctly been named as a subtle form of domination.[57]

The emphasis on the primary obedience to God as ultimate authority is biblically grounded and creates a church committed to finding God's will. However, obedience to God and obedience to human authority within the church can easily be confused. The language of obedience and servanthood has also made it easy to ignore the mediation of human leadership and to deny its exercise of power.[58] Moreover, an idealistic view of authority within the church has discouraged it from wrestling with the needs of leaders and with the various power relationships that are present within every community. Several examples: Mennonites have identified with Jesus and his life and teachings, creating in the process an ideal model for discipleship, but they have failed to include the fallible disciples in that model. They have written an ideal Anabaptist history while ignoring many of the actual Anabaptists. They have promoted an ideal theology of ministry that has hesitated to name the political patterns of relationships in church institutions. Thus, the existence of domination is denied, and necessary authority is undermined.

Suspicion of, and obedience toward, authority can easily become partners in a game, creating an ethos of domination and submission within a community. This is so when these strategies give or take authority from the other on the basis of stereotypes or truth claims that are considered absolute and therefore not open to further insight. These static truths become the justification for creating clear boundaries around the team and for insisting on unquestioned conformity to norms of behavior and belief for all members of the team—a rigid set of rules. Attention is diverted from the variety of ways in which authoritative relationships can be experienced, to a unified ethical system based on obedience to one norm. Thus a game is created in which the dynamic transformation of the team itself is stifled.

This struggle between a transformative impulse and a separatist impulse must be traced back to the understanding of God that informs this theology. Not only is the notion of a uniform church evident in Mennonite theology, but so also is a view of God that can be described in terms that are absolute and uniform. For example, Waldemar Janzen has suggested that the Mennonite tendency to see the Old Testament as superseded by the New Testament is based on the church's not wanting its inner tranquillity to be disturbed by the "realism of the Old Testament in which God's activity cannot be disentangled from history, war and judgment."[59] At times even the picture of Jesus has been stylized in Mennonite theology so that the complex nature of the authority and power of Jesus is hidden in the image of a nonresistant man who willingly gives up power. Jesus' powerful healings and his authoritative leadership of his disciples tend to be ignored when speaking about the "way of the cross." In addition, the dynamic work of the Holy Spirit has often been separated from a static understanding of the Jesus of the Bible. Strong dualisms can often be traced to an oversimplified image of God.

J. Lawrence Burkholder and Gordon Kaufman are two Mennonite theologians who have questioned the separatist direction of the Mennonite theological game. Burkholder, in his discussion of the moral ambiguities

93

created by his strong sense of social responsibility, and Kaufman, in his insistence on the human aspect of all theology, encourage a solidarity with others in the search for strategies that embody positive power and authority.[60] These thinkers have encouraged a dynamic theological game that must grow and change as it engages with a world searching for more humane modes of power and authority. The contrasting directions of transformation and separatism have opened a number of options to players of the game today. Naming the Mennonite theological game "In Search of God's Kingdom Incarnate" might be helpful, for this slogan can remind us that "thy kingdom come on earth as it is in heaven" is a prayer more than a truth claim, and that "the Word become flesh" happens at God's initiative more than ours.

CHAPTER FIVE

The Abuse of Power among Mennonites in South Russia, 1789–1919

JACOB A. LOEWEN

AND WESLEY J. PRIEB

One of the most compelling chapters in Mennonite history involves the settlement of large tracts of land in the Ukraine from the late eighteenth century into the early decades of the twentieth century, when the flourishing Mennonite commonwealth was destroyed in the aftermath of the Bolshevik Revolution and Stalinist collectivization. This chapter recounts in often disturbing detail the ways in which the Russian Mennonite commonwealth compromised Menno Simons' vision of a religious people that operated without the use of worldly "force," a compromise brought on by the institution of a "state" within the faith community and perpetuated by, among other things, an inequitable distribution of land and resources.

Menno Simons objected strongly to four misuses of the sword (power) on the part of both the Catholic Church and the mainstream of the Reformation. These abuses were (1) the use of the sword of iron to defend the truth; (2) the use of the sword to convert people; (3) the use of the sword to impose church discipline; and (4) the use of the sword to protect property and privilege. He called believers into a lifestyle that depended only on the sword of the Spirit. But instead of growing in fidelity to the vision of kingdom, citizens practicing a lifestyle of abstaining from all use of force or coercion, the northern stream of Mennonites—the group that moved from Holland through North Germany, Poland, and South Russia—underwent a series of slippages, adjustments, and compromises that ultimately led to the widespread abuse of power in the Mennonite commonwealth in South Russia. When the Mennonites were given a mandate to govern themselves in the colonies and to become a "development engine" for the country, the former victims of persecution embarked on a new road. They were not aware of the Pandora's box of power possibilities that they were opening. Could the persecuted become the persecutors?

It did not take long to find out. When the Mennonites arrived in South Russia, nomadic tribes still roamed the steppes. These people saw easy booty in the unarmed Mennonite communities.[1] The Mennonite settlers repeatedly appealed to Russian authorities for protection, and the Russian police exercised immediate heavy-handed, frontier-style justice by indiscriminately punishing and killing suspects whenever an injustice was reported.[2] Often Mennonite complaints became the occasion for violent governmental retribution against tribal offenders.[3] Representative justice was often administered—all suspects were flogged so as to teach a lesson both to the guilty and the innocent. Here we see a clear compromise of Menno's ideal that no Christian should appeal to the secular "sword" for protection of personal property.[4]

The Mennonite *privilegium* granted by the czar empowered the colonists to govern their own civic and community affairs. This meant that colony authorities could issue local ordinances and order their own police deputies to enforce them. The typical self-governing civil order in the Mennonite colonies was a village governed by an executive committee composed of an unpaid mayor (*Schulze*), two assistants, and a paid clerk, assisted by one unarmed, unpaid "police" deputy per ten households. The villages were linked under the central authority of the *Gebietsamt*, consisting of a paid mayor-in-chief (*Oberschulze*) and his office staff.[5] The *Gebietsamt* levied taxes, granted travel documents, preserved law and order, issued orders for communal labor, hired herdsmen, and so on. In short, it provided all the necessary functions of civil government. It is ironic that the very Russian law that guaranteed their new colonists privileges also led to the creation of a Mennonite state and to the eventual merger of the Mennonite Church with that state.[6]

Abuses by Mennonite Employers

Many non-Mennonites conducted business or found employment in Mennonite villages and towns. Sometimes colony authorities were forced to arrest, judge, and punish non-Mennonite offenders. The most common offenses were drunkenness, disorderly conduct, and theft. Mennonite deputies soon were flogging increasing numbers of non-Mennonite offenders. But over time Mennonites themselves also came to feel the sting of Mennonite power wielding. During the early years in the colonies, landholders would often provide a small plot of land for a house, garden, and grain for the (Mennonite) landless. Such live-in workers were called *Anwohner* or "adjacent residents." In exchange for such privileges, all the able-bodied members of the *Anwohner* family worked for the landholder, who usually paid them in kind. Soon the *Anwohner* system, which seemed satisfactory, was discontinued, and "slum" sections began to develop on the edges of the larger Mennonite villages. These people were called *Kleinhaeusler* ("little-house people"), or *Armenreihe* ("the poor row"), or even *Einwohner* ("renters") because they did not even own the hovels they occupied.[7]

Totally dependent on finding employment, they did not even have a garden plot or a cow to put on communal pasture. Some were completely dependent on charity. Thus, by the mid-nineteenth century more than two-thirds of all the Mennonites in Russia were landless. They were dependent either on establishing a business, learning a trade, working as day laborers for other Mennonites, or, as a last resort, surviving on private or public dole.[8] Many of these landless Mennonites would have drifted to other colonies or to Russian cities, but the *Gebietsamt* controlled the required travel documents and was not inclined to issue many because it wanted to prevent the loss of cheap Mennonite labor.

It is clear that many Mennonite landholders used their economic and political power to develop a stratified society that clearly compromised Menno's view of stewardship in community as well as equality and brotherhood in the church. In their treatment of non-Mennonite labor, Mennonites opted for the standards of their Russian neighbors. They did not make any effort to improve their wages, nor did most of them create better working conditions. It is true, however, that Johann Cornies (who is discussed below) introduced a labor statute that at least prevented some of the more serious abuses.[9]

Unlike their Russian neighbors, however, Mennonites usually worked in the fields together with their outside laborers, often working as hard or harder than their employees. However, the relationship between the Mennonite worker and his non-Mennonite employees was marked in the social distance that separated the two. Servants did not share the master's table. On returning from their common work, they were strictly segregated: the Mennonite went to a comfortable house, the Russian worker to the workers' barracks or to his sod hovel. The greatest discrepancy was in the inequality of the return each received from their common labor.[10]

The most severe abuse suffered by non-Mennonite labor was punishment for theft. According to one anecdote, a Mennonite once discovered a Russian in his grain bin filling bags with grain. Since it was late Saturday afternoon, the Mennonite simply boarded up the bin with the Russian still inside. On Monday morning he notified the mayor's office, and the deputies came, extracted the thief, and flogged him.[11]

Landlord Hegemony

Only landholders could vote in colony affairs, according to Russian law. As land became scarce, more and more people became landless. The landless were not eligible to vote or to run for office in colony affairs. One landless person said, "One thousand people vote and three thousand others just have to swallow the pill the voters give them!"[12] Another Russian rule was that the property grant entrusted to a colonist was indivisible. Only the youngest son could inherit it. This rule prevented fathers from subdividing their farms. Inevitably the other sons became landless.

During the Crimean War the *Gebietsamt* introduced family-based rather than property-based taxation to supply wagons and drivers for hauling war supplies. Whereas landowners hired servants, the landless had to borrow money to buy horses and wagons and then operate the wagons in lieu of the cash they were unable to raise.[13] Other forms of abuse involved reducing the amount of land *Anwohner* were permitted to cultivate, restricting the number of animals they could put on communal pasture, raising the pasturage fees of the landless, and assessing them with all kinds of new levies, including a school levy, a pasturage levy, and herdsmen levy.[14]

Class System of Mennonite Estates

After 1817 many prosperous Mennonites purchased land outside the boundaries of the Mennonite colonies. At their height, when World War I began, there were about five hundred estates in Russia.[15] These *Khutors* controlled an estimated one million acres of land. The largest estate, that of Wilhelm Martens, is reputed to have comprised about 300,000 acres.[16] These large estate owners represented only 3 percent of the Mennonite population, but they controlled 30 percent of all the land in Mennonite hands. They alone employed 22 percent of the Mennonite population.[17]

The estate owners often aligned themselves with their Russian noble counterparts and became part of the oppressive system of Russian land-ownership. The unhappiness of landless serfs, together with the urban worker dissatisfaction, eventually produced both the 1905 and 1917 revolutions. At one time five out of seven positions on the regional government council in Melitopel were filled by Mennonite estate owners, and two Mennonites even served in the Duma, the Russian parliament.[18] Thus when revolution came, the Mennonites, considered to be ethnic foreigners and part of the prevailing power structure, were singled out as targets by the revolutionaries.[19] On one Mennonite estate three generations of males were massacred by bandits in a single day.[20] Traditionally Mennonites have considered themselves "people of the land." Cornelius Krahn cites a villager in Russia who said, "God is our father, the soil is our mother, nature is our teacher."[21] At a Mennonite anniversary celebration in 1925, Jacob Kroeker said that land may have been a cause of Mennonite downfall because "[We] love the sickle more than the pursuit of peace and the ownership of the earth more than our spiritual inheritance."[22]

The Impact of Mennonite Wealth

Unprecedented economic growth opened new possibilities for land-related industrial development for Mennonites in South Russia. By 1908 there were more than one hundred windmills in Chortitza and Molotschna colonies and another seventy-three motor-powered mills. By 1914 two-fifths of all flour and feed mills in Russia were located in the south, largely on Mennonite lands.[23] The four largest Mennonite mills had an annual production turnover of over 6 million rubles, of which the Niebuhr mill in Alexandrovsk alone produced 50 percent.[24]

By 1914 eight Mennonite manufacturers were producing 10 percent of the Russian farm machinery.[25] By that time Mennonite-made machines were operating everywhere in Russia, from the eastern Ukraine to the far reaches of Siberia.[26] Indeed, they were competing with American giants like McCormack and International Harvester Company—which opened a factory near Moscow in 1912—not only in Russia, but also on the world market.[27] The enormous wealth accumulated by Mennonite industry, the estates, and landed farmers in the colonies made a great impact—both positive and negative—on society and the church community. Whereas estate owners might expect to make 200,000 to 250,000 rubles profit per annum, and a village farmer might make between 2000 and 9000 rubles, by comparison, when we look at the income of the landless Mennonites, we find an enormous difference. An educated teacher's salary averaged about 600 rubles per year, and a good craftsman earned about 500 rubles per annum; but a Mennonite laborer got about 100 rubles annually, and his Russian counterpart got between 60 and 90 rubles per annum. Females received half the amount paid to males.[28]

The rapid increase in wealth, especially among Mennonite estate owners and industrialists, had a very dramatic effect on Mennonite communal solidarity. The super-rich no longer felt comfortable in Mennonite villages. In order to escape community pressures and control, these people now moved their residences to private estates or to nearby Russian cities. The super-rich felt more comfortable with the Russian aristocracy than they did with fellow Mennonites.[29] To the credit of the wealthy, they did not withdraw from Mennonite life entirely. They continued to be willing to invest large sums in better schools, hospitals, and so on. In addition, the tiny minority of the super-rich contributed some 30 percent of the operating costs of programs of alternative service to serving in the military.[30] But there are clear indications the super-rich also cheated in the property values they reported to the colonies for such tax purposes.[31]

The super-rich formed a separate in-group whose members socialized with each other and whose children intermarried, thus creating some vast family fortunes. Ehrt argues that this produced two Mennonite economies, the capitalist economy of the estate owners and industrialists, and the peasant economy of most Mennonite villagers.[32] However, in retrospect we should add two more economies: that of the landless laborers, who were exploited by both groups and who survived at more or less subsistence level, and that of the "poor row," who were dependent on private or public dole.

When we look at the resulting attitudes, we notice that the super-rich were generally very condescending toward their Mennonite co-religionists. However, toward the landless poor they manifested downright disdain. They tended to consider the poor irresponsible and lazy, unwilling to put forth the effort necessary to improve their lot.[33] Estate owners and industrialists also had definite feelings of superiority toward Russian peasants and serfs. They observed a strict class distinction toward their Russian labor. As their wealth increased, the master-servant distinction became increasingly marked. And should a servant ever displease his estate-owning master, he could now expect instant and rough retribution.[34] Observers note that by 1914 the Mennonite elite expected increasing amounts of deference from their laborers and servants.

It should be noted, however, that officially all Mennonites, including the estate owners, were still classed as peasants, even though some of the estate owners functioned as nobility. Just how much solidarity Russian peasants felt toward Mennonites peasants, even when the latter were still poor, has not been documented. But there is no question that when the peasant and worker unrest began at the beginning of the twentieth century, the peasants not only reacted against the Mennonite wealthy, but they also considered the poorer Mennonites to be traitors to the peasant class.[35] John C. Toews points out that especially during the 1905 revolution, nobles made a conscious effort to deflect the revolutionaries' anger away from themselves toward Mennonite "foreigners."[36]

The Mennonite aristocracy exerted considerable influence on Mennonite leadership. When the elite removed themselves physically from village observation and control, they also largely withdrew themselves from the authority of church and colony leadership. This not only weakened overall Mennonite communal solidarity but also greatly increased the insecurity of Mennonite leadership in both church and colony. To combat the erosion of authority that the church and the colony leadership experienced, both now moved toward greater authoritarian control. Before long the church, which had always considered itself the senior partner in Mennonite community authority, was reduced to the junior partner. Eventually, both church and colony leadership worked hand in glove to protect their turf.[37] Several of these dimensions will be explored more fully below.

The amazing shift in the Mennonites' life in South Russia from a people on a pilgrimage, seeking religious freedom and basic human rights, to a stratified class society with economic, political, and religious power vested in a privileged minority that controlled both church and state leaves one almost breathless. But it was also creating increased pressures for a major round of reform.

Johann Cornies

Johann Cornies (1789–1848) was a man of vision, determined to improve the lot of Mennonites in Russia. Through his aggressive leadership, Mennonites became the model farmers and the "development engine" they had promised the czar they would be. In this effort, Cornies was fully supported by Senator Kontenius, the chairman of the Settlement Guardians Committee in Odessa that represented the immediate Russian government authority to which the Mennonite colonies related at that time.[38]

Cornies started a model farm on his own private estate at Juschanle near Ohrloff in 1813. Five hundred *dessiatines* of this land had been a gift from the czar. Some four years later Cornies' personal effort to improve agriculture and animal husbandry became the focal point of an agricultural society that eventually embraced all the Mennonite colonies in southern Russia. By 1830 the Russian government had already elevated this society to the status of a "free academy"[39] and not only named Cornies its permanent head but also made him a lifetime counselor to the Russian government. Backed by the full authority of the Russian crown, Cornies became the "de facto Mennonite Czar" in southern Russia, who could single-handedly issue decrees and force both the Mennonite Church leadership and colony authorities into compliance.[40]

There are many stories about Cornies that illustrate his character. Once Cornies, riding unarmed, discovered an Armenian pasturing his flock of sheep on Cornies' land. The intruder was well armed and rather aggressive. In spite of this, Cornies confronted the man and demanded payment for the use of his pasture land. The Armenian got violently angry, but

Cornies quietly stood his ground until the intruder finally gave him the money. Cornies then invited him to spend the rest of the day and also the night with him, and they became good friends.[41] It is reported that Cornies once said, "I trust no one. I pay no attention to insults. I depend on God as my Savior. There are opportunities here for all. But I want no one cold, no one lukewarm. In God's name work!"[42]

Cornies was not a villain. He was a man who had a vision for the Mennonite people. He was not on an unbridled quest for power. In fact, Cornies refused the noble title offered to him by the czar because, as he put it, "I want to remain a simple Mennonite."[43] It was his utopian dream for an ordered society under God's sovereignty that drove him to become increasingly autocratic. On the whole, the Cornies' period in the Mennonite colonies was a period of unprecedented educational, social, and economic development that raised the overall standard of Mennonite life to a degree that had hardly seemed possible. At first the village and colonial civil authorities cooperated fully with Cornies' reforms, but eventually their patience grew thin, for he was constantly ordering them to enforce all kinds of new ordinances.

Wittingly or unwittingly, Johann Cornies became instrumental in moving the Mennonite colonies farther and farther into the Russian governmental power orbit.[44] The *Gebietsamt* felt the erosion of its authority very deeply. It could execute only those of its decisions which Cornies approved. We can summarize the impact as follows: first, he helped tip the balance of power between bishops and colony administrators in favor of the latter.[45] The bishops were thus forced to become dependent on the powerful *Oberschulze*, who, for all practical purposes, was the local representative of the Russian state. This shift, says Calvin Redekop, moved Russian Mennonites out of the *Gemeinschaft* "meetinghouse" milieu and firmly entrenched them in the individualistic and capitalistic "counting house mentality."[46]

Cornies was also instrumental in secularizing education in the Mennonite colonies. Up to this point teachers had been part of the ministry and thus were considered servants of the church, subordinate to the ministers and certainly to the bishop. After the Russian government gave Cornies full control of education in 1843, schools were effectively removed from church control, and no teacher could be appointed without Cornies' (and hence Russian state) approval.[47] Then, during the Crimean War, Cornies'

Agricultural Union became the driving force that pushed the Mennonite colonies into large-scale participation in the Russian war effort.[48] He also brought Russian government authority, in the form of the Odessa Guardian Committee, into the day-to-day affairs of the Mennonite colonies.[49]

Under Cornies' leadership the prosperity of the landholders, coupled with the rapid population expansion, destroyed the original egalitarian society and produced a three-tiered one. On the top was the landholding and governing minority. In the middle was the landless majority, which was deprived of the vote in civic affairs. And finally, at the very bottom were the non-Mennonite workers and servants employed by the landed minority. These workers, in spite of Cornies' efforts to introduce fair labor practices, often were no better off than the serfs under Russian nobility.[50] There was a breakdown of the brotherhood concept in both church and community. When the landless appealed for redress from their church brothers, the village and colony leaders denounced them as rabble-rousers and revolutionaries.[51] Intense resentment developed among those who felt abused. It is known that Cornies unilaterally terminated farming privileges of farmers he considered irresponsible, released teachers if they did not carry proper credentials, and had bishops removed from office if they did not support his reforms. Thus, the great achievements of Cornies were tarnished. He compromised the vision of Menno Simons because he used coercion to achieve his goals.

Selbstschutz

By far the most tragic departure from Menno's vision in South Russia was the organization of the self-defense army (*Selbstschutz*) during the Bolshevik Revolution. While the church provided some biblical justification for organizing a self-defense army, it was the *Gebietsamt* that organized and managed this military venture by the Mennonites. What was the cause? The treaty of Brest-Litovsk (April 1918) led to the occupation of South Russia by German and Austro-Hungarian troops. Since the Russian revolution had already broken out in the previous year, the anarchy and the destruction at the hands of bandits and revolutionaries was already in progress in South Russia by the time the occupation troops arrived. Some of the largest and wealthiest Mennonite estates had already been plundered, and their owners had been forced to flee.

With the arrival of the Austro-German troops, Mennonite estate own-

ers now saw an opportunity to regain control of their confiscated possessions. Some of them now armed themselves under Austro-German tute-
lage and organized posse-like groups that attacked the rebels and reclaimed
the estates. The rebel leaders were summarily executed.[52] The presence of
the occupation army in the colonies, often quartered in Mennonite homes,
brought to the Mennonite youth full exposure to weapons and military
force for the first time. Many young men and boys became deeply enam-
ored with the military precision displayed by the army units. Some young
men voluntarily participated in the training drills.[53] The Mennonites were
also pressured by other German-speaking settlers—Baptists, Lutherans,
and Catholics—who did not hesitate to use arms to defend themselves.[54]

When the Austro-German army had to withdraw some seven months
later, following the signing of the Treaty of Versailles in November of
1918, a serious power vacuum developed in the area surrounding the Mennonite colonies. The White (czarist government) forces, regrouping in the
south, and the Bolshevik Red Army forces, coming from the north, had
been so far unable to defeat each other. This standoff provided an excellent
opportunity for anarchist bandits like Nestor Machno to loot and plunder
the unguarded Mennonite colonies that lay in the "no-man's land" between
the opposing armies.[55] Each day brought new stories of bloodshed, looting,
raping, and killing. One Mennonite is supposed to have said: "Let them
finally take my property, but if they touch my wife and daughter, I'm ready
to use the axe."[56] The remnants of the occupation army, who remained behind with arms and ammunition, were most eager to organize the settlers
into a defense force.[57] The White Army, amassed south of the Mennonite
colonies, likewise urged the Mennonites to take up arms.[58]

Then, most surprisingly, the influence of the returning alternative service workers supported the move toward self-defense. In the forestry
camps and in the medical service trains, they had been wearing military-
type uniforms and had been operating under a rigid command hierarchy,
using military-type discipline. The result was that some strong leaders
emerged among them. These leaders quickly challenged the parochial and
sometimes lackadaisical leadership in the churches and villages in the colonies. These young leaders were appalled at the growing anarchy and were
determined to stem the tide. Thus they not only influenced public opinion,
but they actually formed the core of the volunteers for reestablishing law
and order.[59]

The erosion of Mennonite loyalty to traditional ideals of peace and nonresistance made it possible for church leaders as well as civil officers to justify self-defense. The estate owners were already committed to upholding law and order, having aligned themselves with the land-owning elite Russians of their day. Once law and order collapsed under revolutionary conditions in South Russia, the emergence of the *Selbstschutz* was more or less inevitable, given the prevailing attitudes.[60]

The Power Struggle between *Lehramt* and *Gebietsamt*

When the first group of Mennonite émigrés left Danzig in 1788, there was no minister or elder among them. During the time the group camped for winter in the Russian village of Dubrovna, they realized to their dismay that they were without servant leadership. They tried to correct the situation by electing deacons and ministers (at Dubrovna) and an elder as soon as they arrived in their settlement area in South Russia. They asked the elders in Danzig to ordain by mail the people they had selected. This was done, but doubts about the legitimacy of these "mail-order" servants lingered.[61] This situation lasted for about three years. Finally two elders from Prussia came to ordain the selected individuals in person. The insecurity of the interim, however, had laid the foundation for long-range problems.

Since the inception of the Anabaptist movement in Holland, the *Lehramt* (church officers, literally, "teachership") had functioned as the maximal authority of the believing group. Now, in Russia, the insecure *Lehramt* felt threatened from two sides. On the one hand, the Russian crown, having negotiated the *Privilegium* (terms of immigration) with Bartsch and Hoeppner, the original "spy delegates," considered these two men the legitimate leaders of the settlers. The czar consulted, extended privileges, and heaped favors on the two men. This resulted in severe tension, especially for the *Lehramt*. This tension increased until the *Lehramt* finally decided to denounce especially Hoeppner for insubordination to the duly installed church authorities and for misappropriating government funds. Hoeppner was condemned, stripped of his property, and sentenced to exile in Siberia. However, the next czar, having realized the internal power struggle in the Mennonite community, exonerated Bartsch and returned all his property.[62]

On the other hand, there was the new *Gebietsamt*. This was established as soon as the first villages of the colony were laid out. It too was basically a church election. All landholders were also church members, so all who voted for the *Gebietsamt* were also church members. The new colony government was recognized not only by the settlers themselves but also by the Settlement Guardians Committee (SGC), the immediate Russian governmental authority to which the Mennonite colonists related. The SGC considered the *Gebietsamt* the legitimate governing body of these self-governing colonies.[63] When unrepentant Hoeppner then leaned toward the *Gebietsamt* as maximal authority, the insecure *Lehramt* also began to react against the *Gebietsamt*.[64]

The Russian colonies thus provided the first occasion for a full-fledged dual governing structure. The *Lehramt*, on the basis of church tradition, considered itself maximal under God. However, the *Gebietsamt* was recognized as the maximal authority by the SGC and the Russian government. This dual governing structure soon ran into conflict. All colonists were church members, and any misbehavior was a church affair, according to the *Lehramt*. However, the *Gebietsamt* was to govern the civil life of the colony according to Russian civil and criminal law. Thus, certain types and occasions of misconduct were defined as the responsibility of the civil colony government. This overlap soon created serious misunderstandings and severe tensions.[65]

A major confrontation between the two governing bodies came to a head in 1806 over a case of public fornication about which history provides only fragmentary information. Al Reimer has given us a fictional account. The account here presented is a composite of historical tidbits and Reimer's fiction.[66] A Mennonite youth was caught behind a haystack fornicating with a Russian peasant girl. The *Oberschulze*'s deputies apprehended the two in the act and gave them a severe lashing as per Russian law. When the bishop learned of this disciplinary event, he was furious. A sexual transgression by a church member was the domain of the church. He considered the mayor's action an infringement on the bishop's authority and demanded a public apology. The mayor countered by stating that this public interracial infraction was a disturbance of the public order for which he, the mayor, was responsible according to Russian law. The bishop, however, continued to insist on a public apology from the mayor-in-chief. When that was not forthcoming, Bishop Jakob Enns used what he considered his bishop's prerogative and excommunicated Klaas Wiens, the offending colony official, for insubordination to his elder/bishop and for using church-forbidden violence as punishment.[67]

Only four years later, however, the very same bishop began to feel that congregational discipline alone was no longer effective to deter deviant behavior among church members. As a result, Bishop Enns, who had earlier excommunicated the *Oberschulze* for having used physical punishment on an erring church member, now appealed to the *Gebietsamt* to strengthen the church's disciplinary actions by meting out corporal and financial punishments to those whom the church disciplined.[68] Consequently, church discipline could now be accompanied by village or colony discipline. The latter could include fines, other economic sanctions, imprisonment, and lashing. In fact, Bishop Enns not only wanted to deliver church miscreants to "secular" colony justice, but he even asked the colony authorities to exile all the members of his own leadership team who opposed his approach to church discipline.[69] Obviously church discipline had lost its redemptive intent and had become a punitive instrument of power. Ehrt sees the landowner-preacher-mayor system—the commonwealth structure—as the crucial factor that robbed Mennonite community life of much of its moral integrity.[70] The church had forgotten Menno Simons' insistence that the sword of government was not to be used for church discipline.

By 1812 a number of ministers were objecting strongly against Bishop Enns's use of force to carry out church discipline. This group called for a "return to Menno Simons," especially in using the ban as a vehicle of redemption rather than of punishment. These ministers called on church people to separate themselves from those who would use the Russian flogging whip as an instrument of the church.[71] The result was the emergence of a new subdenomination, the *Kleinegemeinde*. In order to punish this group, *Lehramt* and *Gebietsamt* colluded and refused to recognize *Kleinegemeinde* ministers as clergy, which forced them to work on communal work projects like lay people, while all the other Mennonite ministers were exempt from such work.[72]

The tension between the two governing entities in the colonies became even stronger when Johann Cornies came on the scene. As we have seen, Cornies effectively became the Mennonite Czar of South Russia. He could unilaterally issue decrees, and the SGC and the Russian government itself would back him to the hilt in their enforcement. The first governing body to challenge Cornies' authority was the *Lehramt*, specifically *Aeltester* (Bishop) Warkentin, who served well over two-thirds of the churches in Molotschna colony. He made a scathing denunciation of Cornies before the SGC, insisting on exile to Siberia as punishment. Since he had been heard out politely, Warkentin assumed victory and announced Cornies' exile on his return to the colony.[73] However, this was premature, because on further investigation the SGC demanded Bishop Warkentin's defrocking on the grounds of opposing legitimate government. Cornies now forced the rest of the *Aelteste* to execute the defrocking.[74]

When Bishop Wiens, one of Warkentin's successors, stepped up the opposition to Cornies, the SGC ordered that he not only be defrocked but that he be banished from Russia.[75] Cornies now stepped up his campaign against the authority of the bishops. In 1843 he convinced the czar to proclaim him the head of all colony education. This effectively removed teachers from *Lehramt* control and secularized them. From now on only those teachers who had Cornies' approval, and hence the approval of the Russian government, could operate. This action caused one *Aeltester* to exclaim in frustration: "Now they have taken everything away from us."[76] Cornies not only went after the bishops who opposed him, but he frequently ordered individual churches to excommunicate individual church members who opposed his reforms. The result was some rather widespread ministerial disapproval of Cornies' autocratic approaches.[77]

The *Gebietsamt* did not launch any special campaign against Cornies. *Oberschulze* Johann Klassen did accompany Bishop Warkentin to Odessa to complain to the SGC, but he himself seems to have taken no overt action against Cornies. However, the *Gebietsamt* did feel the erosion of its authority very deeply. As stated earlier, it could execute only those of its decisions which Cornies approved, and it had to enforce endless decrees unilaterally ordered by Cornies in the name of the Agricultural Union, which Cornies had established under the authorization of the czar.

Cornies' authoritarian rule in the colonies led to a third collusion between Mennonite church and state. When Cornies died in 1848, the two governing bodies decided to field a common candidate for *Oberschulze* so as to be able to wrest some power from the Agricultural Union. They were determined to prevent the development of a dictatorial dynasty in the Agricultural Union. Then in 1851, as part of the *Lehramt's* effort to gain more ecclesiastical control, the *Aelteste* of all the colonies decided to form a bishop's union. This new body declared all the churches in the colonies subordinate (*Untergeordnet*). It gave itself authority to legislate and to speak for the churches without consultation with the church members themselves.[78] This union went against the original "servant" status of the *Lehramt*. It also separated the *Aelteste* from the churches, because until now an *Aeltester* dealt only with the specific church or churches that had selected him. The *Aelteste* were not supposed to make independent decisions, but were to execute the consensual decisions of the congregation. They had had no jurisdiction in other bishoprics and could function there only by invitation and then in purely consultative capacity. With the new consistory all the old patterns and attitudes of servanthood passed into oblivion. Bishops now began functioning just like the Catholic hierarchy, completely independent of the thoughts, feelings, and wishes of the congregations.[79] This launched a series of unpleasant incidents amongst bishops themselves and between bishops and the churches. The bishops had learned from Cornies that one could use outside power sources to get one's way. So bishops began to appeal to the *Gebietsamt* and to the SGC to get their way, as for example in the Halbstadt Church quarrel, in which both bishops involved in the struggle sent delegations to Odessa to the SGC to use its power to get their way.[80]

The emergence of the consistory of bishops (together with a variety of outside pietist influences) precipitated a second and much more powerful renewal movement in 1860. It produced the Mennonite Brethren Church and several smaller groups. The first confrontation between the renewal movement and the *Lehramt* resulted when the newly converted asked one of the *Aelteste* for a separate communion service. When the bishop refused, the new converts decided to secede (January 6, 1860). Instead of following Anabaptist/Mennonite guidelines in church discipline, which called for several levels of admonition before the ban could be applied, the consistory of bishops, not the local congregations, now banned the newly converted without even talking to them. In order to destroy this new movement, the *Lehramt* and the *Gebietsamt* joined hands to use their joint power to destroy the renewal movement.[81]

In their harassment of the new church, the two bodies used their respective rules and laws quite selectively. For example, when merchant Isaak Matthies became a Mennonite Brethren, the mother church immediately excommunicated him, instructing its members to shun him, thereby avoiding payment of the thirty thousand rubles they owed him. Immediately following this, the colony government moved against Matthies with his creditors, to whom he owed fifteen thousand rubles, and his property was sold at a debtors auction.[82] It is only fair to point out that the unwillingness of the leadership of the parent church to dialogue was matched by the Mennonite Brethren Church's own unwillingness to discuss their differences with the church from which they were seceding.[83]

A very similar reaction took place with the Friends of Jerusalem, another branch of the reform movement, which tried to form an alternative Mennonite church in Gnadenfeld but were forced to secede from the Mennonite Church in 1863 because of church and colony government harassment.[84]

The Abuse of Power within the Renewal Movement

No sooner had the Mennonite Brethren renewal freed itself from the arbitrary rule of the self-appointed consistory of bishops than authoritarian ministerial attitudes sprang up inside the renewal movement itself. Several of the newly ordained ministers began to call themselves "apostles." As such they saw themselves as called directly by God. Thus, they needed no confirmation by the church. They could issue decrees and perform excommunications quite independently of any congregation.[85] Fortunately, the new church was able to purge itself of these "spiritual despots" and reverse some of their uncalled-for excommunications.[86]

On the whole, the Mennonite Brethren Church wanted to return to a nonhierarchical church structure. Thus, it soon discontinued the office of *Aeltester* (Russia in 1909, North America in 1920) and instead developed a general conference in which all church people participated in the decisions of the denomination. However, even the Mennonite Brethren movement was not a total return to Menno Simons' ideal of citizenship in only one kingdom. When the new movement got a land grant from the Russian government in the Kuban and settled many of its landless converts there, it perpetuated the church/state compromise by setting up its own *Gebietsamt*.[87]

Already during Cornies' time, due to improved health facilities and the high birthrate, the Mennonite population began to increase dramatically. This eventually resulted in many landless Mennonites. The problem of the landless as such has already been discussed in relation to the *Gebietsamt*. However, there was a *Lehramt* dimension to the problem. The *Lehramt* colluded with the *Gebietsamt* in regard to the landless in a number of ways. For one, as soon as the landless began to seek justice from the authorities—

church and state—the *Lehramt* created a "new church sin," namely, challenging the decisions and actions of the *Gebietsamt*.[88] Secondly, since the
landless outnumbered the landholders, the church seems to have tried to
bolster the landholders' power by granting them two votes in church decisions.[89] When the landless appealed to the *Lehramt* for support in their
quest for justice from the colony, the colluding bishops piously wrung their
hands and publicly claimed that their commission from the Lord limited
them to dealing only with "the heavenly Canaan."[90] When the landless
then increased the pressure on the *Gebietsamt*, and the latter launched two
falsehood-laden denunciations to the Russian government against the
landless as revolutionaries and rabble-rousers, the *Lehramt* failed to raise a
finger in favor of the landless.[91] In Chortitza colony, the *Lehramt* even permitted the landholders to table a resolution forbidding the church to rent
the lands it controlled to the landless. The landless majority, however, was
able to defeat the motion.[92]

Power Abuses in the Wider Church Community

Finally, to give a sense of some of the abuses that occurred within church
and community life, we will draw on accounts recorded in the Jacob Epp
diaries, dating from the 1850s into the 1880s.[93]

As the quality of Christian discipleship decreased in the colony setting,
church people began to become violent toward each other. This often
came in the context of excessive alcohol consumption (386). Most of the
beatings of outsiders were meted out to hired help. Beating of servants,
male or female, when they incurred the employer's displeasure, was common. Such servants could be Mennonites, Russians, Ukrainians, or tribal
people. The Epp diary reports how a group of drinking Mennonites surprised some Jews watching them, so they caught the "spies" and beat them
mercilessly (295). When it came to beating children, the common attitude
in the church was "If you spare the rod, you spoil the child" (Prov. 13:24;
23:13). The common idea was that children were born with a stubborn will
that had to be broken by means of physical punishment. Wife beating
seems also to have been very common, because women in general were
considered *unmündig* (not capable of rational decision) or *unselbststaendig*
(incapable of being independent).[94] Serious wife abuse, however, usually
came in the context of alcohol abuse.

Sexual abuse seems to have been quite widespread in the church and colony family. It involved a wide variety of manifestations. Several authorities have pointed out that because of low female status, men expressed their sexuality with their wives at will. The result was the high birthrate. Some women claimed that once they were married, they never had another menstrual period. For example, one Mennonite prided himself that he and his wife had had 18 children in twenty-one years of marriage. The number of women who complained of being used sexually out of wedlock is frightening (152, 203, 259, 266, 394).

The sexual abuse of children involved several degrees of incest, including fathers impregnating daughters, especially stepdaughters, and brothers impregnating younger sisters (203, 394). Maids, who tended to be poor Mennonite girls who were virtual slaves in Mennonite homes or Russian girls employed in the home, were also sexually abused. Epp's diary lists a case of a young Mennonite maid constantly being raped by the three older sons of the house in which she was employed. When she appealed to church and colony authorities for redress, nobody paid any attention to her complaints (394). Diarist Epp also lists several women who were used sexually by ministers (266).

Violence could be fatal. Two men were drinking together. They were married to sisters, and one of them was a known wife-beater. When the latter returned home and began beating his wife, the other man who had followed him home stabbed him (259). In a case of a family murder-suicide, a man killed his wife and children and then committed suicide (415). A man, known to be *Jähzornig* (given to violent temper) drowned his wife in a fit of anger.[95] A number of illegitimate children were exposed at birth and died (399).

Diarist Epp sums up the Russian Mennonite situation as follows: "Our Mennonite people think that if we refuse to go to war we are fine Christians. They forget that their hearts can be full of malice, vengeance and revenge. Everywhere there are quarrels, disputes, strife and violence. Our people have not let God's Word establish roots in their hearts" (91).

Conclusion

The abuses lamented by Epp may well be considered as the accompanying consequences of the abuses of power exhibited by the community leadership, both the *Lehramt* and the *Gebietsamt*. While the extent of the power abuse should not be overstated, the widespread institutionalized use of the "sword" during the commonwealth period of Mennonite social history—to defend "the truth," to impose church discipline, and to protect privilege and property—has been demonstrated in this study. The descendants of the early Anabaptists had, during the Russian period, accommodated their beliefs and practices to the beliefs and practices of the society around them. In the process they lost the vision of a peaceful lifestyle to the point of engaging in armed defense of property and privilege. By losing their focus on a Christ-centered and community-based exegesis, they let their disciple-ship slip, and along with it their Christian identity. The abuses of power that accompanied these changes shadowed the economic and social prog-ress of the Mennonite colonies and, at a crisis point in Russian history, left them open to identification with the oppressors.

How the history of the Mennonites in Russia would have been different if the Mennonites had retained Menno Simons' original vision of a citi-zenry of the kingdom of peace remains a matter for the imagination. Fidel-ity to Menno Simons' vision might well have led to persecution and a much more restricted lifestyle. It is hard to escape the conclusion, however, that the twentieth-century fate of the Mennonites in Russia—to be at-tacked as a privileged and propertied class and dispersed into the Gulag—is at least partially a consequence of the loss of that vision.

CHAPTER SIX

Power under the Cover of Tradition
A Case Study of a "Plain Community"

JOEL HARTMAN

Whereas the preceding chapter approaches the abuse of power from a broad social and historical perspective, this chapter presents an individual case study from the present. The author recounts a heartbreaking story of how a conservative, "plain" Anabaptist community was unable to come to terms with HIV/AIDS, resulting in the unnecessary infection of a woman and her child. Viewed within the context of the maintenance of communal norms, the story becomes one of how power can be exercised in the name of tradition and in the maintenance of authority with disastrous results for individuals, particularly for women.

In the opening chapter of this volume, J. Lawrence Burkholder points out that power is an integral dimension of community life. It would follow that the more important the continuing existence of a strong, viable sense of community is to a group of people, the more important the exercise of power becomes in the dynamics of the political, social, and religious maintenance of the community. Historically, two characteristics of Anabaptist culture have reinforced an emphasis on a strong and highly integrated sense of community such as we find among the smaller, more conservative Mennonite/Amish groups: (1) the importance of being nonconformed to the world—and, therefore, culturally distinct from the larger, surrounding society; and (2) the emphasis on unity and consensus in carrying out that witness of nonconformity. To maintain such a highly integrated and homogeneous culture requires considerable energy and effort by those in the community who are vested with the responsibilities of leadership. In other words, it requires a significant exercise of power.

However, most Anabaptists have perceived the exercise of power to be a "worldly" phenomenon. Historically, says Burkholder, Anabaptist/Mennonites have assumed that Christians can live together in community "without the exercise of power, that is, power in the form of compulsion and force." So power's "reality is hidden under the deceptive cover of tradition." Thus hidden, it can be denied, even by those who are involved in exercising it. What is overlooked, of course, is that wherever there is a hierarchical social structure, power is inherently a part of the social reality—no matter how well hidden under the cover of tradition, no matter how much its existence is denied, and no matter how willingly those in the subordinate positions of the community submit themselves to it.

Power has been defined simply as the ability to bring about desired results, to determine outcomes even against opposition. Implicit in the exercise of power, however, is the fact that if one person or group obtains their desired outcomes, other people's desires will most likely be frustrated or denied. Under some circumstances the stakes for such denial are very high: life itself, or at the least one's physical well-being, which, as Burkholder suggests, is in effect having one's "power of being" destroyed. Who, then, assumes responsibility for this destruction of life or being? Who sits in judgment on the act of destruction, particularly if the authority to exercise power is rooted in sacred tradition? How is the justice of one desired outcome weighed against the justice of an opposing desired outcome, particularly if neither is consciously articulated? Does that lack of conscious awareness absolve the wielder of power?

Burkholder suggests that if we are to examine critically the exercise of power, we must also consider the criteria by which power should be judged—which leads us (taking a page from Paul Tillich) to the matter of justice. As we said above, one person's authority to exercise power may well be another's oppression; and beyond the question of "right" or legitimacy to exercise power that so frequently bogs us down in endless debates is the question of accountability. For Tillich, as Burkholder points out, this was the crux of the matter: in the existential situation, raising the question of legitimacy has little practical utility. The situation is what it is. But each individual has the responsibility of being accountable for the power that he or she has the authority to exercise. This chapter attempts to raise precisely this question of justice in the exercise of power. In a socioreligious tradition undergirded by hierarchical structure—leadership by bishops, subordination of women to men, and so forth—the question is not whether power is exercised or even whether the power wielders have a legitimate right to do so. Rather, the crucial question often becomes that of justice and accountability.

What follows is the story of the response to HIV/AIDS in a "Plain Community" (i.e., Conservative Amish/Mennonite). The purpose for telling this story is not to understand or analyze the responses of community members to HIV/AIDS per se, but rather to see those responses within the context of several latent power-wielding patterns inherent in the structure of the community's sociocultural environment and to examine to what extent that power was exercised with a sense of responsibility toward its objects. Although I will discuss the specific wielders of power and their roles in the incident, I will focus on the sociological and theological components of the cultural setting that provided the legitimacy for the particular exercises of power and attempt to understand how the actors weighed their own sense of accountability in what they did.

Methodology

This is a case study. The methodology, as such, is that of participant observation. I use the term *as such* because I did not enter into the situation with the intent of analyzing its outcome. That came much later, and the present articulation is more an attempt to bring some sort of understanding to what happened, both for my own benefit and for that of the others involved in the medical response team. I was a volunteer with a regional medical center, available for counseling with Amish and Mennonite patients and their families. At the time of the events described here, I had no idea I would eventually attempt to stand back and analyze what happened. Consequently, I did not put on my "sociologist's hat" until long afterwards.

This may well be a limitation of the interpretation I have given the situation. A true participant-observer is consciously aware of that role from day one and always keeps one part of his or her brain in an analytical mode.

There is also the matter of professional ethics with respect to the confidentiality of the counseling relationship. As a result, only that information is revealed here that was aired publicly by the people involved. However, this is a very personal story, and for purposes of confidentiality, the specific community will not be identified, either geographically or within the spectrum of Amish-Mennonite groups, other than to say that it is a small, geographically isolated, and relatively conservative community. The names of all individuals and locations in the account have been changed.

Crisis

Aaron Miller, a young man in his twenties, had been treated several times since childhood at a regional medical center, hereafter referred to as the "Center." During the course of those treatments, Aaron had received blood products. At his last visit, as a result of the awareness of the contamination of the blood supply, a sample was taken to be tested for the presence of the HIV virus. When the sample tested positive, the Center contacted Aaron to come in for consultation about the results of the test. However, unaware of the nature of the consultation, and since he felt no specific need for any kind of treatment, Aaron ignored the requests for him to report to the Center until shortly before the planned date of his marriage almost a year later.

For several years Aaron had been courting Sarah Burkholder from Oak Tree, a settlement somewhat distant from his own. One of his siblings was married to one of Sarah's siblings, and both families were looking forward to a heightened alliance between them—especially since another romance seemed to be brewing between another set of siblings. With the financial backing of Sarah's parents, Aaron and Sarah had purchased a small farm, and considerable time, energy, and resources were being invested in improvements so that the farm would be ready for occupancy by the time of the wedding. Aaron finally responded to the request to report to the Center for consultation on the results of his blood test. Sarah accompanied him to this meeting. In a private session, he was informed by a physician that he was HIV-positive. Then the center's social and educational workers at-

tempted to counsel the two of them about the implications and consequences of his HIV condition for their planned marriage.

Needless to say, the basic information conveyed to the couple that day
had somewhat of a traumatizing effect on them. HIV/AIDS was not an
unknown subject to them. In fact, it had been discussed rather widely, at
least in Oak Tree.[1] However, that discussion had been decidedly negative
in that HIV/AIDS was perceived to be "a plague visited by God upon the
perverse people of the world."[2] Numerous tracts and reprints of newspaper
and magazine articles elaborating this general motif had been circulating
within the community almost since the time HIV/AIDS had become a
media topic within the larger society. Most of this material was published
by small religious presses (some of them with Anabaptist connections) or
came from journalistic enterprises specializing in sensationalism and/or
pseudoscience. This material had two basic foci: it claimed that HIV/AIDS
was the consequence of sinful life choices, primarily the sin of sodomy/
homosexuality; and it warned (erroneously) of the dangerous communicability of the HIV virus, including everything from casual contacts with
infected people, to using "unsterilized" tableware and toilet seats in public
settings, to mosquito and other insect bites.

In addition to the traumatic effect of discovering that Aaron was HIV-
positive, much of the content of the counseling in this initial session was
contradictory to Amish/Mennonite social and religious norms and expectations for marriage and family life (for example, being informed of
the necessity of using condoms in conjugal relations). Neither Aaron nor
Sarah knew quite how to respond to the specific recommendations of the
counselors. Consequently, a second counseling session was set up in which
the couple would be accompanied, at their request, by their parents and
other adult members of their families, including Aaron's grandfather, a retired bishop now living in Aaron's home community. Although this second
session provided an opportunity for the medical staff of the Center to convey a considerable amount of basic information about HIV/AIDS to the
members of both families, the Center workers were very much aware—
frustratingly so—that the two groups belonged to entirely different cultures. As a result, the Center recommended that both families contact me
for further counseling.

On the way home from this meeting, the two families decided they
were not ready to "go public" with the information that Aaron was HIV-

positive. Although nothing was withheld from other members of their immediate families, the information was not shared with anyone else in their respective communities, including church leaders. Both families felt they needed time to integrate this new information into their own lives and to try to deal with its implications for them before they would be ready and able to deal with other people's responses to it. However, by an unfortuitous circumstance, the bishop at Oak Tree gained knowledge of Aaron's condition and felt constrained to confront the family, seeking clarification as to whether the information was indeed true. The Burkholder family felt inadequate in attempting to deal with many of the questions raised by the bishop, and they referred him to me. The family prevailed upon the bishop to agree that for the time being the information about Aaron's condition be kept confidential, although he insisted that this was a matter that eventually had to come before the church.

Response

This confrontation with the bishop spurred Sarah's mother to decide their family should avail themselves of further counseling, and despite her husband's rather strong reluctance, she contacted me. At the same time, the bishop also contacted me.[3] As a result, I began my involvement with the Oak Tree community at two levels simultaneously: counseling with the bishop and with Sarah's family.

Initially, the bishop's major concern was the communicability of the HIV virus. For all practical purposes, Aaron was already a part of the Oak Tree community. The first thing that occurred to the bishop was the possibility of transmission of the virus, particularly through ritual acts such as the holy kiss and the shared communion cup. But other common casual behavior—simple tactile contact, coughing and sneezing, sharing of eating utensils, and so on—were of great concern.[4] Once his anxieties in these matters were somewhat allayed, his concerns turned to the implications of Aaron's condition for the conjugal relations of the couple and the prospects for parenthood. He was greatly disturbed that unprotected sexual intercourse was strongly contraindicated in their case, although his concerns seemed to be oriented more to the implications for potential parenthood than for the possible life-threatening risk that conjugal relations had for Sarah.

Although Sarah and her family had some questions about the communicability of the HIV virus through casual contact, they were quick to move on to other issues. The major concern of Esther, Sarah's mother, was the risk to her daughter's survival if she were to enter this marital union. Numerous times during the discussions she voiced the opinion that Sarah would be "committing suicide" if she went through with the marriage plans. And if the couple were to have children, Esther was concerned that the children would be born with AIDS. For whatever reason, however, Sarah's father, Henry, did not seem to share his wife's great concern about their daughter being at risk through conjugal relations. He seemed unwilling to integrate that concern into his thinking; he was more concerned about the potential ostracism of Aaron by the community. He also seemed unwilling (or unable) to accept the terminal nature of Aaron's condition: more than once he expressed the opinion that it would be only a matter of time before medical researchers found a cure for AIDS, and then the situation would be "normal" again.

Two of Sarah's older siblings vocally reinforced their mother's concerns. Both had left the local community and now lived and worked in less-conservative Anabaptist communities in other states. But despite their physical distance, they were in and out of the family circle frequently during the course of these events. Both had access to wider sources of information about HIV/AIDS. Their major concern was for Sarah if the marriage were to be consummated, and they strongly reinforced their mother's fears.

For a period of four to six weeks, I met frequently with the bishop and with Sarah and various members of her family, individually and in family groups. (Aaron's family did not request any consultation, and Aaron himself refused to meet with me.) During these sessions I attempted to emphasize three points: First, it was important not to ostracize Aaron. Although Aaron was asymptomatic and relatively healthy at this point, the psychological and emotional impact of knowing he was HIV-positive (and would eventually develop AIDS) was traumatic; he was in need of a strong support system. There was no danger or risk to anyone in the faith community through casual contact with Aaron. However, all indications were that his condition would become terminal within a three-to-six-year time span, and until then he deserved to be able to live as normal a life as possible. Second, under normal circumstances, unless adequate precautions were taken, Sarah would be very much at risk once marital relations were initiated. Even with the use of high-quality condoms, there was the risk that the HIV virus could be transferred from Aaron to Sarah during intercourse. And third, with very disciplined care, HIV can be lived with in a conjugal relationship. I pointed out that there were couples in which the husband was HIV-positive, and they were able to maintain the wife's HIV-negative condition. But this is accomplished at a very high level of vigilance, and it is primarily the husband who must accept the responsibility for the well-being of his wife.

During the course of the counseling sessions with Sarah and her family, I made several specific recommendations. These were made in sequence, that is, each subsequent recommendation was made after the previous recommendation had been rejected. My initial recommendation was that the couple should put their decision to marry "on hold" for at least one year. I suggested that the short time remaining until their planned wedding date was simply not long enough to allow them to fully comprehend and consider the implications of Aaron's condition. Sarah's mother, Esther, strongly urged the couple to consider that option, and Sarah indicated she would be willing to think about it. However, she later reported that Aaron rejected that recommendation out of hand, and she said she felt bound to honor her original commitment to marry him.

When it was obvious that the couple was going to go through with the wedding, I suggested they consider committing themselves to a celibate relationship, at least until they had time to deal with the gravity of the potential consequences. I pointed out that there were couples under care of the Center who had opted for this alternative out of concern for the well-being of the noninfected spouse. I tried to emphasize how high the stakes were with respect to risk of life for Sarah. Again, Sarah indicated she was willing to consider this option, but she reported later that Aaron was not.

The third recommendation, which eventually appeared to be acceptable to all parties involved, including the bishop, was that the couple would engage only in "protected" sexual relations, using high quality condoms, which the Center offered to supply at no cost. Although this would preclude the possibility of parenthood, it seemed to be a "reasonable" compromise to the dilemma.

It is interesting that the Oak Tree bishop was willing to agree to this concession at this point—albeit after considerable discussion and debate—

although it was obvious he was rather uncomfortable with it. Whether his willingness to go along at this point was out of a genuine concern for the risk to Sarah of the group's traditional position on birth control or out of a belief he still harbored that the wedding would not occur is not known. Several times in our conversations he expressed surprise that the grandfather of the groom (a retired bishop) did not stop the entire affair. He himself had occupied the office of bishop less than a year and tended to defer to the judgment of his older colleague. Also he expressed some disappointment that Henry, Sarah's father, had not (yet) withdrawn his consent to the marriage. The bishop was aware of Esther's strong objections, and he seemed almost to hope that her objections would influence her husband.

During the wedding service, however, the bishop did an "about face." Although the bulk of his sermon was conventional in the content of its message, the last fifteen to twenty minutes was a vehement condemnation of the worldliness and evils of birth control. He confessed that he had earlier agreed with the couple and their families that under the circumstances of this union the use of birth control measures might be appropriate. However, he reported that "a revelation" he had received the previous evening called him back to the truth, and he exhorted the young couple not to be seduced or compromised by the corruption of the world and succumb to its teachings: "God's will works in mysterious ways; we must allow that will to work, and not attempt to thwart it by imposing our own wills." It is not known what prompted his revelation, whether it was a matter of coming to terms with his own conscience, since he truly had had difficulty agreeing to the compromise, or whether it was the result of questions raised by one of the other ministers or elders of the congregation, since the subject of recommended "protection" in conjugal relations in the face of HIV infection (even though not accurately understood) had become a topic of discussion among members of the community. Despite the bishop's admonition, however, the couple—at Sarah's insistence—did practice "safer sex" through the early months of their marriage. There is reason to believe, though, that it was a point of contention within their relationship.

During the first year of their marriage, Aaron and Sarah received information through the informal network of Anabaptist communities that there was a nonmedical health practitioner in a distant metropolitan center who had a substantial Anabaptist clientele, and who could possibly help Aaron. The couple made a trip to visit this practitioner and returned, reporting that he had assured them he could help Aaron, if not completely cure him. This person put Aaron on a strict dietary regimen, and the couple made periodic visits to the clinic for special treatments there. There is little doubt but that the couple was convinced that these treatments and the dietary regimen were having a positive effect on Aaron's general health and well-being. After eight or ten months of these treatments and adherence to the special diet, they reported the practitioner had "tested" Aaron for the HIV virus and informed the couple that Aaron was "completely cured—that his body had no traces of the virus anymore, and that there was no reason for the couple to continue practicing protected sexual relations."[5]

Prior to this time, the bishop had suggested that Aaron submit to the ritual of anointing. This was done, and although the bishop made no claims for the effect of this ritual, he told the couple that he felt confident God would cure Aaron of his condition. This sentiment was reinforced by numerous other people in the church. Following the anointing and the practitioner's "cure," there was considerable social pressure from many sources for the couple to begin "having a family." By this time, almost everyone in the community knew that, despite the bishop's admonitions in the wedding service, the couple was practicing birth control. Now, however, everyone was convinced that a cure had been effected and that there was no reason to continue these protections. Even Aaron's family, who had great faith in modern medicine—as opposed to Sarah's family, who were generally quite skeptical about science and modern medicine—began to encourage the couple to have children. In the interim since her own wedding, several of Sarah's married siblings had either become pregnant or had already had a child, so Sarah felt a strong urge to have children of her own. The only holdouts in this sphere of social influence around the couple were Esther (Sarah's mother) and the two siblings who had initially raised objections to Sarah's getting married.

Not surprisingly then, within a short time Sarah was pregnant, and eventually she gave birth. Out of a sense of loyalty and respect to their family physician, a rural general practitioner, Esther confided in him about the probability of Sarah's being HIV-positive. A blood sample drawn at the time of the delivery verified that Sarah was indeed HIV-positive. Although the baby was initially HIV-negative, when retested around three years of age, the child had contracted the HIV virus, probably during the process of breast feeding.[6]

Within several months of the birth of their child, Aaron's health began to deteriorate, and when the baby was approximately six months old, Aaron died of AIDS-related complications. That Aaron contracted the HIV-virus through contaminated blood products is indeed tragic. Along with thousands of others in the larger society, he was a victim of a series of failures in the health-care delivery system. However, that Sarah should also fall victim to this terrible disease is also tragic, since it was in large part the consequence of the failure of the traditionally institutionalized authority within her culture to wield its power with respect to her just claims for life and well-being.

Discussion

Calvin Redekop notes that most discussions of power are Weberian in orientation, seeing life as a continuous succession of power plays between the "controllers," who have the authority or power, and those who are in varying degrees able (and, since the exercise of power is essentially a "reciprocal" relationship, to some extent willing) to be influenced or dominated. Redekop goes on to point out that power manifests itself in various forms.[7] Examples of the exercise or manifestation of power are generally quite complex and involuted, involving more than just the inequality existing within a situation of one actor vis-à-vis another. Quite frequently, especially when one considers the situation of the person being controlled, there is a complicated network of relationships within a larger segment of the societal system in which the person is located. Often the controls and influences that operate through these different networks interact with one another with respect to the way in which that control impinges on the individual's life space. A full appreciation of the mechanisms of control, then, suggests tracing the loci of power-wielding within the system. Certainly, it may be neither possible nor desirable to identify all of the loci of power. In attempting to understand the outcome of the situation examined here, it seems to me that three loci of power-wielding appear to be rather salient.

Aaron and Sarah's Relationship

First, let us examine the exercise of power in the relationship between Aaron and Sarah. Obviously, power is often a relational issue between individuals, but generally it is oriented toward some "thing" external to either or both of the actors. The "thing" in this case is their planned marriage (and the establishment of a family). Marriage and family are overriding goals within the Anabaptist worldview, particularly among more traditional Amish/Mennonite groups. In these groups adulthood is not a matter of age but a matter of baptism, marriage, *and* parenthood. Success in life is often equated with having contributed to the perpetuation of the church and the society, not only through one's personal work or contribution but also through producing a family of children who in turn produce families of children who grow up within the society.

In contracting HIV and in having his planned marriage to Sarah placed in jeopardy, Aaron's dreams for adult fulfillment are threatened. Not only is he faced with potential ostracism because of the reaction of people to HIV (in this sense he is no different from members of the larger society who are similarly afflicted), but his aspiration to be the head of a household (and eventually a father) is also threatened. If the relationship between Aaron and Sarah were egalitarian, then the outcome at this point might be a matter of negotiation. One might argue that inasmuch as the female in a traditional Anabaptist courting situation has the power to say No, there is equality. Even there, however, the courting proceeds in a cultural context in which the female is a *passive* partner. She cannot take the initiative in expressing interest or developing a relationship: she is dependent on the initiation of interest by the male. But in this case, Sarah had already said yes, her father had given consent, and the couple had invested jointly in a farm. One might say that she was "as good as married."

With some notable (and for the most part early) exceptions, traditional Anabaptism tended to define the women as being subservient to men, especially to the husband. The strength of that belief is indicated by the continuing importance of the symbol of the woman's head-covering among the more traditional/conservative groups. As a matter of fact, although the Oak Tree church does not practice "shunning," the few young adults who left the community and moved to other settlements had been urged, at the risk of excommunication, to affiliate with groups that maintain the woman's covering. And in the Oak Tree church women were forbidden even to ask questions in Sunday school, because it was seen as a behavior unbefitting their position of subservience and maintaining silence in the church. Donald Kraybill refers to this power differential between men and women as a "tilted balance of power" and quotes one young Amish woman as saying, "The joke among us women is that the men make the rules."[8]

This inherent bias toward male superordinance manifests itself in numerous ways among more traditional Anabaptist groups, particularly during adolescence and young adulthood prior to marriage. Boys often appear very self-centered in their relationship to girls. This is frequently manifested at large gatherings and picnics, when adolescent girls are often the last to have access to foods, especially desserts. Boys will often overindulge or go back for second helpings even when they are aware that their overindulgence will deprive their female counterparts of a reasonable fair share. I have frequently observed this assumed superordinance manifesting itself during recreational activities, for example, during softball or volleyball games, when the males will dominate the play at the obvious expense of the girls' participation.

In light of this culturally conditioned tendency to dominate relationships with females, it is not surprising that Aaron refused to participate in the process of negotiation that could possibly result in his being deprived of attaining his culturally instilled life goals. Sarah had consented to marry him; now she should be subservient to him and his decisions. He refused to participate in the counseling sessions. He rejected the recommendation to put the decision to go ahead with the wedding on hold until they could fully consider the consequences of his recently discovered medical condition. He rejected the option of a celibate relationship and only very reluctantly agreed to use condoms in the forthcoming marital relationship. Even though his insistent behavior had a high probability of inflicting a life-threatening condition on Sarah, he was unwilling to surrender his superordinate position in their relationship. And since he refused to participate in the counseling sessions, all of the suggestions to bring some resolution to the situation were introduced by Sarah, contradicting the culturally expected dominance of the male within the relationship. Aaron's insistence on controlling Sarah in the situation was legitimized by the traditional authority inherent in the male-dominated cultural expectations for the marital couple, even though, in this case, the marital relationship had not yet been formally established.

Very important is the fact that there was no support in the structure of the sociocultural tradition for Sarah to protect what she might have felt was her own "just due," so to speak. Her mother and two of her siblings encouraged her to act for her own self-interest—in this case, possibly her own survival. But their concern was perceived as being "personal," and her own interests were very easily cast in terms of "self-interest"—which, of course, bordered conceptually on selfishness in that setting. The theological worldview of her religion, which demanded subservience and reliance on her mate's responsibility to care for her (as God cared for him); the cultural expectations of her society's norms; and the weight of social pressure—all these weighed heavily against her and gave her no support to make her claim for justice.

Henry and Esther's Relationship

Second, let us turn to the exercise of power that took place in the relationship between Henry and Esther Burkholder, Sarah's parents. At first glance, this might seem to be a replay of the differential power relationship existing between Aaron and Sarah. In part it is, except that here Esther had the benefit of many years of experience in dealing with the role of subservient wife, which Sarah, of course, did not have. However, in this relationship there is another very important dimension. My observations indicate that, although the "power-wielding" here is a manifestation of the superordinate-subordinate relationship called for by traditional Anabaptist religion and culture, the dynamics of the process reflect more the separation of male and female subcultures that is characteristic of many traditional societies and that is certainly the case in traditional Anabaptist groups. For example, Hostetler and Huntington describe well the cleavage between the male and female subcultures in Hutterite society.[9]

Perhaps this division is not quite as stark among many Amish and Mennonite groups; nevertheless, such a cleavage does exist and is in part a reflection and function of the strict division of labor and segregation of social roles on the basis of gender. Outside of the family a considerable proportion of formal and informal activity occurs in gender-segregated settings. Even within the context of the family circle, more time than not is spent in gender-segregated activities, especially if one includes household and farmwork activities. Although inequality is certainly one of the consequences of this gender segregation, it leads also to differential expectations and perceptions of those things that people think about or concern themselves with—things such as family matters, church affairs, and community events. For a significant proportion of their lives, in terms of time, males and females exist in two different worlds.

This is evidenced in the manner in which men and women segregate themselves during informal social events. Women will gather in the kitchen; men will congregate somewhere else. But more important, they generally discuss different things. In situations in which the physical space is limited and both groups are in the same room, there is attentional and interactional segregation. Although some intergender communication may occur, intragender communication prevails. Consistent with the power differential between the genders, men are much more likely to ignore what the women are discussing than vice versa. In fact, my observations in these settings are that women, even while holding forth on their own discussions, generally have one ear tuned to the men's conversations. From time to time, one of the women may even encroach on the men's dialogue. I have never observed the opposite: men simply are not interested in women's conversation. Men perceive women's matters to be of little import, which only serves to reinforce the males' sense of superordinance. This is not unusual or unique to Anabaptist settings. In any social situation in which there is great inequality, subordinate statuses and their concerns are characteristically of little import to those in highly superordinate positions—unless, of course, the presence or services of the subordinate incumbents are needed.

Another consequence of this cleavage between the men's and women's subcultures is that loyalties tend to be divided, particularly among the men. Men experience competition between their loyalty to other males (and male concerns) and loyalty to their female family members, particularly with respect to family matters involving primarily females. These tendencies were exemplified on numerous occasions in the events described in this case. During family discussions, it seemed many times that Henry and Esther were operating on different wavelengths. Henry was concerned about the possible ostracism of Aaron. He appeared much more sympathetic to Aaron's frustration over possibly not attaining family and parenthood than to the possible risk to his daughter's life. In fact, at times he seemed unwilling to accept the reality of the seriousness of that risk. The idea seemed almost to upset the order of his worldview. At the same time, he felt a strong bond with Aaron. They had worked together closely for some time, both on his farm and at the new farm the couple was preparing for occupancy. Sarah's younger brothers also exhibited this bond and sense of loyalty to Aaron. Although they never participated in the discussions, they manifested an expectation that the wedding would occur.

One obvious manifestation of these power and attentional differentials was that Esther never confronted Henry with her differing opinions, at least not in my presence. When she expressed her thinking, she laid out her thoughts in the form of questions. He then had the option of considering the question and answering it or of deflecting the question completely. On numerous occasions he seemed to ignore her questions, acting as though he hadn't heard (or hadn't been listening). When Esther stated her opinions declaratively in Henry's presence, she usually did so in conversations with other persons so that her statements were not addressed to him, but it was very obvious to whom she was speaking. In almost all cases he gave the appearance of not hearing her. Even in their sessions with me, when Esther asked questions or stated opinions in the discussion, Henry very seldom picked up on any of them. Esther and one of Sarah's older siblings frequently discussed the situation of Sarah's "predicament" in Henry's presence, but his typical response was not to hear. It was as if they existed in separate dimensions of time and space (and I suppose they did).

It was understood by all, including Henry, that he had the authority to stop the wedding. But his only acknowledgments of that power were comments to the effect that he could see no reason to call it off. Esther continued to encourage Sarah to assert "her rights." It was also well understood that if Sarah had stated "her case" strongly to her father, he would have acceded. But Sarah was so dominated by Aaron that that approach was futile; and eventually Esther's pressing of the point began to alienate Sarah. Finally, Esther gave up.

This was the final verification of the power differential between Henry and Esther. She realized somewhat earlier in the process that she was not going to influence Henry. And all along it was apparent that Henry knew by his ignoring Esther's concerns and wishes she would eventually subordinate herself. There was, essentially, a sharing of expectations for the other in the drama that played itself out. Those expectations were culturally determined as part and parcel of the power inequalities between the men's and women's subcultures. Whenever there is a significant inequality in the relationship between two groups or categories, individuals in the subordinate category tend to be treated as mere elements in the environment rather than as participating actors. Over time, specific patterns of conduct, such as the way one responds to another's concerns or questioning, becomes habitual. Esther had acquiesced before, and she would do so again.

The Bishop's and Community's Relationship

Finally, let us examine the actions of the bishop. We recognize, of course, that the position of bishop in the community is vested formally with authority to exercise power. Therefore, the question is not that he wielded power to "control" aspects of the situation. Rather, the question becomes why and how he used his authority to articulate the specific actions he took.

The evolution of the bishop's concerns and actions are interesting. His first response to learning about Aaron's HIV-positive condition was to view it as an "outside" danger that had potential for threatening the stability of the ritual life of the community—unless Aaron were to be "quarantined," so to speak. His next concern was the implications of HIV/AIDS for the integrity of family and parenthood. His initial understanding was that the couple could not have children. When he realized that the real concern was they *shouldn't* have children, it raised a question about the appropriateness of consummating the marriage. He seemed to comprehend, to some extent, the inherent risk of conjugal relations to Sarah's life, but that certainly did not become a priority issue. His reaction to all these concerns was a conviction that the wedding should not occur; but there was no guidance in the cultural tradition or in his own brief experience in the office to advise him about how to handle the situation. He looked to Aaron's grandfather to intervene, but that did not happen. He looked to Henry to exercise the father's prerogative to withdraw consent, but that did not occur either. In the interim, then, he reluctantly agreed to the compromise plan for the couple to use "birth control measures" (condoms)—clearly contrary to tradition and the teaching of the church.

By the time of the wedding, however, the bishop found himself facing what he probably perceived to be a serious threat to the stability of the social order of the faith community. The very fact that HIV/AIDS was at the center of the issue had already had a destabilizing effect on the community. Aaron was neither a drug addict nor homosexual, and there was never any question about that in the minds of community members. Nevertheless, the association of AIDS with the so-called "perverse" elements of the larger society, coupled with the almost hysterical fears about its transmission, had threatened the emotional and interactional stability of the community. In addition, although the Burkholder family had not advertised the

intent of the young couple to use condoms in their conjugal relations, that
information had spread among the members of the community as part of
the explanation of how Sarah would be protected from contracting the
deadly disease. (Within such a high-context cultural setting, information
does not long remain only among those to whom it is initially imparted.)
Not surprisingly, then, numerous members of the community were seriously disturbed by this departure from a long-held proscriptive norm, and
they were equally disturbed by the fact that the young bishop had con-
doned that departure.

There is a strong probability that this sequence of happenings became
a very pointed message to the bishop about the potential fragility of the
community's socioreligious order. This particular community of people
had migrated to this isolated rural area precisely to insulate themselves
from liberalizing influences of other Anabaptist groups as well as from the
larger society. If the integrity of their culture were to be maintained, vigilance was required. Not to act was to make a concession to the forces for
change that were impinging upon them. In a traditional society, traditional
ways are usually seen as the answer to threats from the outside. So the
bishop retreated to the traditional position on birth control, sacrificing any
concern he might have had for Sarah's individual claim to life and well-
being.

After the wedding, the bishop again retreated into tradition. It had become common knowledge in the community that the couple was using
condoms in their conjugal relations, despite the bishop's admonition in the
wedding service. The bishop appealed to them to conform to the traditional norm of eschewing all forms of birth control. Following Aaron's
death and the general awareness within the community that both Sarah
and her child were now HIV-positive, the bishop indicated that his intent
had been to implore the couple to adopt a celibate relationship. However,
at the time there seemed to be considerable ambiguity about what he was
actually advocating. In light of the "cure" by the health practitioner, reinforced by the traditional ritual of anointing, many community members
provided strong social support for an interpretation of the bishop's appeal
as calling for, or at least condoning, unprotected intercourse. In any event,
this wielding of power by the bishop can be interpreted as a perceived necessary action to protect the integrity of the traditional culture. Allowing an

obvious rejection of an important cultural norm had far too much potential for initiating social change.

Summary

We have examined what I feel are the three central examples of power-wielding in this situation. In each instance the authority to exercise power was legitimate according to the longstanding tradition of the culture. Aaron's exercise of power could be termed "coercive influence" and might be seen simply as an individualistic exercise of power over Sarah as a stratagem for obtaining his own ends. He seemed to be unwilling to confront the reality that his medical condition might have forfeited his "right" to fulfill the traditional goals of marriage and/or parenthood. Certainly, by refusing to meet with me to discuss the implications of his condition, he avoided being confronted with the very significant risk to which he was putting Sarah. To be sure, Esther confronted him. But as a woman, what she said seemed to have little impact on Aaron. There is little evidence to suggest that he gave any consideration to Sarah's well-being or that he even ever acknowledged to himself the serious consequences for Sarah.

In the actions of both Henry (Sarah's father) and the bishop, the power-wielding was not direct coercion or influence. In fact, they both seemed to stand aside from the situation. Their power in both cases was derived from the fact that they had the authority to define the meaning of the situation in which they would act, and their authority to act was rooted in their cultural tradition. In fact, we might well call their behavior a "nonpersonalized exercise of power," to use a term coined by Georges Balandier, the French political anthropologist. Balandier contends that much power-wielding within all social systems, but particularly within traditional systems, can be characterized in this way. It follows simply "from the need to struggle against the entropy that threatens (the social structure) with disorder."[10]

For Henry that order had to do with the traditional process of courtship: his giving consent, the preparation of a new farmstead, the integration of a new son-in-law within the family and community—all of which in effect had begun to occur, even though the formal marriage had not. It had to do with the traditional Anabaptist faith in the working of God's providential hand. Because of his traditional conditioning, Henry was totally unable to accept the terminal nature of Aaron's condition or the possibility that Sarah would be at risk. He frequently said, "God would not let that happen!" On numerous occasions he accused Esther of exhibiting a lack of faith by her opposing the marriage.

The bishop, on the other hand, was concerned with a "larger" order: he perceived the faith community that had been entrusted to his care to be literally disintegrating. He became almost desperate in his attempts to restore order. But the only alternative he saw at the time was to retreat to the authority of tradition. He accomplished this by defining the situation in such a way that the tradition would dictate the response. For example, when his agreement that under the circumstances the couple would use condoms to protect Sarah from contracting the HIV virus created controversy and ambiguity within the community, he redefined condoms back to a mechanism of birth control. Now there is no ambiguity: tradition dictates how to respond to the situation. Within this redefinition of the situation, there is no room for concern for Sarah's well-being. Responsibility for Sarah is delegated to God.

Conclusion

What we have seen in this case is a series of circumstances in which the traditional order of a communal society is threatened. Not only is the source of that threat (HIV/AIDS) a manifestation of the corruption of the "world," but it is perceived in and of itself to be a terrifying and horrible reality. How does one protect oneself, both individually and societally? One answer is to retreat to the authority of tradition, which has little or no flexibility to accommodate anything new. The cultures of long-lived, stable, traditional societies are tightly integrated, all the cultural pieces fitting together in a highly cross-referenced structure. This is what gives a traditional society its stability, its strength. But this is also its fragility, for its structure may be likened to a "house of cards"—remove one card and it could easily fall in upon itself. Some change can be accommodated, but that takes time to allow for gradual adjustments to the intricate parts of the whole. With respect to Sarah's predicament in this situation, there simply was not time.

It should be acknowledged that Sarah, like most women in conservative, traditionalist Anabaptist communities, had not been socialized to take control of her own life; so in a sense she was a willing subject of control. She was socialized to be submissive to her parents (in this case, her father), to her (future) husband, and to her bishop. Her mother and two of her older siblings urged her to assert herself. But she had not been prepared to take such responsibility for her own life. She had been socialized to delegate that responsibility, primarily to males.

Undeniably, at the center of Sarah's having her "power of being" destroyed is the theological imperative within traditional Anabaptist faith for women to be subservient to men. Although this does not necessarily demand that women's concerns be ignored entirely in favor of men's concerns or of larger systemic needs, it does mean that women's concerns are much less likely to be entered into whatever power equation is being factored at any particular time.

This brings us back to one of Burkholder's central concerns with the exercise of power: *justice*, which, as the prophet Micah recognized, cannot be separated from mercy and love. Within our human enterprise, and especially within the community of faith, we tend to focus on who among us has the legitimate right to exercise power. Yet in the Gospel parables in which Jesus describes the exercise of power, he hardly ever raises the question of the right or authority of the power wielder. He seems to be much more concerned with the just and responsible exercise of power.

CHAPTER SEVEN

Mennonite Culture Wars
Power, Authority, and Domination

STEPHEN C. AINLAY

In this chapter the author employs the concept of "culture wars" to analyze power differentials between groups of Mennonites. Noting that "Mennonites have their own collective myths, symbols, identity, and institutions," the author argues that "Mennonite culture wars have been fought — just as those of a more national character have been — over the ability to define those myths, symbols, identity, and institutions." The chapter focuses on the modernist-fundamentalist controversies among American Mennonites during the first several decades of the twentieth century as instances of "Mennonite culture wars" and concludes by "mapping" the contemporary Mennonite power-knowledge system.

Mennonite culture wars may seem an odd juxtaposition of terms. Mennonites are often known (especially by non-Mennonites) for their "pacifist" stance, a stance rooted in a tradition of nonresistance dating to the Reformation.[1] The language of war seems curiously inappropriate in the face of this tradition. An image of Mennonites at war seems almost provocative, but it is useful if it forces us to think about a topic that has been difficult for Mennonites to deal with candidly and openly—the topic of power (and, as will be seen, the attending concept of conflict). Beyond being provocative, however, the notion of Mennonite culture wars is intended to bring recent work in the sociology of knowledge to bear on the analysis of Mennonite life.

I do not mean to suggest that Mennonites have not dealt with issues of power. As Chapters 3 and 4 make clear, Anabaptist/Mennonite thinkers since the Reformation have tried to discern the appropriate relationship with state government and have often resisted its coercive power. I would emphasize at the outset that my interest here is not so much in what Mennonites say or do about power differences in the world around them. Rather, my interest is in better understanding power differences *within* the Mennonite world.

Mennonites and the Problem of Power

As Paul Harrison noted some years ago, power has long been a difficult concept to deal with for all those religious movements associated with the "Free Church" tradition.[2] There are at least three prongs in the Anabaptist/Mennonite cultural tradition—the ideas of the "priesthood of all believers," submission (*Gelassenheit*), and humility (Pietist influence)—that make it difficult to talk about power.

Calvin Redekop claims that "unquestionably, the 'body of believers,' or 'the priesthood of the laity,' gave the Mennonite tradition a starting point."[3] Early Anabaptist/Mennonites conceived of themselves as a *Gemeinde*, a body or community of people who voluntarily joined to share a common life. Harold Bender, writing on the Anabaptist conception of the church, noted: "One of the most characteristic features of Anabaptism is its church concept. The church (*Gemeinde*), according to the Anabaptist, is a voluntary and exclusive fellowship of the truly converted believers in Christ, committed to follow Him in full obedience as Lord; it is a brotherhood, not an institution. It is completely separated from the state, which is to have no power over the church; and the members of the church in turn do not hold office in the magistracy. There is to be complete freedom of conscience, no use of force or compulsion by state or church; faith must be free."[4] Bender concludes that this Anabaptist emphasis on church as "brotherhood" carries an "anti-hierarchical emphasis," which means that the clerical nature of church offices is minimized, and lay participation and responsibility are given a high priority.[5] Thus, the egalitarian emphasis of the idealized Anabaptist/Mennonite church organization makes it difficult to discuss power, a concept that confronts us with inequality.

Although it has had many meanings, the term *Gelassenheit* (yieldedness) has come to signify much of the early Anabaptist/Mennonite spirit. Donald Kraybill suggests that the theme of *Gelassenheit* was a pervasive and shared theme in the social, cultural, and religious experience of all Anabaptist-related groups.[6] Robert Friedmann noted that "self-surrender," "resignation to God's will," "yieldedness to God's will," and "self-abandonment" are among the numerous expressions of the concept. It was intended to communicate both a submission to God's higher authority and the submission of the individual to the group. Hans Denck may have popularized the idea among early Anabaptists and summarized the idea effectively when he said, "There is no other way to blessedness than to lose one's self-will."[7] *Gelassenheit* provided a language for understanding martyrdom and the costs of discipleship in the early Anabaptist experience.[8] On the social level, it meant that individuals were to resist selfish ambitions and embrace the qualities of meekness and lowliness.[9] *Gelassenheit*, like the idea of church as *Gemeinde*, is a concept, a way of living, which makes it difficult to discuss power—other than understanding the interests and power of the group over against the interests and power of individual members.

Humility theology has been another important ingredient in the Anabaptist/Mennonite worldview, and it may have given *Gelassenheit* a somewhat different meaning than originally intended. Theron Schlabach has noted that adequate research on the roots of humility theology remains to be done.[10] He notes, however, that there is no doubt that its roots go back to the Pietism that Mennonites brought with them from Europe. So important was the Pietist influence on Mennonites that "by 1800 Mennonites and Amish had accepted so much from Pietism that ever since, many perceptions of what is 'Mennonite' are probably at least as Pietistic as Anabaptist."[11] Their embrace of Pietism and its humility theology meant that Mennonites lost much of the confrontational mood of early Anabaptism. It also became an important way for Anabaptist/Mennonites to set themselves apart from the individualism, enterprise, and aggressive nationalism they found in America. Schlabach notes that making humility a central theme in their life allowed them to prove themselves separate from "human greed, self-aggrandizement, and war."[12]

Like the priesthood of all believers and *Gelassenheit* themes, the humility theology that runs through Mennonite life makes power a difficult issue with which to grapple. The power of one individual to exercise her or his will over another simply cannot be reconciled with the notion of humility. To even argue the power of the group over against other groups borders on group aggrandizement, an idea that proves troublesome as well.

A Tale of Two Approaches to Mennonite Life:
Social Control versus Power

While it may be true that Mennonites have had difficulty with the concept of power, social control has proved to be a friendlier concept. In discussing this concept, sociologist Peter Berger notes that "in the background of any system of social control there is a set of assumptions concerning the range of conduct that is deemed permissible, that is, against which social controls will not be applied. The scope and character of this permissible zone of conduct vary from society to society."[13] Social control, thus understood, implies some sort of *unified* social system that tries to keep individuals and groups within its bounds.

Power is a concept that goes beyond social control. Here we can accept the classic Weberian definition, that is, power refers to the probability that an individual or a group will be able to carry out its will even against resistance.[14] Power suggests that in many instances the interests of individual or group over against the interests of another individual or group *conflict*. Parenthetically, we should note here that Weber is speaking of what some contemporary social theorists have described as "power-over" rather than "power-to"—two fundamentally different understandings of power. Thomas Wartenberg—building on the work of C. B. McPherson, Hannah Pitkin, and others—argues that this distinction is important.[15] *Power-to* refers to people's ability to use their own capacities. *Power-over* refers to people's ability to use or direct the capacities of others. Power-over speaks of domination (either individual or collective), whereas power-to speaks of energy, capacity, potential.

Of course, the distinction between social control and power is not always as clear as we might wish. While sociologists commonly use both terms as if they had different meanings, the distinction between the two can be messy. As Berger has noted, both power and social control can in-

volve coercion against recalcitrant individuals or groups.[16] He points out
that oftentimes the usage of the two words says more about the sociologists
using them than about either the words' conceptual precision or the phenomenon they address. Referring to the same phenomenon, sociologists
who stress the consensual nature of a group or society are more likely to
discuss "social control," whereas conflict-oriented sociologists will use
"power." Dennis Wrong, in advocating the conceptual advantages of the
concept of power, notes with some dismay that sociological treatments of
social control often seem to miss the asymmetry in seemingly consensual
relations.[17] He notes, for example, that many sociologists (and Berger is one
of them) stress that social control is often accomplished de facto through
the socialization process.[18] If social control works well, in other words,
community norms, standards, and boundaries are internalized through the
socialization process and there is no need for sanctions. Wrong argues that
this view minimizes the power differentials inherent in human relationships, suggesting that it represents an "oversocialized conception of humans." He points out that socialization itself involves power asymmetry—
between socializers (e.g., parents or teachers) and socializee (e.g., children
or students). Social control accomplished through socialization may, therefore, involve more power relations than sociologists have typically acknowledged.

A Preference for Social Control

Given the Mennonite reluctance to discuss power differences generally, it
is not surprising that Mennonite sociologists, in their commentaries on
Mennonites and other Anabaptist groups, frequently turn to social control
rather than power in their choice of concepts. Hostetler and Huntington,
for example, in describing the "genius" of Hutterite society, clearly assume
a consensual model wherein socialization has done its work. "Each individual," they note, "knows what is expected of him; he wants to follow these
expectations and, in most instances, is able to do so. He identifies ideologi-
cally and emotionally with the colony system. There is a strong aversion
to the ways of the *Draussiger*, the outsider, who is a child of the world. The
Hutterite looks at himself as belonging not to a world created by Newton,
Beethoven, Sartre, or Einstein, but to the model described in the Bible.
The colony is for him, as for certain other ascetic Christian groups, a para-

dise surrounded by vast numbers of unconverted human beings whose destiny is determined by God and whom he will not judge."[19]

Theron Schlabach (a historian) has correctly anticipated how sociologists might look at humility theology, noting, "A sociologist might say that Mennonite and Amish leaders used humility for boundary maintenance and social control. Clothing and other humility symbols marked who was in the group and who was out. Calls to humility were often calls to obey and be subordinate to the group."[20] In his classic study of the Old Colony Mennonites, Calvin Redekop points to the high degree of conformity among members and notes that "the deviant is the exception rather than the rule."[21] Redekop's work also focuses on the concept of social control, examining both positive and negative sanctions that are used to form social identity and compliance. Redekop's work is distinctive in that he explicitly addresses the issue of power. However, it is the power of the collective (e.g., kinship group or village) over against the isolated deviant that concerns him rather than power differentials between groups—a distinction that requires additional explanation.

Power and the Analysis of Mennonite Life: The Concept of Culture War

Let us consider some of the ways in which our analysis shifts if we substitute *power* for *social control* as the starting point in our approach to Anabaptist/Mennonite social life. Let me begin with a reexamination of church discipline, something that Anabaptist/Mennonites have discussed openly since the sixteenth century. Is church discipline a matter of power or of social control? The historical and theological origins of church discipline are fairly clear. Separating themselves from the Lutheran and Zwinglian churches, which originally disciplined only for heresy, the early Anabaptists attempted to establish a church "not having spot or wrinkle or any such thing." Menno Simons' list of those to be excluded was lengthy: "Exclude," Simons insisted, "according to the Word of God, all adulterers and fornicators, drunkards, slanderers, swearers, those who lead a shameful and inordinate life, the proud, avaricious, idolatrous, disobedient unto God, whoremongers and the like, that you may become the holy, Christian church which is without spot or blemish, which is a city built upon a rock."[22]

Harold Bender, speaking about the relationship between discipleship and discipline, clearly saw the role played by social control in church discipline. "Since the Anabaptist conception of the church is ultimately derivative from its concept of Christianity as discipleship, i.e., complete obedience by the individual to Christ and the living of a holy life patterned after His example and teachings, an essential idea in it is that the church must be holy, composed exclusively of practicing disciples, and kept pure. It is a church of order, in which the body determines the pattern of life for its members and therefore has authority over the individual's behavior. It controls admission of new members, requiring evidence of repentance, the new birth, and a holy life, and maintains the purity of the church through discipline."[23] Understood as a problem of social control, church discipline is a simple matter of taking the *deviant*—a term that assumes that the majority of people (so-called normals) agree—and subjecting him or her to appropriate sanctions in order to insure compliance to group standards or, for the deviant who refuses to comply, expulsion so as to insure the well-being of the community.

How might we otherwise conceive of church discipline? If one substitutes *power* for *social control*, church discipline becomes more a matter of conflict than of deviance from the consensual authority of the group. An analysis of church discipline viewed through the lens of power would suggest that community standards are continually contested, with the losers of that contest labeled as "deviant" and the winners retaining "normal" status.

James Davison Hunter's recent work on the contemporary American "culture war" allows us to more generally frame this understanding of church discipline as power relations. Peter Steinfels, reviewing Hunter's book *Culture Wars: The Struggle to Define America*, succinctly states the central point of the culture war thesis, noting that "two opposing world views are locked in mortal combat on the battlefield of American culture."[24] For Hunter the contemporary culture war (singular not plural) is one between the "progressive" impulse (i.e., those who tend to resymbolize historic faiths according to the prevailing assumptions of contemporary life) and the "orthodox" impulse (i.e., those who are committed to an external, definable, and transcendent authority). For the progressive, truth is a process and reality is ever unfolding. For the orthodox, truth is "capital T" truth and is for all time. People of the two impulses take sides against one another on a range of issues: homosexuality, abortion, education, and so on.

Hunter believes that the current struggle between progressive and orthodox has replaced the "old culture war" that has all but disappeared—a war between Protestant America and the waves of Jewish and Catholic immigrants who came to this country in the last half of the nineteenth and first half of the twentieth centuries. In fact, the alignments of the new warring parties cut across the old divisions. Hence progressive Protestants, Catholics, and Jews find themselves aligned with one another and at odds with orthodox Protestants, Catholics, and Jews.

Hunter suggests that the more general lesson to be learned from all this is that "cultural conflict is ultimately about the struggle for domination."[25] The conflict between the competing visions (whether you are speaking of the new or the old culture war), in other words, is about power—the power to define reality, to interpret society's collective myths, its symbols and national identity, and its basic institutions like family, work, school, and politics. Mennonites have their own collective myths, symbols, identity, and institutions; and Mennonite culture wars have been fought—just as those of a more national character have been—over the ability to define those myths, symbols, identity, and institutions.

Who has determined the shape of Mennonite myths, symbols, identity, and institutions? Here again, Hunter instructs us as to where to look. Drawing on the work of Antonio Gramsci, Hunter insists that within societies there is always a struggle for "cultural hegemony." This refers to the dominance of a single group in shaping the prevailing worldview that gives a people an interpretation of the age. Those who come to shape that worldview, those who dominate, are called "cultural elites." Hunter suggests that the cultural elites in modern America are not, by and large, intellectuals. He suggests that debates about such things as "postmodernism" and "deconstructionism" have little effect on the culture war. Hunter insists that the American cultural elite is to be found in "knowledge workers" like public policy specialists located in think tanks, special interest lobbyists, public interest lawyers, community organizers, clergy, religious administrators, and journalists. As Hunter puts it, "collectively . . . their efforts constitute the heart of the formation and maintenance of public culture."[26]

Once a group of cultural elites comes to dominate, they establish their sense of the world as the right one, the normal one. Unseating the prevailing worldview proves difficult for those who would try because the cultural elite also controls the rules of debate. Sue Curry Jansen, in a recent study of censorship, notes that cultural elites have the capacity to create the illusion of consensus through their control of public discourse. Jansen argues that "the powerful do not just have the first and last say. They do not just control access to the podium, presidium, or press room. They also determine the rules of evidence, shape the logic of assertion, define the architecture of arguments. The powerful are not just talkers. They are makers and shakers who draw the lines in language and life which others dare not cross."[27] Jansen refers to the "lines" that are drawn by the powerful as "power-knowledge." Understanding the cultural war, the cultural elites and the knowledge systems they generate and defend, then, is not simply the sociology of knowledge but rather the sociology of power-knowledge, a concept that has its contemporary roots in the work of Michel Foucault (see Chapter 2).

Mennonite Culture Wars over the Past Century

Like the cultural elites of any society, Mennonite cultural elites have established the very boundaries of Mennonite community life. The struggle for this ability to set the boundaries, to draw the lines, is at the heart of Mennonite culture wars. Thomas Wartenburg notes that there are two strategies that individuals or groups—the cultural elite—can pursue in their quest for domination. The first strategy is to use force or coercive power to establish domination over others. The second is to use ideas.[28] Clearly, Mennonite culture wars have been waged with ideas more than force, but a fair amount of coercive power has also entered into the conflict. For example, careers have been at stake: college administrators and teachers associated with Mennonite schools have lost their jobs, and ministers have been "silenced" or removed.

To pursue a power analysis of Mennonite life, the parameters of the culture wars must first be defined. What is the established power-knowledge system? How has it changed? What are the competing power-knowledge systems that are vying for hegemony? Who are the cultural elite who seek to advance one power-knowledge system over and against another? These are critical questions. For present purposes, a brief sketch of some promising ways in which these questions can be answered will have to suffice.

I would suggest that we look at the modernist-fundamentalist controversies of the first several decades of the twentieth century. This is a good place to begin, not because it is the only place where power elites have operated, but because the competing power-knowledge systems that operated then are fairly easy to see, and a fair amount of work on the period has already been done.

While George Marsden may be correct in noting that Mennonites did not, as a rule, get caught up in the formal fundamentalist and modernist movements of the early twentieth century, his observation is a little misleading because Mennonite life was shaken to its very foundations by fundamentalist-modernist debates quite similar in tone and concept to those taking place at the national level. Marsden observes that at the national level "fundamentalism was a loose, diverse, and changing federation of co-belligerents united by their fierce opposition to modernist attempts to bring Christianity in line with modern thought."[29] As Marsden cautions, we should not fall victim to the mistaken impression that fundamentalism was a simple-minded defense of a dying way of life, a mere manifestation of "cultural lag" that would be eliminated once the laggards caught up with the modern world. Nor was it a product of psychological pathologies. However shrill its rhetoric became, fundamentalism was a movement well grounded in a genuine doctrinal tradition.

Paul Toews observes that "fundamentalism among Mennonites was as much an effort to redefine the relationship between culture and Christianity as a crusade to root out theological modernism—and perhaps it was even more the former than the latter."[30] Mennonite fundamentalists differed from those debating modernism at the national level in that their concern was not so much about the drift of the modern culture but rather about the drift of Mennonites toward the alien ideologies of that culture. As a result, Mennonite fundamentalists often found themselves suspicious of, or at odds with, those who neared the modern world in pursuit of higher education or ecumenical dialogue.[31] Toews finds little evidence of true modernist theology among those dubbed as such by Mennonite fundamentalists. What they imported was cultural modernism: "new fashions, new modes of conversation, new aspirations, new forms of church service, new educational degrees." James Juhnke observes that "like historic fundamentalism, [fundamentalist] Mennonitism was an uneasy coalition of diverse groups who found it difficult to cooperate or to speak with a common voice."[32] They were able to cooperate effectively enough, however, to orchestrate major changes in the church and dictate the tenor and tempo of the Mennonite power-knowledge system of the 1920s and 1930s. Norman Kraus points out that the fundamentalists codified church doctrine, centralized church authority, and rigidified cultural nonconformity.[33]

Juhnke argues that the fundamentalist-modernist conflict among Mennonites was given its clearest shape in the (Old) Mennonite Church.[34] The Mennonite colleges provided perhaps the most fertile ground for the Mennonite culture war of the 1920s and 1930s. As Juhnke describes them, Mennonite colleges were "crucibles of contradiction": "They stood not only between traditional, German-speaking Mennonitism and progressive, English-speaking Americanism but also in the midst of the double transition from farm to town to city."[35] Fertile ground indeed for Mennonite culture wars—it is no wonder that they frequently were at the center of controversy.

The most dramatic instance of controversy was the closing of Goshen College in 1923. Preceded by the Elkhart Institute of Science, Industry and the Arts, Goshen College opened its doors for business during the 1903–4 academic year.[36] While the school had its critics, Goshen College opened with grand visions for its future. Announcing its motto to be "Culture for Service," Goshen's first president, Noah E. Byers, spoke of preparing young men and women for service to their communities and their church.[37]

Over the next two decades, such optimism was confronted with financial difficulties and opposition from various church leaders and constituencies. Some of the criticism was aimed at the "liberal" atmosphere at the college and focused on things as seemingly insignificant (in the present context) as students who participated in sporting events and wore short-sleeved shirts, and the existence of works of modern fiction on college library shelves. Some of the criticism focused more squarely on the character of the college and its faculty and administration. As Susan Fisher Miller notes, certain individuals associated with school became "lightning rods" for criticism (particularly the first president, Noah Byers, and his successor, John E. Hartzler).[38] A sure measure of the struggle was the fact that after Noah Byers' term as president (1902–13), Goshen went through five presidents in ten years.[39] While financial woes no doubt played a small part in the college's closing, it was due in larger part to doctrinal and cultural concerns. Its motto, "Culture for Service," seemed an oxymoron to fundamentalist critics (if by "service" was meant Christian service).

By 1923 "Goshen had come to symbolize Mennonite disunity."[40] The language for understanding the divisions was supplied by the fundamentalist-modernist controversies that were operative in the larger American culture. A number of Goshen College faculty and administrators were charged with theological modernism (and what Miller calls the "frightening academic bogeymen" of "the new theology" and "higher criticism"). Critics of the college were viewed as embracing fundamentalist ideologies. While it is probably true that the labels attached an ideological clarity to the positions that was not deserved, they were telling of a divide within the Mennonite world—a divide that spoke volumes about a struggle to control the definition of what it meant to be Mennonite.[41] According to Miller, the underlying question being contested in the conflicts leading to the college's closing was whether the academic estate would one day rival the ecclesiastical establishment for authority.[42]

Understood from a social-control perspective, the closing of Goshen College and the events leading up to 1923 can be understood as individual educators who—by virtue of their unique socialization experiences (e.g., educated at non-Mennonite "secular" universities)—found themselves at odds with the prevailing Mennonite ethos as applied by church leadership. Understood from the perspective of culture wars, power elites, and power-knowledge systems in competition with one another, the closing of Goshen College becomes less an issue of deviance and more a struggle over the definition of a group's identity.

This struggle was not only fought out on college campuses. The Mennonite culture wars of the early twentieth century were also fought in the area of publishing. In his 1989 book *Knowledge Is Power*, Richard Brown provides a fascinating account of the impact of print publications on the power-knowledge system operating in Boston, Massachusetts, at the close of the seventeenth century. Brown's analysis of information networks in Boston and the impact of print publications is instructive if one wishes to better understand some of the conflicts and power struggles among Mennonites. Brown details the way prominent families and clerical leaders maintained a power base in Boston through their use of "information networks." Focusing on Samuel Sewall, an individual who is remembered for having served as a judge in the infamous Salem witchcraft trials, Brown shows how a circle of family and professional and social contacts controlled information and hence exercised considerable influence in the city and Massachusetts Bay Colony. Brown suggests that Sewall's information network was enhanced by his frequent "information transactions" with clerical leaders (such as Increase Mather and his son Cotton). What is perhaps most interesting, however, is Brown's suggestion that the appearance of print publications in Boston diffused information, making it more widely available and thereby reducing the influence of the information networks (and power) of people like Sewall and his clerical contacts. At the same time, Brown points out that those who controlled the new print media came to play a critical role in the newly emerging power-knowledge system.[43]

Mennonites have been in the publishing business for a long time. This is the case even if one focuses exclusively on the U.S. experience. The first Mennonite book in America, a widely accepted confession of faith, was published in 1727, and in 1748 the Ephrata colony in Pennsylvania handled the first U.S. printing of the *Martyrs Mirror*.[44] The Ephrata colony published other Mennonite writings during the colonial period, but it wasn't until the second half of the nineteenth century that Mennonite publishing really came of age.

In 1864 John F. Funk began printing the first regular publication of the (Old) Mennonite Church, the *Herald of Truth*. As a young man, Funk had worked on his father's farm. Then, after a brief stint in teaching, he entered the lumber business in Chicago. While in Chicago, Funk became involved in various church-related activities, including teaching Sunday school and distributing and writing tracts. Funk became committed to a churchwide publication and ultimately established a Mennonite publishing house in northern Indiana, leading James Juhnke to call him a "denominational entrepreneur."[45] Funk and his partners in publishing tried to walk a middle line between the "new" Mennonites on the left and "old order" Mennonites on the right. By 1890 Funk had convinced many Mennonites that the *Herald of Truth* was indeed "their" paper. In many ways, Funk's publication did facilitate Mennonite unity. It also catapulted Funk into a position of considerable power and authority.

The year 1890 was significant for other reasons. In that year Daniel Kauffman—then a twenty-five-year-old school teacher—was converted through the preaching of John S. Coffman. Over the next several decades,

Kauffman was to become one of the most powerful leaders of the (Old) Mennonite Church. His ascendancy was in no small part attributable to the role he assumed in Mennonite publishing. During the (Old) Mennonite general conference of 1898, there was a struggle for control over various church institutions, including Mennonite publishing.[46] Kauffman was pitted directly against Funk, and the latter resisted. In what proved to be a very stormy period of transition, Funk's influence waned and the center of Mennonite publishing moved (along with Kauffman) from northern Indiana to western Pennsylvania. Kauffman and other young leaders founded a church-owned publishing house and a publication board and began publishing the *Gospel Herald*.[47] This marked more than a physical movement of church publishing. It marked a profound shift in the control of Mennonite media and, correspondingly, the lines of the power-knowledge system were redrawn.

In 1924 a group of Mennonite "progressives" established an alternative publication to Kauffman's *Gospel Herald*. Titled the *Christian Exponent*, the periodical was edited by Vernon Smucker, a 1915 graduate of Goshen College and the one-time editor of the *Christian Monitor*. The periodical attempted to affirm its connection to Mennonite theological sensibilities but also offered a clear criticism of some church leaders. Herein, James Juhnke notes, was its "radical challenge." In describing the significance of the *Exponent*, Juhnke suggests that "at age thirty-five Smucker was only a few years younger than Kauffman had been in 1905. If history were to repeat itself, a new generation would come to power and 'old' Mennonite authority would shift away from Kauffman and Scottdale to a new center—perhaps to Bluffton in western Ohio. Daniel Kauffman and his generation of conservatives would not rest easily until this 'anti-church publication,' as Kauffman called it, went out of business. There appears to have been an intergenerational struggle for power as surely as for orthodoxy and cultural stability."[48]

By 1928 the *Christian Exponent* ceased publication. In 1929 a conservative quarterly, titled the *Sword and Trumpet*, was born. Published in Virginia, the periodical was edited by George R. Brunk, who set out to correct what he saw as the "drift" among Mennonites toward "liberalism, worldliness, and Calvinism."[49] While careful to suggest that it was "intended to supplement every other loyal paper in the Church and supplant none," Brunk was not only watchful of those progressives who clearly manifested the "drift." He was also mindful, and at times critical, of the main church publications such as the *Gospel Herald* and its editor, Daniel Kauffman.[50]

It may be, as Juhnke suggests, that the *Christian Exponent* was "too far ahead" of the thinking of most Mennonites.[51] However, it would be a mistake to reduce the publication's existence to a matter of individual initiative or misguidedness. So too would it be unfortunate to see the *Sword and Trumpet* as the result of conservative excesses. While it is tempting to see the likes of Vernon Smucker or George Brunk as aberrations or deviants from some prevailing Mennonite worldview and in need of sanction, they can alternatively be seen as spokespeople for sides in a contest. Indeed, Juhnke describes the *Christian Exponent* as a "mouthpiece for the 'old Goshen' group."[52] Yet to the extent that the debates over Goshen College, its control and its future, are to be understood as manifestations of a larger struggle between groups contesting Mennonite identity, the same can be said of publishing disputes in the 1920s.

John Graybill has appropriately suggested that the *Christian Exponent* must be understood as well in terms of the fundamentalist-modernist debates within the Mennonite church. "The *Christian Exponent* was only one expression of the conflict between progressives and conservatives; it was not the cause," Graybill observes. "The progressive group which organized and published the paper had been quarreling increasingly with the mainstream group. The closing of Goshen College seemed to give the final push to the progressives. What they now needed was an organ to express their views. The *Exponent* provided the forum. As Lester Hostetler said in a 1982 interview: 'The aim was to have a platform for our side of the case.'"[53]

While the specific agenda varied between publishers (in terms of relations to the "mainstream group"), the same could have been said of the other publications of the day. Correspondingly, the tensions between Daniel Kauffman, Vernon Smucker, and George Brunk can be best understood as a struggle to give media voice to various factions in this culture war. Interestingly enough, these editors and others who wrote for their respective publications may have seen the power implications to these struggles more clearly than have most sociologists. An Ernest Gehman and George Brunk cartoon appearing in the October 1930 *Sword and Trumpet* captured the essence of the culture war, using images of the Mennonite "fort," or "stronghold," taking shots at modernists while being undermined by "world-lovers, laxitarians, and liberals" within the gates of the Mennonite camp (see figure).[54]

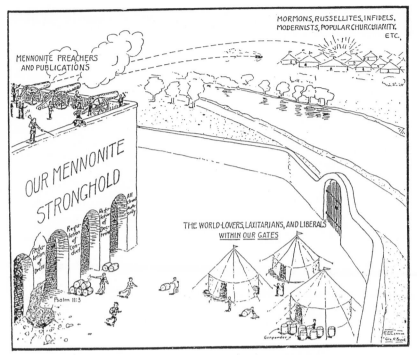

Brethren, we must also fight the nearest foes, OR WE ARE LOST!

Similarly, the editors of *Christian Exponent* understood that they were in the midst of an ideological struggle for the future of the Mennonite church. As Lester Hostetler commented in the first issue of the periodical in 1924, "The so-called unrest within the church may prove to be the birth pangs of better things. At least one likes to hope so. But we must recognize that there are possibilities in either direction. We have special problems to meet in our day as our forefathers did in their day ... It is the aim of the *Exponent* to help define and clarify the so-called church problems and questions and issues which are coming so thick and fast that they threaten at times to completely overshadow Him who came in order that the life in us might be full and joyous and abundant."[55] The *Christian Exponent* was to provide a vehicle for other points of view—other than those expressed in the official church publications.

Daniel Kauffman was, in many ways, caught in the middle. Trying to hold the middle together during these times of great turmoil, he was seen by the fundamentalists as being a "laxitarian" who associated too freely with liberal elements in the church. At the same time, he was seen by liberals as standing in the way, through his unquestioned control of the major church publications, of the free exchange of ideas and the inevitable movement of the church and its institutions. All this must have seemed somewhat bewildering if not ironic to Kauffman, who as a young man had undoubtedly harbored similar feelings about John Funk.

The culture war was also waged on the congregational and conference levels. Lester Hostetler had been involved in one such battle at Walnut Creek in Ohio.[56] The experience of the culture war in the congregation taught one lesson very well: when one side of the culture war succeeds in establishing domination, this does not mean that those who lose will acquiesce. Robert Dahl distinguishes between the "potential for control" and the "potential for unity."[57] He suggests that the two may vary independently from one another. Controlling a population does not guarantee its unity. One only need look as far as the congregational membership figures for the College Mennonite Church around the closing of Goshen College to see Dahl's point. The College congregation became deeply embroiled in a conflict with the leadership of the Indiana-Michigan conference, and J. C. Wenger reports that of the 213 members listed in the *Mennonite Yearbook* in 1923, only 15 remained by 1924.[58]

I would suggest that schisms—within congregations and within conferences—as well as the conflicting views of Mennonite life offered by various parties during this entire period of Mennonite history need to be looked at from the standpoint of competing visions of community life. The fundamentalist-modernist struggles of the 1920s and 1930s gave shape to the Mennonite power-knowledge system of the day. They also shaped the worldviews and strategies of both the transitional generation of Mennonite leaders (those with one foot in the old and one in the new worldviews) and a new generation of Mennonite cultural elites that would, in its day, usher in a new power-knowledge system.

The new power elite, which had moved into positions of power in congregations, conferences, educational institutions, and publishing houses by the 1940s and 1950s, was far more highly educated and cosmopolitan in character (having traveled both to the cities of the American East Coast and those of Europe) than the previous cultural elite. They developed a power-knowledge system that tried to "recover" the Anabaptist vision within Mennonitism, thereby undermining the truth claims of fundamentalism. Thus, for example, by 1951 J. C. Wenger was able to give new (modern, postfundamentalist) meaning to "nonconformity." Wenger observed that

> even the members of the so-called nonconformist Christian groups need also to deepen their understanding of the Biblical meaning of separation. All too often the meaning of the word "world" has not been clear. It has sometimes been a failure of nonconformist Christian bodies to distinguish between those who are not born again and those who are not members of the so-called "plain churches." While it is true that there is all too much worldliness in many Christian denominations today, the fact remains that by the term "world" the New Testament has in mind those who belong to Satan, together with all their ways of thinking and living, their evil attitudes, and their rebellion against God and His Christ. Members of the Mennonite Church and of similar groups need to clarify their thinking in reference to the concept of worldliness. Being nonconformed to the world is not a matter of rejecting science and inventions, nor is it the maintenance of a cultural *status quo*, nor is it difference for its own sake. One cannot be nonconformed to the world by adopting a few symbols of nonconformity while remaining carnal and unspiritual in heart. Nonconformity to the world is the natural outcome of having been born again and of being alert to the spiritual issues which confront Christians in a given culture.[59]

Had Wenger drawn such conclusions in the 1920s, he might have faced a fate similar to those who had been branded "liberals" and "modernists" (the likes of J. E. Hartzler, Paul Whitmer, N. E. Byers, and others). By 1951, however, the culture war was shifting in favor of the forces of education, ecumenism, and greater (if not complete) cultural assimilation. This is not to say that skirmishes were over: battles over wedding rings, life insurance, plain coats for ministers, and head coverings continued to be waged throughout the 1950s and into the 1960s.

Mapping the Contemporary Mennonite Power-Knowledge System

One of the most pressing questions for historians should be: How does one map the power-knowledge system of various historical periods? Similarly, for sociologists working on Mennonite life, the question must be: What are the parameters of the power-knowledge system today? Who are the power elite, and what system of power-knowledge currently dominates Mennonite life? I suspect that the answers we will find will look similar to the answers that are being given as sociologists try to understand North American society as a whole.

Following the work of Abercrombie, Hill, Turner, and others, we may find that there is no "dominant ideology" or power-knowledge system among Mennonites today.[60] This could be due to a sort of "postmodern" reasoning, that is, Mennonite society has become so fragmented that the coherence of any ideology escapes it.

If Mennonite society is truly fragmented, and no single power-knowledge system works today, this may be due to a sort of "leadership void" similar to that which you sometimes hear or read about as an explanation for our current political woes. That is, after the early 1960s, with the death of people like Harold Bender, Orie Miller, and other power brokers, there was a failure of a generation to supply a new cultural elite. What the assassinations of the late 1960s were to the American political scene, the lure of newly opened opportunities to work in non-Mennonite educational institutions, business, private foundations, and even government may have been to (potential) Mennonite cultural elites.

This problem of leadership has been complicated by a growing ambivalence about giving Mennonite leadership too much "say." This is a genie that Harold Bender let out of the bottle when he reshaped the power-knowledge system through his "recovery of the Anabaptist vision." Calvin Redekop notes that, especially since the attacks led by the Concern Movement[61] in the late 1950s and early 1960s, institutionalized leadership has become problematic. Citing Urie Bender's *Four Earthen Vessels*, Redekop points out that Mennonite leaders have, on the one hand, found themselves expected to preserve the historical faithfulness of the Mennonite heritage; while on the other hand, they have been practically powerless in terms of the authority and leadership functions that would enable them to carry out their mandate. If Redekop is right, this calls for a closer examination of the sources of legitimation available to current Mennonite leaders.[62]

In the end, Wartenberg is certainly right: power *is* one of the central phenomena of human life. To account for it, to develop our analysis of it, both as part of the Anabaptist-Mennonite critique of secular non-Mennonite culture and as part of our understanding of social relations within the Mennonite world, should be one of our highest priorities.

CHAPTER EIGHT

Power and Authority
in Mennonite Ecclesiology
A Feminist Perspective

DOROTHY YODER NYCE

AND LYNDA NYCE

One of the most salient issues concerning the use and abuse of power among religious groups in general, and Anabaptist/Mennonitism in particular, is gender. This topic, which has already emerged in a number of the foregoing chapters, is the center of attention in the present chapter. The authors present a wide-ranging theoretical and practical discussion of power and gender in relation to Mennonite ecclesiology. The discussion combines scholarly analysis and critique with a call for change.

Power, which is inherent in all social relationships, actively shapes church life, whether church members and leaders own, confront, deny, or ignore the extent of its influence within ecclesial settings. When traditional, unbalanced power is legitimated, church experience resembles certain sixteenth-century modes of Roman Catholic leadership. Early Anabaptists protested against those forms of church polity, and prophetic word is still needed today against them. Many forms of worldly power and authority have shaped church practice. Historians, sociologists, and theologians have identified the believer's church in various ways that presuppose strong biblical ethics, yet as Rosemary Radford Ruether notes, "All patterns of church polity are relative and historically developed, patterned after political and social patterns in the culture."[1]

Most normative exercise of power in Christian churches has centered in a few men. Though rarely named, such exercise accentuates gender divisions. By *gender* we refer to the social roles linked to masculine and feminine that are largely produced through culture, whereas *sex* refers explicitly to biological distinctions between women and men. Just why a pattern becomes normative and who exercises power to determine that designation is a subject that needs attention.

The fact that men are socialized for more public roles and are identified as more authoritative does not prove that the patterns have merit. In fact, such stereotypes unduly bless some, while limiting other individuals. Reinforced by male language and a male priesthood for God, the Jewish-Christian heritage credits men with more qualities of the divine. This limits God's breadth of being as it blesses men's practice of power. As women exercise disciplined skills with biblical texts and risk dissent from traditional views that restrict their strengths, more equitable channeling of power may follow. Faithfulness, marred for centuries, will occur when power finds equitable expression and when authority emerges from within each person. Commonweal—the common or public good—could then shape leadership consistent with Jesus' radical call for wholeness (salvation) for all.

The Concept of Power

Max Weber's definition of power is an important touchstone in contemporary Western thinking about power. Although Weber's notion of power has been translated differently, it is typically understood by social scientists as "the probability that one actor within a social relationship will be in a position to carry out his own will despite resistance, regardless of the basis on which this probability rests."[2] Using this definition, the "powerful" are seen as those who have power *over* others—whether via access to resources, positions of prestige, or wealth. Power-over creates a social relationship wherein a power differential exists between the dominant and subordinate actors. It implies "the ability to advance oneself and, simultaneously, to control, limit, and if possible destroy the power of others."[3]

Many views of power have influenced believer's church ecclesiology since the mid 1500s. Today Mennonite women scholars turn to feminist writers like Elisabeth Schüssler Fiorenza, who explains feminist intentions to change systems of domination and subordination. Patriarchy has generally conveyed a separation between men, who dominate or have power over subordinate, less powerful women. But rather than limiting the discussion to man's rule over woman, Schüssler Fiorenza has introduced the neologism *kyriarchy*. By this she means "rule of the emperor/master/lord/father/husband over his subordinates." This points to the multiple "interstructuring of systems of dehumanization."[4]

Patterns and attitudes related to power among believers' church members often reinforce domination and submission. This in part stems from faulty biblical interpretation. For example, creation texts in Genesis reveal how God shared dominion with the first human beings. Whereas dominion in that context meant "responsible care," it has been interpreted as justifying power *over* created life, including other people. Or, in another example, the verse in Ephesians 5 that calls for wives to submit to their husbands has been interpreted in denial of the overarching radical call of verse 21 for mutual submission between husband and wife. As long as imbalance of power marks this primary human relationship, other expressions of power within the church are destined for inequity. Jesus spoke for people restricted by social power, warning those with more power to share it more selflessly (see texts surrounding Matt. 18:1; Luke 7:44; 11:46; John 11:27; 13:14).

The Historic Position of the Free Church on Power

Several years ago, when approached about the extent of his power, the CEO of a major Mennonite agency responded, "Oh, I don't think of myself as having power." Such a denial should alert those who might be under his influence. Traditionally, Mennonite leaders have tended to downplay how positions convey power. Whether appointed or chosen by lot, they have expressed suspicion toward the exercise of power. Because it is thought to reflect sinful pride from the world beyond the church or is known to have the potential for coercion and force, personal power has been minimized by church leaders. Fear of accepting power and its harmful consequences to others at times prompts its subtle use. As Julia Kasdorf observes, "Traditional injunctions to be humble have at times served to silence the voices of some while protecting the authority of others in the Mennonite community."[5]

S. Loren Bowman notes Church of the Brethren leaders' reluctance to admit the presence of ecclesial power. Because of the dictum "Power corrupts," to talk about the use of power and authority is "not nice." Leaders close their eyes to it, yet they use their positions to gain privilege.[6] While some leaders willingly enable church members, others prefer not to recognize their responsibility for power. Still others seem unwilling to admit that their actions may block able members from exercising their power. For example, rather than endorse qualified women for the task, a few (Old) Mennonite Church men controlled much of the written discussion about women and the church during the 1970s and early 1980s.

Looking to historic origins, Gordon Zook identifies the first generation of Anabaptist leadership (1523–1561) as "charismatic." Leaders challenged the dominant, interrelated system of church and state hierarchy. Through personal power of convictions, they adapted the style of leadership to particular situations. But the "free-floating and ad hoc" early New Testament pattern of leadership began to give way to "more settled" structures.[7]

So how did early Anabaptist women's authority express itself? Lois Barrett translated and examined the longest extant document (33 pages) written by an Anabaptist woman—Ursula's "77 visions." Five years after the movement began, Ursula explains, "The glory of the Lord approached me and unfolded." During that charismatic era, and perhaps because women were less encumbered with "official" authority, they were more prone to or open to visions. As both artists and exemplars, visionaries used their power to teach, counsel, and heal. Through them, people were strengthened to "grow internally, change the world, and take direct actions."[8]

The Anabaptist emphasis on the end of this world and individuals' hope for the next world affected leadership too. Because many leaders died for reasons of conscience, the turnover rate precluded dynasties of leaders from emerging. Yet kyriarchy shaped their praxis. Convincing egalitarian attitudes did not replace previous Roman Catholic Church patterns. Historian Joyce Irwin finds little evidence "that women's status in sixteenth-century sects was more free and equal than in established churches."[9] Keith Sprunger, in his study of Anabaptist women, concurs: "It is hard to find in the Anabaptist writings any distinctive or innovative trend regarding women."[10]

Yet, historian Linda Huebert Hecht's study of the Tirol area reflects a premise from Schüssler Fiorenza's study of the early church in Acts: since women's accounts of ministry survived androcentric history writing, we can be sure that even more were significant leaders. Huebert Hecht's data also confirm Max Weber's hypothesis: "Women have always been more involved and more visible in the early stages of religious movements . . . until relationships in the community become routine and regimented."[11] Using court records of 238 women from the Austrian territory, Huebert Hecht discovered four major categories of women's leadership within a several-year span: 172 were *believers* whose only crime was rebaptism; 10 were *missioners* who actively brought others into the movement; 7 were *lay leaders* who preached, baptized, and hosted meetings (one unnamed female leader of the Ziller Valley allegedly baptized 800 people); and 49 were *martyrs*, most of whom had been arrested at least twice.[12]

Consider Helene of Freyberg, rebaptized sometime before March of 1528. Her castle became a house-church and a refuge for Anabaptists. Her example and teaching, her profound confession and testimony, and her letters influenced believers. These aroused suspicion of her long before she was exiled from Augsburg. Also competent in theological debates, she served as intermediary between Pilgram Marpeck and Caspar Schwenckfeld.[13] Clearly, women were among charismatic leaders of the Anabaptist era.

By 1561 Mennonites adopted a threefold ministry pattern called "the bench." In so doing, early Anabaptists followed a pattern common among many religious sects: the movement to more structured church, social, and religious arrangements. First-generation rigor and radicalism gave way to the demands of the second generation for growth in membership, accumulation of wealth and status, and education of the young.[14] A related shift occurred within the early church, as recorded in Acts and Timothy. The pattern clearly reverted to a more hierarchical scheme, like that practiced prior to Jesus' new, more equitable community. Spanning four centuries, the Mennonite triad of bishops or elders, preachers or ministers, and deacons was ordained to lifelong leading. Surely, variations rose and waned. Even the term "threefold pattern" sounds contemporary for what likely formed or de-formed over time.

Zook identifies the single-pastor pattern as emerging after 1950. Its cabinet-style coordinating group, followed by the addition of a body of elders, preceded shifts that included salaries and the present team-

leadership concept. Within the single-pastor and team-leadership patterns, women have had a greater voice than before but not without resistance. Many church members fear women's increased self-definition and
personal control. Or the wife of a male leader may still be praised for stay-
ing "behind the scenes." The question emerges whether defining women
in relation to men distorts the image of both. Such distortions, related to
gender and power within the church, no longer go unnoticed, however.

Historian Arnold Snyder raises further questions: Can the present
North American church, from its position of privilege, truly follow the call
to serve Christ in the world? Does being part of a powerful northern nation counter the gospel's vision of a worldwide church? Will believers resort to conformity and silence rather than lose privilege? Has the church
that is structured in bureaucracies of control (led by a professional, elite
class that expects members to be submissive) not misused valid power?[15]

Leadership

A central theme in early Anabaptist/Mennonite writing is "the body of
believers" or "brotherhood," a relatively egalitarian entity. According to
historian Harold Bender, the Anabaptist emphasis on the church as a
brotherhood is antihierarchical; it minimizes the role of clergy and church
offices and places emphasis on lay participation and responsibility.[16] Kniss
and Ainlay note that the egalitarian emphasis of this "idealized Anabaptist-
Mennonite church organization seeks to make members full participants,
to level inequalities of status or power, and to de-emphasize conflict in
interpersonal and intragroup relationships."[17] Yet for many church leaders
this remains only an ideal; the practice of power in leadership has not made
most members full participants.

Some leaders, thinking they might minimize the corruption of power,
choose to add the concept of *service* to leadership. To attach "servant" to
power fails, however, to attack the root stance of "power over" within
churches. For as Schüssler Fiorenza observes, "As long as actual power relationships and status privileges are not changed, a theological panegyric
of service must remain a mere moralistic sentiment and a dangerous rhetorical appeal that mystifies structures of domination."[18] To claim to be a
servant leader, yet retain rather than reinvest authority given by others,
makes hypocrisy of the "servant" role. To cause another to be dependent

robs that other of worth and personal authority. The weakness of leaders who depend on others to be dependent upon them cannot be disguised as "service," for to serve another or to truly share power means to delegate it and to exchange roles.

Another manipulative feature of faulty servant leading is expressed when a leader carries out tasks, notably in the public arena, in place of others who are either fully qualified or who deserve to have the experience in order to improve their skills. Leaders who fail to empower those who have invested their personal authority in them do the investors a disservice. Authentic servant leading, woven into the fabric of an institution, entails the regular exchange of roles. As David McClelland states, "To be an effective leader, one must turn all so-called followers into leaders."[19] For leaders to become followers further reveals authenticity.

A context for mutual service presents itself with the planned merger of the General Conference Mennonite Church and the Mennonite Church denominations. Time will reveal how these two groups will agree, or agree to disagree. As Rodney Sawatsky notes, General Conference Mennonites have "rejected the authority of Mennonite bishops who sought to maintain a traditional Mennonite identity premised on sectarian separation from the world."[20] Some distinctive features of General Conference Mennonites pointed out by Sawatsky include: authority of individual religious experience (for Christian freedom and against group discipline); congregational autonomy (decentralized); value of acculturation (borrowing from others); centrality of authority (identity impossible without authority); high view of biblical authority (preaching). With more validation of the individual, the move toward the ideal of exchange between followers and leaders might materialize.

Creative, enabling church leadership waits to be reborn. But authentic "priesthood of all believers" continues to be aborted as long as the rite of ordination distinctly blesses a few. Some people believe that because men are ordained for leadership tasks, equity requires that women also receive that blessing. For others, being radical and equitable requires an end to the selective rite of ordination.

A consistent believers' church model would hold that *all* are ordained, as part of personal commitment in adult baptism, to the prime task of sharing the good news of God's inclusion. That rite initiates ministry. To re-ordain in essence discredits priesthood for all. Therefore, ministry, and the power endowed through it, needs to be credited to, and claimed by, every believer. Defined more broadly than tasks performed by "ordained" individuals, ministry, in its basic and inclusive sense, describes every believer's service to Christ, the church, and the world.[21]

Several biblical texts give direction. Matthew 23 begins with a challenge for leaders to avoid vanity. Because all people are brothers and sisters, special titles distinguish only the divine. Members of Jesus' immediate circle of followers were expected to avoid human hierarchy. Not being God, believers had no basis for being authoritative or for forming a Christian elite class. Piety for the sake of honor expressed hypocrisy. To be set aside through a rite, or to expect others to call them "Master" or "Great One," went against their common priesthood.

Luke 22:24–27 also addresses leaders of the Christian community. Issues noted include strife among believers over power, betrayal within the circle of the covenant, interpersonal humility when believers sit at the "Lord's Table," "office" or position that counters the integrity of community, and failure of authority figures to follow the pattern of Jesus' life and passion. Matthew's account (20:20–28) of contention among leaders adds striking features. It portrays the mother of James and John requesting a position of honor, attributing such "small mindedness" to a woman. Without condemning ambition, Jesus clarifies what accompanies her request: suffering, service, and forgiveness. The request for honor is deemed inappropriate, for only God determines who will be exalted. Similarly, only God decides who is worthy of inclusion in God's commonweal. So among people of God's kingdom, washing others' feet qualifies a leader rather than dominion or prestige.

These texts do not negate the reality or validation of power in Scripture. In most religions, power is an important quality of divinity. Those with faith in the One God are to express that power, as did Jesus, by bringing glory to God and by enabling the marginalized of society to renew their strength. Numerous acts of power beyond Jesus' miracles appear in texts. Ruth exercised power when she assisted Naomi's reversal from deep bitterness, an expression of power from within. Esther, with power and courage, approached the king on behalf of her marginal Israelite people. The Syrophoenician woman expressed power when she countered Jesus. Her sense of personal authority influenced him to change his plan. He then agreed to extend salvation (a message of power) to the Gentiles. Peter also gained new power to include others. Whereas Cornelius was already a convinced believer, Peter's conversion to accepting those he had thought were "unclean" transformed him into a new, authentic witness.

Need believers' church members, therefore, hesitate to claim power or inherent authority? Or might caution about it imply guilt for abusing valid power? What alternative beliefs about, or practice of, power lie dormant within church settings? Perhaps a first response involves protest against past developments, against consent primarily to "things as they are." Leaders may fear change, but kyriarchal power will decline only when members refuse to approve faulty patterns. Rosemary Radford Ruether argues that "it is precisely at [the] point of assent and economic support that Catholics need to subvert hierarchical power."[22]

Judith Plaskow, a Jew, also expresses dissent. Jews must reject the historic Jewish idea of chosenness (without denying that Israel is a distinct religious community). The purpose of being chosen was to tell others of God's *inclusion* of all people. Yet the "chosen" idea has come to exclude others or to imply superiority. Plaskow calls Jews to view election as *duty* (not privilege), as *service* open to suffering (not reason to be exalted).[23]

Jesus set a standard for action. Asking for baptism, Jesus willingly showed his solidarity with people in their need. The "heavens were opened," and Jesus was endowed with power, wisdom, and holiness. Chosen by God, he took on the mission of offering wholeness to all people. In order to begin his ministry, Jesus set a precedent. In the rite of water and Spirit baptism, he was "ordained" for all of the leading, healing, calling, and forgiving that he would practice. In that rite, he established a true "priesthood of all believers."

Authentic adult baptism, then, bestows the power to minister on each believer. No further rite to distinguish some who minister from others who minister is justified or encouraged by the radical Jesus. To bless a few can detract from all believers being responsible with the power invested in them in baptism. To do so blesses hierarchical division. Letty Russell reiterates this point: "Many women would like to see the sacraments return to their communal function with baptism of all members for ministry . . . Women notice the basic issue . . . to transform the church structures that divide clergy from people and obscure the meaning of ministry as the work of Christ that is shared by all those who are united with him through baptism."[24] For Russell, there are never too many leaders. She believes that power and leadership gifts multiply when shared. Rather than endorse power accumulated at the expense of others, she affirms styles of leadership based on a partnership paradigm of shared authority in community. Leaders share power and authority; they inspire others to lead. "Effectiveness is related to how well the leader empowers those who are assigned marginal roles." The task begins with opposing and exposing social and ecclesial patterns that sanction over-under categories or that interpret ministry as service while blessing clerical privilege and exclusion.[25]

The Radical Reformation was strongly anticlerical; to confront today's leaders about clerical power entails a similar risk. The historian Arnold Snyder predicts that "the desire of the powerful to dominate and utilize the ministry of the church will remain constant." He concludes that if we were to imitate "the Anabaptist impulse towards a more equal ministry," we would curtail a clerical class. Our "faith parents" desired "a church in which every believer is a minister, a servant, and disciple of Christ."[26] Such a vision will fail to be actualized, however, if church leaders resist relinquishing their "credentials." If all believers fully endorsed all as ministers, no need would exist for the terms *clergy* and *laity* that inappropriately divide followers of the Radical One who lived and died to empower *all*.

Power is measured by its ability to control or to mobilize people and institutions. Worship services and church events also foster either a dependency on the "leader" or significant empowerment of the majority. Group process enables one or several of the following: goal achievement, policy change or implementation, behavior that benefits or harms, renewed or altered patterns, and the dispersal of power.[27] To the extent that leaders or members abuse, downplay, or ignore these options, effective influence is bypassed.

God's power is entrusted to believers; "it belongs to us, to the extent that we pass it on."[28] For Christians to have faith means that they believe in God's power through Jesus. When Jesus said to the woman who touched his garment, "Go in peace, your faith has healed you," he acknowledged her power in what occurred. To re-create power in those disenfranchised by church or society further multiplies God's good power.

This is not to say that all church leadership has "failed." Exceptional pastors truly enable all members; and members, through personal authority, expect to be faithful ministers to others. But the reciprocal task is not simple. Increased sensitivity to God's mission has transpired at times, but church people need not deny the existence of problems. Nina Colwill suggests that a person competent in organizations must be extraordinary, visible, and relevant.[29] Within church life, the extraordinary may counter community, and the drive for visibility may foster pride or fail to empower others. However, to be relevant never hurts.

A Broader Look at Power

Thus far we have noted that theorists, as well as those who have wielded power, have often accepted a classic Weberian understanding of power without reference to a broader meaning of the term. In German, *power* is both *Macht* and *Kraft*. *Macht* implies might or use of strength; *Kraft* means by virtue of, to be in operation, efficacy, or energy—"power exists as potential."[30] If seen as *Macht* and not as *Kraft*, power intrinsically prescribes social relationships of dominance and inequality. Thus the other face of power, as indicated in the previous chapter, is *power-to*[31]—a very different concept than *power-over*. Power-to invokes the usage of *Kraft* and has been termed "empowerment" by many feminist writers. Power-to can be used in a positive manner to encourage others to rise from a position of comparative powerlessness to one of comparative equality.

The predominant kyriarchal expression of power has been *power-over*. This sanctions power at another's cost. One person gains strength or definition, while another's is reduced. One participates more fully, while another loses voice. One holds onto rather than reciprocating that which truly enhances. *Power-to*, on the other hand, expects each individual to stand firm and free. Rather than being coercive, it promotes partnership. Rather than needing categories like dominant and subordinate, rulers and servants, high class and untouchable, haves and have-nots, clergy and laity, power-to knows mutual suffering and glory. In believers' church ecclesiology, whether for efficiency or for more nefarious intent, power has been exercised as *Macht* rather than *Kraft*. However, the believers' church ideal implies that the early Anabaptist church felt that *Kraft* was essential.

As we have seen in Chapter 2, for Michel Foucault power is productive and strategic. Power as negative or repressive is a direct antithesis to strategic power. As repression, power is a force exercised over the body that denies its real "essence." But as a productive force, power produces reality; it produces realms of objects and discourses of truth.[32] When Foucault conceives of productive, strategic power, he notes that power is exercised in techniques, functions, and tactics but is not a possession. Furthermore, power relations are not limited to confrontations between social classes or between citizens and the state, but they exist at the most basic level of the social domain.

Society writ large is imprisoned in a mode of conceptualizing power that originated within the context of early Western industrialism. This factor has created an obstacle to effective analysis of contemporary power relations. For Foucault, each historical era legitimizes a particular discourse of power/knowledge. The establishment of a structure of power within society or a group in society is correlated with the production and circulation of "true" discourse: "Power produces knowledge (and not simply by encouraging it because it serves power or by applying it because it is useful) . . . power and knowledge directly imply one another . . . there is no power relation without any correlative constitution of a field of knowledge, nor any knowledge that does not presuppose and constitute at the same time power relations."[33]

Following this logic, feminists attempt to be more "up front" about power, their own included. Free to critique abuse of power—whether by force, coercion, or political and economic might—they are determined to avoid repeating mistakes. They also expect to be constructive through power, to bring about greater justice through exercising it. They describe the neutral quality of power in terms like "the ability to act," "the capacity to effect change," "a person's present means to any apparent good," and "the ability to mobilize resources."

In *Gyn/ecology*, Mary Daly focuses on the importance of discourse in building reality—a truth of women that has been denied and repressed.[34] Yet feminists have increasingly recognized that there are multiple truths of women (for example, that of white and nonwhite women)[35] and thus multiple practices of power. Foucault's emphasis on the material or basic level of power relations may lead to new awareness of power differentials among women of various race, class, and age groups. As women continue to recognize their diversity and to rediscover their own relations of power, knowledge, and discourse, they wish to avoid "the romanticizing assumption that acknowledgment of women's historical involvement in social discourse will somehow be the key to success in rebuilding a world with equality for women."[36]

Generally defined or shaped by those who control it, power within patriarchy left oppressed men and most women at a disadvantage. Feminists reinterpret power by focusing on empowerment. Throughout the recent World Council of Churches "Decade of Churches in Solidarity with Women," feminist women of the church boldly expressed their vision. Ready to reclaim dignity rather than succumb to being victims, they took initiative to reconstruct theology and spirituality. They endorsed societal and familial changes that foster relationships based on equitable authority.

Elaine Graham identifies three dimensions of gender: (1) Individual characteristics and personality traits shape a person's sense of self, or *identity*. (2) Gender *relations* involve multiple factors and roles, including customs and cultural expectations concerning marriage, position within law, education, or government, sexual divisions of labor, and how wealth, opportunity and rewards are distributed. (3) Gender *representations*, coming from deep within structures of culture, affect the metaphors and binary distinctions that order and shape our complex perceptions.[37]

Open to such new ways of thinking, women's discussion of power related to leadership will first test views through the direct experience of women. Personal charisma matters more than office. Determined to be creative, women will both accept and challenge traditional sources of religious authority. They will, for example, critique religious ideas and practices that distinguish mind from body in to order to reinforce hierarchy or exclusive separation. The historic Mennonite posture of *sola scriptura* will be scrutinized also, for never has Scripture alone been our source of authority.

Secondly, according to Durka, women are changing the style of religious leadership.[38] Intent on being more collaborative, shaped by direct religious experience, and influenced by having been on the margins, sensitive women ask new questions: Why simply move into ordained ministry models meant to exclude women? How do openness, pluralism, and dialogue reshape ministry? Writer and professor of theology Letty Russell calls the church to host a round table where all gather around God's table as a household. With no space on a circle for a "head," each member claims, extends, and receives authority. Those whom society rejects will be invited; faithfulness to Christ depends on that. Those empowered at the margins participate from there assured, or they join the center. From either location, they talk back. They confront and disturb those who have presumed a central location. All work to cancel divisions of margin and center.[39]

The Christian church has rarely achieved true community or shared partnership. Those features are diminished within a framework of authority as domination and subordination, as powerful and powerless. "People of the Way" or *koinonia*/community described the early Christians prior to *ekklesia*/church. Today justice-oriented Christian feminists call believers to side with the poor of every circumstance and to witness to God's liberating action. They understand spirituality to be connection—with self, others, and God—within varied religious traditions. Spirituality affirms the full humanity of all people while rejecting dualisms and hierarchies.[40] Attention to gender brings all such dimensions to a discussion of power.

Legitimacy and Authority

As with power, authority shapes all relationships. It depends on perceptions, especially of those more influenced by power through relationship. Within organizations, Colwill concludes that "people who *feel* powerful *are* powerful, and people who *are* powerful *feel* powerful."[41] Within churches, to the extent that leaders deny either statement, all people under their influence are endangered rather than empowered.

Diverse kinds of authority—also called "weight"—originate from diverse sources. Authority might be conferred by consensus on a person respected for clear insight. Professions confirm competent people in their field. Previous effective functioning might endorse a person's "people skills." Agreement might confer on a person the right to speak for a community. Due to ex officio position, tradition, or custom, an older person might be extended authority.[42] Legitimate authority in a Weberian understanding is granted to leaders or groups via traditional claims (patriarchal custom or inheritance), charismatic claims (an individual holding "divine grace"), or rational/legal claims (appeal to rational rules, procedures, or structure rather than qualities inherent in any given individual).

Power holders have an interest in securing the legitimacy of their authority over those who are expected to obey them, for legitimate authority is less costly than coercive or reward-based authority. Therefore, what is essential to an understanding of authority is the claim to legitimacy, where leaders cultivate a belief in their own legitimacy among the led. Per Weber's definition and use of the terms *power* and *authority*, traditional and charismatic leaders could only be men. We would argue that he also viewed leaders within the rational/legal structure only as men. Hence, if only men define power, they do so to legitimate their own power position. However, redefinition of power also must be done cooperatively by both women and men.

Authorities (who establish and interpret the rules and norms that constitute a tradition) have traditionally excluded women, and the rules and norms on behalf of which authorities act have traditionally excluded values and practices considered feminine or maternal. Yet women have always employed power in their traditional roles. This power takes the form of fostering the growth of others, using power to empower others. Women have also been seen as the keepers of tradition, yet without legitimate public outlets for that knowledge. In our everyday actions we all participate in the reproduction and interpretation of some tradition, hence we all have prudential knowledge. Nevertheless, because of our different locations within the relational network of society, we participate differently and develop different stocks of knowledge. The problem is that the knowledge that some of us have developed has no voice in the public world; it has no authority.

Lois Janzen Preheim writes about needing to develop voice and authority: "For years I was the recipient of the church's power. I neither had to understand the overall picture or feel responsible for the outcome . . . To be an effective person in the congregation, I have had to make the transition from recipient of power and a learner of how it all works to a user and a respecter of authority. For me that meant finding my voice, learning to use my verbal skills in honest and loving ways."[43] An example of gender legitimacy occurs when a woman expressing an insight in a Sunday school class receives no response, only to have a male "authority figure" a few minutes later make nearly the same statement and be publicly credited for his good idea. Little vision or progress results, however, if women gain voice or position primarily because they cater to male leaders or established patterns. Radically different approaches need to be implemented to overcome past habits of power imbalance blessed by church life.

A 1959 paper by French and Raven notes six bases of power: reward, punishment, legitimate, expert, referent, and information. All of these characterize church life, though their expression may differ compared to other institutions. Not only might a church leader reward or punish a member, but the leader also portrays God (and not the church leader) as the arbiter. Legitimate power is conferred when a person's legitimate right to influence another is recognized by the latter. For one to perceive another's expertise differs from the referent type, which extends power because of identifying with another. At times church leaders have also been known to withhold information valuable to others.[44]

Authoritative exercise of power can be construed to legitimate the pursuance of self-interest. Some church leaders reveal an inner need to be a savior figure for others. Because Jesus saves, they think that to practice in his stead warrants that others will perceive them as essential and indispensable. Or a leader of a congregational business meeting may feel a need to translate what others say through his or her own lens without remaining faithful to the speaker's original words or meaning. With paternalism or "father knows best" implied, less-defined people will give assent rather than assert their own power.

Change

Rarely have Anabaptist/Mennonites been radical enough regarding power and authority. To "go to the root" would credit each child of God with being created in goodness and endowed with authority. Each retains throughout life the responsibility to choose in whom to reinvest a portion of authority for a particular period of time. To the extent that the recipient of another's authority reinvests (in due proportion) this power in those who have extended it, she or he proves to be worthy of the investment. Such constant exchange reimages power and authority.

As this concept is instilled in each young child, woman, and man, each becomes a more faithful steward of divine authority. Doing so could revolutionize the concepts of obedience and discipleship for *all* believers. It could help to counter the sin of violence and abuse that has thrived within structures that discriminate based on gender, class, age, or race. It could replace corrupt power of office with the power of each believer's primary accountability to God. Such changed expressions of authority could promote justice and power for all.

Sally Brown Geis notes three areas of significant change for redefining religious leaders' status and role: the "sacredly masculine" image of the

ordained leader, the separation of clergy and laity (replacing it with ministry of "the whole people of God"), and the image of clerical authority as
interpreter of religious truth. She contrasts controlling power as bad, and
life-giving power as good, observing how both St. Paul and Carter Heyward reshape Christian community around views of power: "For both,
power is relational, incarnational and generative of new forms of human
connection and community."[45]

Women have always made major contributions to church life. Their
power, authority, and influence have shaped the church. As their secondary
posture and compliance with male rule have diminished church effectiveness, less faithful membership has resulted. Both women and men will
need to change. For women to assume more leadership roles is a partial
solution, providing they intentionally counteract kyriarchy. Since radical
change disturbs "things as they are," neither mediocrity nor conformity to
established male patterns will move the pendulum. Only with power and
authority truly reimaged by all will ecclesial energy express divine potential.

Moving toward that goal, what can be expected? Already Mennonite
and free church women in leadership roles have brought genuine passion
and compassion to pastoral tasks. An MCC Women's Concerns *Report* asks,
"Have women leaders made a difference in worship?" Articles that follow
answer *yes*. The proof expresses itself through more hospitable space and
refined timing of services, attention to symbols and visual elements, inclu-
siveness, scriptural variety, validation of the whole being, collaboration,
and flexibility. Repeatedly, stronger preparation by women is noted. Re-
marking that when women are more visible in the congregation's public
life, it changes a congregation's sense of what it means to be a people of
God, Rebecca Slough sees women becoming blessed by gaining empowerment through leadership. "We have voice. We have authority. We know
ourselves as embodied spirits of God. We are changed."[46] The church is
being transformed through women's leadership.

Resistance also occurs. At the 1981 Mennonite Church General Assembly in Bowling Green, Ohio, major discussion focused on leadership
and authority. An ad hoc group of church women had met in advance to
strategize on how to address the theme from the floor and how to communicate in settings with only women present. Male leader anxiety took several turns with one obvious result: only delegates were permitted to speak

at subsequent Assemblies. When women mobilized the power within their reach, leaders responded to the challenge to their power with backlash or tightened control.

As reported by Mary E. Hunt following Re-Imagining (a conference to promote the World Council of Churches' Ecumenical Decade of Churches in Solidarity with Women) held in Minneapolis in 1993, backlash distorts, confuses, and distracts. That conference provoked negative judgments from people who did not attend. Mennonite women who were present left the life-giving experience inspired to more disciplined, faithful study of biblical texts and were freed to responsibly reimagine basic categories of theology. Hunt describes the common thread for the two thousand diverse participants as "a willingness to revisit, reconsider, and reshape fundamental dimensions of the Christian faith tradition."[47] Effective leadership empowered all present; shared authority reinforced each participant's integrity of being.

Who knows how long the wait will be for women leaders to instill radical insight into power through full ministry within the free church tradition? Pamela Dickey Young observes, "The appropriate form of leadership is one that promotes the work of the gospel without denying the possibility of full participation for all its members in all its functions."[48] A current movement called Women-Church calls for authentic, political community through exodus from patriarchy. To cooperate with "the enemy" is no longer satisfactory for men and women committed to a revitalization of "being" and "doing" church. Renewed personal and corporate faith will form around such tasks or needs as "advocacy, self-identity, transformation of the church, [and a] new practice of spirituality."[49]

Faithfulness to the gospel calls for more power from within free church groups to creatively reorganize both church and society. Counter to most church trends to become more ingrown and less world-aware, faithful leaders will challenge believers to pursue in-depth analysis of the root causes of deepening poverty, for example. Limited Western concepts of development will no longer suffice. To politically transform patterns of violence calls for convincing authority within individuals and groups.

Free church members' concern for social ethics has a lengthy and venerable history. But renewed vision from leaders on issues of sexuality and poverty are still needed. The Roman Catholic record of risk taking on behalf of the oppressed in non–North American countries speaks for itself.

The willingness of Catholic nationals to express power through political confrontation of injustice sets an example for Mennonite and related free church groups. The Radical Reformation legacy of separation of church and state led to an isolated worldview, and pacifist convictions likely restricted believers from public defense of justice.

The imitation of secular forms of power imbalance lingers on. Although centuries of teaching about being *in* the world but not *of* it shaped a certain stance toward authority for many Mennonites, new insight into this stance comes from Letty Russell: "[Presbyterians] recognized a need to be *in* the world but not *of* the world, serving those in need, but they did not recognize that they themselves were *of* the world, holding to a view of reality that looked upon persons who were victims of injustice as 'others' who 'bring these things on themselves' by their actions . . . The problem or sin was the churches' conformity to the unjust norm of compulsory heterosexuality and gender inequality."[50]

While free church members preach love of neighbor, they also often support a social status quo that fosters oppression. Furthermore, Christians teach God's preference for the church and claim exclusive powers of salvation through baptism and the Eucharist. These teachings in turn sanction ecclesial power and clerical privilege. Such inconsistencies abound, making the need for attention to issues of personal and social justice more prominent.

For free church people to "aspire to join the movers" as J. Lawrence Burkholder suggests in Chapter 1, they must learn from others, including Two-thirds World leaders, who increasingly call for rainbow power patterns rather than traditional kyriarchy. Rooted in struggles for liberation and understood best by oppressed peoples, global as well as local efforts for change can no longer accommodate patterns of power-*over*. Mennonites and other Christians can draw on feminist insights to radically reform their understandings of authority and power-*to*.

CHAPTER NINE

Power in the Anabaptist Community

CALVIN REDEKOP

In this final chapter we return the discussion to a point near to where it began: a broad philosophical perspective. The author identifies a basic paradox in the Christian message, the inherent contradiction between "being" and "doing," and proposes that the Anabaptist movement attempted to solve this problem. The discussion identifies the implications of the Anabaptist/Mennonite movement vis-à-vis the exercise of mundane power, takes account of the movement's shortcomings, and proposes an alternative to secular views of power consonant with the original Christian message and the Anabaptist promise: "pro-humana" power.

Power, we probably all agree, is a universal reality. It lies at the foundation of all human societies and civilizations: power is an all-pervasive presence. Most thinkers who have expounded on power allude to its imperious and assertive nature—people love power and are enthralled by it.[1] Power is self-energizing, aggrandizing, and self-justifying, hardly capable of being conceptualized and objectified, much less dealt with from an ethical perspective.[2] Throughout history people generally have desired power and used it. This very imperious nature of power seems to explain why most histories have been written almost exclusively from the perspective of the powerful. Given such a perspective, the question of power's legitimacy is obscured.[3]

A Brief Analysis of Power

Max Weber's analysis and definition of power, already alluded to in some of the preceding chapters, has become generally accepted as foundational: "We understand by 'power' the chance of a man or of a number of men to realize their own will in a communal action even against the resistance of others who are participating [acted upon] in the action."[4] Weber then makes a significant distinction: power is the application of force without necessarily gaining the consent of the recipients, while the *potential* use of power that is considered legitimate by those acted upon, is called authority.[5] The perceptions and reactions of the person(s) acted upon determine whether power is legitimate—that is, exercised with due authority—or if it is power defined simply as force—that is, coercion. As a consequence, Weber's analysis has resulted in a basically descriptive or analytical approach that, ethically speaking, is relatively neutral.

The basis for achieving, distributing, and allocating authority, according to Weber, is derived from three sources: traditional authority (based on heredity and historic practice), charismatic authority (based on the individual's ability to convince followers that he or she has the *right* to power), and legal/rational authority (developed as expressions of established social values and norms, such as public and democratic elections).[6] But the evaluation of how power was achieved and its conformity to social values— that is, the ethical problem of the illegitimate usurpation of power—was not extensively examined or treated by Weber or by social scientists in general.[7]

A brief comment must be made about the forms of power before we move to an ethical analysis. Legitimate power (authority) or illegitimate power (coercion) is incarnated in a variety of forms, each of which comprises a critical sector of human existence. One of the most pervasive and oppressive sectors has been political.[8] Another is economics. There is almost universal agreement that one of the most effective expressions of power is the ownership or control of wealth or resources.[9] Whether in interpersonal relations, family systems, institutional contexts, political structures, or international contexts, the achievement of access to resources and money and its utilization encompasses a vast arena for the exercise of power, often exploitative and oppressive.[10] One painful example of the effects of unequal access to power via economic institutions in the history of

Mennonites is the landless class that emerged in the Russian Mennonite commonwealth (see Chapter 5).

Another form of power is embedded in religion itself, especially in its institutional aspects such as the clergy and sacerdotal ceremonies. The control of access to the supernatural deity and salvation, and control of belief generally, has played a major role in the application of power to religious adherents as well as to officials in the religious structures themselves. The authoritative and hierarchical religions are by no means the only systems that utilize power to control, dominate, and oppress. Equally brazen, or possibly even more so, are sectarian or cultic religious groups, as well as utopian groups that have applied power in many forms deriving from self-imposed communal disciplines and rules. A recent example is the Society of Brothers, a movement of Anabaptist filiation, which envisioned total communality and equality yet became embroiled in incredible applications of coercive power.[11]

The institution of marriage and family is another form in which power is applied. The historical structure of marriage and family has codified the locus of power in the family patriarch. It is almost redundant to argue or illustrate this point. Power has been pervasively and perniciously asymmetrical in reference to the female sex throughout history. It is generally accepted that early Anabaptism gave women relatively equal status and function. Nearly a third of early Anabaptist martyrs were women. But asymmetry in male and female power began to emerge relatively early. Most Mennonite religious groups and conferences have excluded women from any voice in religious affairs since the late sixteenth century and until well into the twentieth. It could be argued that in some ways Mennonites have been more oppressive of females than most other religious groups, as for example in expressions of nonconformity, where women have been the bearers of separation from the world via dress and other aspects.[12] Children have also been the focus of illegitimate expressions of power in Anabaptist communities.

Another form of power application (though by no means exhausting the list) is personal or charismatic power. Weber proposed that some people have the personal ability to influence or even coerce others to submit to them even against their own will. Although this form has not been very pronounced in the Anabaptist/Mennonite tradition because of the communal seat of values and beliefs, it has on occasion expressed itself. For example, the "Great Trek" of Mennonites from the Ukraine to eastern Asiatic Russia resulted largely from the personal ability of Claasz Epp to convince a substantial number to families to follow him. The human suffering and disorganization that resulted reached epic proportions.[13]

Returning to an analysis of the ethical approach to power, it is evident that Max Weber "resolved" the problem of the ethical dimension of power by assuming that the illegitimate use of power was by definition an unstable sociological form bound to disappear by self-destruction, rejection by cultural evolution, rebellion, revolution, and the like. Subsequent social-scientific analysis has expanded the analysis of power into the areas of subconscious and conscious suggestion and influence, intimidation, manipulation, use of threats, and physical restraints and violence; all of these are normally subsumed in the discussion as coercion, which implies a normative position.[14] But in most of these discussions, the *ethical* aspects of these situations have not been very explicitly addressed.

Thus, although sociological analysis provides us with the basic conceptual tools to evaluate the broader issues presented by the phenomenon of power, since social science cannot by definition engage in ethical analysis,[15] a comprehensive analysis demands a philosophical or normative set of guidelines regarding power. I believe that despite its shortcomings, the Anabaptist/Mennonite tradition can provide (along with some of the theories just mentioned) useful insights in formulating such guidelines.

An Alternative View of Power

The universally self-aggrandizing nature of power described above has typically been assumed to be normative. On the political level, power is often rationalized as supporting a lofty "national purpose" while providing a convenient mask for the personal arrogation of power. An alternative perspective deriving from Anabaptist/Mennonitism suggests that power can be used constructively for agreed-upon ends for the common good of all—what I will call the "pro-humana" view.[16] I define *pro-humana* as that behavior which maximizes the subjective and social worth of each person in the context of social and cultural life. In contrast to understanding cultural and social history as exhibiting the tendency for individuals, groups, and institutions to use power for their own ends, which are assumed to be legitimate, this alternative view approaches the study of human history from the perspective of how the actors and institutions consciously utilized power in a pro-humana sense.

To help visualize this perspective, I propose a model of power usage based on a continuum stretching between two poles. Pole A represents the traditional orientation, which assumes the attainment of power is for the purpose of achieving and expressing *personal* or rationalized political goals. This is the universally legitimated "natural" view of power: power is there for the taking and use, and may the most ambitious and *strongest* person or organization win.

Pole A: Natural View		*Pole B: Pro-Humana View*
Power is for the taking	⟷	Power is limited for the common good

Pole B represents the position exemplified by Augustine, who, while agreeing that power is present in the order of creation, understands the City of God as being based on using power only for the collective benefit of others: "But in the family of the just man who lives by faith and is as yet a pilgrim journeying on to the celestial city, even those who rule serve those whom they seem to command; for they rule not from a love of power, but from a sense of the duty they owe to others—not because they are proud of authority, but because they love mercy."[17]

This is a helpful definition of the "pro-humana" view of power, which Augustine clearly derived from the life and teachings of Jesus, who rejected all forms of application of power and gave his life for his followers, and whose constant reminder to his disciples was, "You know that in the world, rulers lord it over their subjects, and their great men make them feel the weight of authority; but it shall not be so with you. Among you, whoever wants to be great must be your servant . . . like the Son of Man; he did not come to be served, but to serve and to surrender his life as a ransom for many" (Matt. 20:25–28).[18] The significance of this position has probably never been fully addressed or even understood, and clearly has not been implemented. But attempts to achieve this "pro-humana" approach to power have included nameless followers of Jesus through the centuries, such as the monastic groups and a variety of separatist and communal groups as well as individuals.

It might be maintained that the followers of Jesus Christ have presented an impressive record regarding the "pro-humana" view of power. But the Christian church that Augustine so staunchly defended was not up to resisting the temptation of unlimited exercise of power. Addressing the question of "why the Gospel was in grave danger of being lost [in the first centuries] among those who professed adherence to it," La Tourette concludes that "from the very beginning, pride of place and the desire for control in the Christian community were chronic temptations."[19]

The Dilemma for the Alternative View of Power

Let us briefly reflect on the fundamental reasons why the alternative view had difficulty in achieving its ideal. Philosophers and theologians have suggested that power can be conceived on two levels: pure being, and pure being acting on other things. In Chapter 1, J. Lawrence Burkholder proposes that from a philosophical perspective *being* is the consequence and expression of power—level-one power. Hemmerle says, "To exist is the most universal and primordial form of power." Power at this level is "pure being," expressed in the ability of preserving being in the present and into the future. On the second level, "[b]eing can determine not only itself, its own form, but can also determine what is other than itself which comes to exist by it, yet without its originator's ceasing to be one with itself and to endure." It is in this way that power becomes "productive, creative power of being itself."[20]

It is obvious that the second level of being, which is achieving one's own will over others, ipso facto becomes a moral and ethical issue. For when one being acts on another, the issue of "rights," legitimacy, and, of course, ethics emerges. The idea or phenomenon of power for the purpose of promoting "pure being" does not raise moral or ethical problems in itself. When individuals or groups and movements are concerned about achieving ends beyond their own pure being, however, moral and ethical issues arise, for this normally implies changing the status or relations between plural beings without full individual consent.[21]

This being/doing dilemma creates problems for any person or institution concerned about level-two power—achieving future ends beyond mere personal being. Augustine was aware of the two levels of power: the City of God was not only pure being but had certain goals, so power would need to be applied to achieve its end state. But the dilemma was that mundane power, necessary for achieving ends, would not or could not by definition always be legitimate.

The leader and founder of the Christian movement took a new view toward power that illustrated the paradox. On the one hand, he enunciated personal salvation and membership in the kingdom of God as a *state of being:* "I am the vine, and you are the branches. He who does not dwell in me is thrown away like a withered branch. If you dwell in me, and my words dwell in you, ask what you will, and you shall have it" (John 15:5f).[22] But Christ also enunciated the second dimension of the message of the kingdom—achieving the goals of the kingdom. "Full authority in heaven and on earth has been committed to me. Go forth therefore and make all nations my disciples and teach them to observe all that I have commanded you" (Matt. 28:18–19). A new status and a new eschatology was fundamental to the new gospel; this new status or condition is also applicable to most religions.

But the *doing* dimension or dynamic tends to undermine the *being.* There is thus great irony for the Christian movement, because it exhibits two seemingly contradictory factors: a personal *status* (a new status in the kingdom through salvation—a gift, with no effect on others involved), and a *goal* (achieving the goals of preaching, teaching all peoples the message of the gospel). This is dramatically illustrated in Acts 6. In the course of spiritual fellowship in the new covenant, there was a complaint that "widows were being overlooked in the daily distribution. So the Twelve called the whole body of disciples together and said, 'It would be a grave mistake for us to neglect the work of God in order to wait at table. Therefore, friends, look out seven men of good reputation, and we will appoint them to deal with these matters, while we devote ourselves to prayer and to the ministry of the Word.'" (Acts 6:1ff). Some theologians have proposed that at this critical juncture the essentials of the Christian gospel were compromised. Brunner, for example, has argued that Christianity was pure being (fellowship or *koinonia*) and that when the early church instituted the dispensing of the sacraments, Christians "began to receive the body of Christ, rather than being the Body of Christ."[23]

The problem with the emerging Christianity was not that Christians could or must be in one state or the other. The paradox was that the new status in Christ required both: pure being, the spiritual *koinonia*, and achieving specific goals, an eschatological orientation, which required goal-oriented work. This welds the two levels of power into an inseparable, contradictory union—personal salvation (pure being) and doing (acting on other beings). The early church tried to harmonize these two contradictory tendencies, but the achievement of its goals tended to degenerate into the use of power (force); this undercut the new status of pure being operating on level-one power.

The Christian movement was soon abusing its authority and hence operating with level-two power. The most convincing evidence for this position is the numerous revolts against the early church and later the Roman church. By the time of the Reformation, rebellion in the Christian community was epidemic. And while the rebellions were reactions to a variety of conditions, a vast number of revolts rejected the perversion of authority by the church as it became a locus of naked personal power. Many people suffered and lost their lives in those forms of rebellion. Over time power was accumulated in European civilization by the Catholic Church, and its alliance with secular governments and institutions loosely defined as the Holy Roman Empire was supported by an extensive theology and philosophy. Unfortunately, the Reformed and Lutheran Churches also cannot be excused from this complaint.

The Anabaptist Contribution to the New Paradigm

We come now to the Anabaptist contribution to solving this basic dilemma. The Anabaptist rejection of the way power and authority were employed in the secular and religious institutions in the early 1500s as described by Stayer in Chapter 3 is very suggestive and instructive. Stayer points to the central issue or problem for the Anabaptists and their persecutors: When and in what way was the Roman Catholic Church ultimately authoritative? And when was it acting illegitimately? In other words, when was the Roman Church, as a spiritual institution, exercising power legitimately, and when was it asserting power illegitimately, being deeply allied with the various European kingdoms and principalities?

What was the Anabaptist basis for questioning, challenging, and in critical instances rejecting the Roman Catholic and princely authorities? The critical factor was their insistence that the Roman Catholic Church and the state were uncritically integrating the two levels of power—being and doing—into one. Anabaptists maintained that the power of pure being is legitimate and cannot hurt others; however, they also said second-level power is acceptable but only when the recipients see it as good and legitimate. Though they did not express it in these words, they maintained that when a force or act is imposed on others, the pure being[24] status of the others is threatened and violated; in fact, this almost always hurts the other. Thus the moral/ethical dimensions of power were raised by the Anabaptists and other nonconformist groups who asked the question "By what authority do you do these things?"[25]

A contemporary way of describing the Anabaptist position would be to ask, "By what rules are we playing the game of social order?" This is a fundamental question that is at the heart of organized social and cultural life. How compliance is achieved to create order in society is a question philosophers since antiquity have attempted to answer. Hence power as such is not the problem, it is rather the understanding of the rules by which we play the game of power. That is, is the source and purpose of power for the benefit of some or for all, and on what basis? Furthermore, who decides? And finally, how is power controlled—how is the *being* of persons protected from violation by the consequences of *doing?* Anabaptist scholar John Howard Yoder, who has written extensively on power from a theological perspective, states the case simply: "The Powers cannot simply be destroyed or set aside or ignored [but] their sovereignty must be broken."[26]

What is the "bottom line" as far as a positive and redemptive Anabaptist/Mennonite approach to power is concerned? A clue is found in the statement regarding the role of the state in the Schleitheim Confession: "The sword [the state] is an ordering of God outside the perfection of Christ. In the law the sword is established over the wicked for punishment and the secular rulers are established to wield the same. But within the perfection of Christ only the ban is used for the admonition and exclusion of the one who has sinned."[27] The Anabaptists viewed power as legitimate—as long as it remained within its boundaries (legitimate power, hence, "authority" according to Weber). Power is necessary and positive when it operates according to the "rules of the game." When some of the players do not play by the same rules, the game in that context is over, and another set of rules apply.[28]

James McClendon, a Baptist scholar with strong Anabaptist sympathies, has recently proposed that "a theory of the game may provide the best analogy to control the 'evil powers' that exist in the universe around us." McClendon proposes that (1) a game must have a goal logically prior to the goal of winning; (2) strictly limited means are to be employed; (3) rules are necessary because they constitute the nature of the game; and finally (4) participants must want to play the game.[29] McClendon applies this concept to theological and ethical analysis using sociological theories and suggests that this conceptualization "makes possible the discrimination of a distinctively social strand in the moral life of Christians." Tracing his thinking back to Alasdair MacIntyre and Bernard Suits, McClendon proposes that this approach is superior in that "it shows the structures of biblical social morality in ways that are clearer or more revealing than alternative theoretical approaches."[30] The usefulness of this approach has already been demonstrated by Lydia Harder in Chapter 4.

The "game" paradigm can be very helpful in analyzing religious understandings of power when applied theologically to the kingdom of God.[31] In large measure, the Anabaptists maintained a worldview congruent with such a perspective in their understanding of the way God wanted his creatures to act during their earthly sojourn. This is indicated by the fact that the Anabaptists generally accepted the two-kingdom understanding of history in which there was the earthly, worldly kingdom and the kingdom of God, each with a specific set of "rules of the game." Those who accepted membership in the heavenly kingdom accepted the divine rulership and submitted themselves to the rules of the game as decreed by God (element 3 of the game theory). They further accepted the fact that they must voluntarily agree to play the game (element 4). They also agreed that those who chose not to submit themselves to obedience to God were either not playing by the rules of the game and thus were liable to discipline and excommunication, or they belonged to a different kingdom (element 2). And finally, the individualistic approach was rejected totally: playing the game in order to "win" was out, for Anabaptists expected that their own membership conform to a morality higher than that of the "world" (element 1).

These "rules of the game" were implied in the earliest Anabaptist church order, which very concisely states the rights and limits of the state to use its power: "The rule of the government is according to the flesh, that of the Christians according to the Spirit."[32] The state *can* use power, *if* it is for the benefit of its subjects within the designated sphere. This new language explicating the limitations of power was posed and broadened in many ways and in many locations during the early phases of the Anabaptist movement. Dirk Philips (1504–68), an Anabaptist leader, presents the case dramatically: "From this it is evident that no church may exercise dominion over the consciences of men with the carnal sword, or seek by violence to force unbelievers to believe, nor to kill the false prophets with sword and fire. With the Word of God she must judge and expel those in the church who are found wicked. What is done over and above this is not Christian, nor evangelical, nor apostolic."[33] The kernel of the Anabaptist view was the *legitimacy* question, not the power *reality* and *use* questions. In relation to the state, the question of its mandate to "punish the wicked" and protect the innocent was "Is the state going beyond its mandate in this regard?" The challenge extended to the persecuting territorial churches as well.

Menno Simons (1496–1561) discussed the issue of the legitimacy of power and its authority in bold terms: "You may understand from these Scriptures that you are called of God and ordained to your offices to punish the transgressors and protect the good; to judge rightly between a man and his fellows; to do justice to the widows and orphans, to the poor, despised stranger and pilgrim; to rule cities and countries justly by a good policy and administration not contrary to God's Word, in peace and quiet."[34] Because Menno observed that the Anabaptists were oppressed by the Roman Catholic bishops and the reigning princes who were not conforming to their "legitimate role," he wrote: "You see, dear sirs and rulers, this is really the office to which you are called. Whether you fulfill these requirements piously and faithfully, I will leave to your own consideration. No dear sirs, the thing is now in reverse gear. The scale of justice is so badly out of balance. The policy is to punish the good and to protect the evil. We see daily that of which the prophets complained."[35] As we saw in Chapter 2, the state and the religious institution were almost imperceptibly identified and interdependent until the period of the Reformation. The legitimate power of the state to punish the "evildoer" was subtly misused by the Roman Catholic Church and subsequently by Reformed and Lutheran institutions when they cooperated with the state to punish and destroy "heretics," in the process exercising what Russell calls "naked" power.[36]

The grisly heresy hunting and inquisitions, and the resulting martyrdom of the nonconforming Waldensians and Hussites, among other groups, was later visited on the Anabaptists, Huguenots, and many others. The idea of the freedom of religious belief and thus the disestablishment of religion (as a source of power) resulted from this refusal of persons and groups to accept the illegitimate enforcement of the religious will of those in power on others. This conflict was of great historical significance. Roland H. Bainton states, "The Anabaptists anticipated all other religious bodies in the proclamation and exemplification of three principles which are on the North American continent among those truths which we hold to be self-evident: the voluntary church, the separation of church and state, and religious liberty."[37] The issue for Bainton, though not explicitly stated, was the right use of power, according to the rules of the game.

For Anabaptists the crucial point of dissent was when individuals or religious institutions imposed their will on others without their consent or involvement in establishing the rules. They did not challenge the right of individuals or institutions to use power of being (first level) nor the power of doing (the second level) as long as they acted legitimately according to rules assigned to its sphere by those affected. When authority was abused, that is, when the rules of the game were broken, it became illegitimate and coercive power, which ultimately destroyed its victims. The individual must give his or her assent if any power is to be legitimized and transformed into authority, which theoretically serves all the individuals in its sphere.

For the Anabaptists, authority, backed up ultimately by power of excommunication, resided in the local fellowship of believers, the *koinonia*, a totally voluntary banding-together of fellow believers. This was a collective level-one power of being with mutually accepted "rules of the game." By rejecting the power of the state and religious institutions upon their lives in specific areas, the local covenanting members authorized the congregation to be totally authoritative (and hence all powerful) in almost all areas of life, including the authority to discern the meaning of Holy Scriptures, to pronounce on ethics—that is, to define the nature of Christian obedience—and to command conformity and obedience. This resulted in a complex system of discipline, punishment, or even excommunication, and the ban of obdurate members. And when one individual imposed his or her will over others, collective level-one power of *being* was displaced with coercive discipline. This discipline resulted in numerous schisms that plagued Mennonites for generations.

Ernest A. Payne, a scholar of the free church idea, proclaims that the Anabaptists were "the forerunners of the free church conception" and suggests that "the Anabaptists were challenging what had been the basis of ecclesiastical theory and practice since the time of Constantine. For them the church had become a fellowship of believing people, entered by baptism on personal profession of repentance and faith, committed to aid one another in their discipleship."[38] By voluntarily offering one's power of being to the rule of the fellowship, the *doing* aspect (the goal orientation) of Christianity for the Anabaptists was theoretically subordinated to level-one power and protected from coercion. Theologically, as Yoder states, "the church does not attack the powers: this Christ has done. The church concentrates on not being seduced by them."[39]

The Anabaptist heritage contributed to an emerging view of power that maintained that power is everywhere, even in sacred institutions, and that it can destroy as well as protect the innocent. Power that is used positively—that is supportive of personal and common well-being—was authority, and they gladly submitted. But power that was injurious of personal or common well-being was not authoritative and was resisted. The most critical Anabaptist contribution to the reevaluation and thus "redemption" of power was the establishment of structures to define and limit authority (the rules of the game) and hence diminish its abuse so that uncontrolled power could not emerge.

The first and most effective structure was a congregational ecclesiology in which the religious or spiritual authority and power of any individual was limited to his or her own congregation. Even today no Mennonite minister or leader technically has any religious or spiritual authority beyond his or her congregation. But this position has eroded through time with the development of conferences and regional organizations and institutions that have developed sources of power that are not controlled or limited by local congregations.[40]

A second structural control has been the principle of voluntary membership. Those who wanted to "follow Christ" did so on a voluntary, mature basis. It was a conscious adult volitional act that made clear that personal regeneration and restitution had taken place. Each person who became a follower of Jesus voluntarily committed him- or herself to become a member of the fellowship of believers and accepted all the rules operative in the fellowship. All of the members were thus equally bound to submit to the others as well as to participate in the binding of the others to the covenant.[41]

A third structural principle was the lay nature of Anabaptist biblical discernment. All persons are theoretically equal in the sight of God and called upon to know, obey, and exegete the meaning of the Holy Writ for the Christian community, the so-called hermeneutical community. In ideal conditions this structure tends to prohibit the emergence of false prophets and individualism, although there have been serious breaches in Mennonite history.

Finally, the fourth and most effective, yet most controversial and hence unstable, structure in Mennonite history to control power has been the principle of congregational discipline culminating in excommunication. Thus the congregation exercised authority by virtue of the voluntary principle above, but if individuals would not conform, authority was backed up by power, namely, the power to excommunicate an individual and ban him or her from membership. The validity of this principle has been hotly debated in Anabaptist/Mennonite communities from the beginning, and some painful and violent congregational conflicts have resulted. But a principle is not invalidated because it has often failed.

Anabaptism and Structural Limitation of Power in Practice

To conclude on the basis of the arguments presented so far that the Anabaptists "solved" the problem of controlling the corrupting influence of power would be a denial of reality. Anabaptists and succeeding Mennonite bodies have succumbed to many misuses of power. This book itself delineates many unfortunate and often heartbreaking examples of the abuse of power within Anabaptist/Mennonite faith communities. Mennonites throughout their history have often avoided and capitulated to the reality of power and its misuse in their corporate religious, communal, economic, familial, and gender relations.[42]

How could a movement that introduced a significant, morally and ethically innovative view and practice of power slip into the "worldly" approach to the use of power in other areas of life? Initially the Anabaptists expressed a strong stress on the *doing* aspect of faith, obeying the teachings of Christ regarding the missionary commission, along with an emphasis on discipleship. Little information is available as to whether power was abused. This emphasis declined rather early, Anabaptists becoming mainly concerned with the *being* level—survival—due to extreme persecution and even martyrdom as they struggled to preserve and maintain their religious community by separation from the world and quietism.

But the *doing* aspect of the Christian gospel slowly reasserted itself in the heart of the community as toleration increased. Consequently, the faith community began to need structures to carry out its communal needs, such as mutual aid and church order, as well as missionary outreach structures. This resulted in the creation of organizations that began to amass and centralize increasing amounts of power. The Mennonite commonwealth in Russia, existing from the late eighteenth century into the early twentieth, and the Mennonite commonwealth in Paraguay, established in the 1920s, are probably the two most celebrated examples of this trend.[43] The late nineteenth and twentieth centuries have been rightfully defined as the time of Mennonite organization and institution building. The Mennonite Central Committee, a worldwide relief and service organization, is probably the best example of this phenomenon.[44] Mennonite communities thus became more aggressive participants in the *doing* dimension, which involved organizations and institutions, and with it came the concentration of power in institutions and bureaucracy.

It cannot be denied that institutions and organizations have wielded great authority as well as power. But why did Anabaptism fail to practice "pro-humana" power, neglecting the structural restraints to power misuse? Even though we have assumed that the "lust" for power can probably not be explained, we may need to take a brief look at the psychological and personal dynamics of power. One study of the motivation for power suggests that it can be derived from three sources: (1) an irrational impulse; (2) role behavior, motivated by the expectations of the roles we perform in society and institutions; and (3) a universal personal drive, "the induction of behaviors in others [that] can be instrumental in obtaining rewards for oneself."[45]

These three are certainly enough to suggest that to define the power dilemma as basically social and institutional ignores the egotistical and even evil tendencies in individual human beings. In one way, the easiest way to solve the problem of misuse of power in Mennonite society (and in general) is to deny the human desire for power and the tendency to misuse it, or to insist that use of power is unavoidable, and that potential misuse in the institutional dimension in society (the doing) is in the nature of things. This approach answers the problem of "falling short" by appealing to grace and forgiveness to cover the sins of power abuse. This position has been developed by Reinhold Niebuhr and others and has been widely applied.[46]

But this approach does not seem do full justice to the Anabaptist view of power. The pro-humana understanding of power does not assume that the misuse of power is normal and that a well-meaning church official, because he is simply caught in a structural (*doing*) dilemma, is thereby exonerated for misusing his power. Anabaptism flatly rejects the exemption of the individual from accountability for his or her actions regarding *doing* aspects in the kingdom of God. The Anabaptist perspective assumes that the person wielding social power as a voluntary member of the kingdom of God is personally committed to its rules; the compromises normally assumed to exist between two incompatible choices inherent in the human structures and institutions are not license for unaccountable actions.

In other words, *individuals*, when they are tempted to extend their authority rooted in *being* so that it becomes acting on others and hence coercion (level-two power), are culpable for their behavior. The implementation of power in a social context such as the business world can be, and often is, exacerbated by personal temptation and motives. Here the secular philosophers described above and in Chapter 2 have been more honest— they assume that persons will grab power when they can, although they have tended to avoid ascribing moral dimensions to this issue. If it is true that power tends to corrupt individuals, then the personal experience in using power needs to be taken seriously by Anabaptists who, as followers of Jesus, operate by his rule; that is, those who would rule must take the servant stance. This places the responsibility squarely on the individual as well as on the structure. To maintain that compromise is inherently necessary, and the approach that those in authority should merely behave as ethically as circumstances allow ignores the full significance of the Anabaptist alternative view of power where individual responsibility is also structurally limited.[47]

However, granting the argument that the individual has a central responsibility in using power, I would still maintain that the source of most of the misuse of power in Anabaptist/Mennonite congregational and community life lies in the fact that the structural restraints of power (rules of the game) were developed and applied mainly in relations with the state and political institutions. Structural restraints were less developed in the family, communal, and business life of members. That is, the structural restraints on individual temptations to misuse power in domestic relationship like marriage and the family were not developed in Anabaptist/Mennonite theology and ethics. Anabaptist/Mennonites were not sufficiently concerned with the fact that power exists in the Mennonite community and is as prone to be misused as in matters of the state.[48]

This unconcern has been unfortunate because there is an inherent asymmetry of power in human relationships. If everyone were endowed with equal status and power no matter how it was defined or derived, the problem of misuse of power would be diminished if not totally exterminated. But this, unfortunately, is not the case. The social scientist Richard Schermerhorn stressed this idea long before the current fashion, maintaining that even if power were originally distributed equally between humans, experience shows that power never remains equally distributed, whether one is talking about conjugal relations, communities, or institutional structures. Thus, because power asymmetry is "normal," conflict and power misuse will probably not be eradicated.[49] In this context it is clear that Anabaptist/Mennonite structures of accountability were never developed to deal with the realities of power asymmetry even in congregational life, much less in community and domestic life.

Ironically, the theological idea of equality in the Anabaptist movement, based on the congregation as the seat of authority in which everybody had equal status and meaning, was not applied generally in "real life." Family members, members of congregations, and employees of conference organizations or other institutions in the Mennonite community never possessed totally equal power.[50] And exacerbating the failure of the Anabaptist solution to asymmetry of power in the congregation and community has been the *Gemeinschaft* nature of Mennonite congregations: they are basically collectivities of families and communities where genealogical relationships, intermarriages, and interpersonal relationships and friendships tend to counteract the operation of the "structural restraints" controlling power assertion and its misuse, thus supporting personal favoritism and privilege.[51] The world of business and economics illustrates this. Whether in earlier agrarian communities such as the Mennonite commonwealth in Russia with its very successful farmers, or in contemporary North American communities where business and financial successes have created great wealth, there has been an immense increase in the power held by wealthy families both in the congregational life and in the community.[52] Hence, the development of structural restraints on the use of power *within* the Anabaptist/Mennonite faith community, according to Anabaptist principles, remains a pressing task.[53]

Conclusion

As has become apparent in this book, Anabaptism has never achieved the level-one application of power on the congregational level, much less in the interpersonal and social spheres. But because this likely cannot be achieved in any human situation, it would be churlish to expect Anabaptist/Mennonites to completely "solve" this issue. For Anabaptist-Mennonite communities, the difficulty regarding power was failing to relate the principle to life beyond the conflict of religion with the state and national life. Power issues on the family, interpersonal, congregational, and economic levels have not been addressed by the development of structures of accountability and limits equal with those that were created for the state and political life.

The Anabaptist restraints on medieval social and ecclesiastical misuse of power was path-breaking and was a signally important historical event. There is increasing agreement that Anabaptists were instrumental in changing the approach to power because they were among the first to establish conscious rules and structures to control its use and abuse. Refusing to submit to the heresy hunters because they were not legitimate representatives of state or church power was clearly an overt act of redefining legitimate power while defying illegitimate power. Refusing to put on the military uniform in present-day circumstances is putting present limits on the definition and exercise of power.

But in the subsequent evolution of the Anabaptist tradition, the theological restraints on power were not translated into the basic social parameters regarding how power can be limited to its legitimate sphere in mundane and domestic life of the Anabaptist fellowships. The irony is that the Anabaptist/Mennonite community has been far more successful at challenging the legitimacy of power in the larger body politic than it has been in its own internal congregational life and in the domestic and economic sphere. It seems that it was much easier to define and limit the power of the "pagan" world than that of members of a congregation who live in intimate contexts. The heart of the problem for the Anabaptist (and Christian) use of power becomes not merely admitting the reality of power and its misuse societally and structurally, but focusing on how power is defined, distributed, and allocated; and above all, how it is monitored and disciplined on the personal, interpersonal, and congregational level.

There are a variety of human and social contexts in which every human being is expected to play according to the rules of the game. When the rules are flouted, power is misused. What complicates issues even more is that there are numerous social systems that impinge on each other or overlap. Thus, for example, Christians living as members of the kingdom of God are also members of the secular world. Members of both systems need to be careful to respect the rules of the game regarding power over members of the respective communities.

Anabaptists indeed were instrumental in introducing a new paradigm concerning power and authority—a new game with a new set of rules regarding power—into the bloodstream of Western society. But if Anabaptism is to complete the transforming challenge to power in all dimensions of human existence and offer an alternative to the use of power for religious groups as well as groups in general, it will need to work heroically to develop and nurture structures of accountability in its domestic, community, and church life.

Notes

Introduction

1. Robert Bierstedt, *Power and Progress* (New York: McGraw-Hill, 1974), 222.
2. Kenneth B. Clark, *The Pathos of Power* (New York: Harper and Row, 1974), 71.
3. Charles H. Page, "Introduction," in Richard A. Schermerhorn, *Society and Power* (New York: Random House, 1961), vi.
4. Bierstedt, *Power and Progress*, 220–21.
5. Meredith B. McGuire, "Discovering Religious Power," *Sociological Analysis* 44, no. 1 (1983): 1.
6. Richard A. Schoenherr, "Power and Authority in Organized Religion: Disaggregating the Phenomenological Core," *Sociological Analysis* 47 (1987): 53.
7. See Joachim Wach, *Types of Religious Experience: Christian and Non-Christian* (Chicago: University of Chicago Press, 1951).
8. Liston Pope, *Millhands and Preachers* (New Haven: Yale University Press, 1942).
9. J. Milton Yinger, *Religion and the Struggle for Power* (Durham: Duke University Press, 1946).
10. Paul M. Harrison, *Authority and Power in the Free Church Tradition: A Social Case Study of the American Baptist Convention* (Princeton: Princeton University Press, 1959), 207.
11. Schoenherr, "Power and Authority in Organized Religion," 65.
12. See J. Lawrence Burkholder, *The Problem of Social Responsibility from the Perspective of the Mennonite Church* (Elkhart: Institute of Mennonite Studies, 1989). An edited collection of articles in honor of Burkholder has also recently been published. See Rodney J. Sawatsky and Scott Holland, eds., *The Limits of Perfection: Conversations with J. Lawrence Burkholder* (Waterloo: Institute of Anabaptist-Mennonite Studies, 1993).
13. James M. Stayer, *Anabaptists and the Sword* (Lawrence, Kans.: Coronado Press, 1972), 21.
14. See J. Richard Burkholder and Calvin Redekop, eds., *Kingdom, Cross and Community* (Scottdale, Pa.: Herald Press, 1976).
15. Keith Graber Miller, *Wise as Serpents, Innocent as Doves: American Mennonites Engage Washington* (Knoxville: University of Tennessee Press, 1996).

16. Perry Bush, *Two Kingdoms, Two Loyalties: Mennonite Pacifism in Modern America* (Baltimore: Johns Hopkins University Press, 1998).

17. Fred Kniss, *Disquiet in the Land: Cultural Conflict in American Mennonite Communities* (New Brunswick: Rutgers University Press, 1997), 6.

18. Roland Bainton, "The Anabaptist Contribution to History," in *The Recovery of the Anabaptist Vision*, ed. Guy F. Hershberger (Scottdale, Pa.: Herald Press, 1957), 317.

19. Ibid., 321.

20. Leo Driedger and Donald B. Kraybill, eds., *Mennonite Peacemaking: From Quietism to Activism* (Scottdale, Pa.: Herald Press, 1994), 13.

21. Ibid., 33.

Chapter 1. Power

1. The Seven Articles of Schleitheim (1527) were promulgated by Anabaptist leaders in the wake of the Peasants' War. They called for Christians to separate themselves from "the world" and to eschew participation in violence. For more on this subject, see Chapter 3.

Chapter 2. Power and Religion in the Western Intellectual Tradition

1. In this chapter I speak mainly about "power," and I allow the various meanings of the notion to emerge from extensive citation of original sources. This narrowing of focus is necessary in order to achieve the kind of broad survey I have in mind (and which I have been unable to find elsewhere). Nevertheless, as the other chapters in this collection demonstrate, the notions of "authority" and "domination" are crucial features of the exercise of power.

2. *The Republic of Plato*, trans. Francis Macdonald Cornford (Oxford: At the Clarendon Press, 1948), 17–18.

3. Plato's allegory of the cave encapsulates the movement from the world of appearances to an apprehension of the Good, which provides a vision of truth and justice that serves as a template for ordering earthly affairs. See ibid., 226–28.

4. Aristotle, *The Politics*, ed. Stephen Everson (Cambridge: Cambridge University Press, 1996), 169–70.

5. See Stephen Everson, "Introduction," in ibid.

6. Aristotle uses power (*dunamis*) in this sense of potentiality. See Aristotle, *The Politics*, trans. Carnes Lord (Chicago: University of Chicago Press, 1984), 278–79.

7. St. Augustine, *The City of God*, in vol. 16, *Great Books of the Western World*, ed. Mortimer J. Adler (Chicago: University of Chicago, 1990), 579.

8. Ibid., 589. For Aristotle on domestic power relationships, see Aristotle, *The Politics* (1996), 27ff.

9. St. Augustine, *Confessions*, in vol. 16, *Great Books of the Western World*, ed. Mortimer J. Adler (Chicago: University of Chicago, 1990), 63.

10. Ibid., 710.

11. St. Augustine, *City of God*, 591.

12. Ibid.

13. St. Thomas Aquinas, *The Summa Theologica, vol. 1*, in *Great Books of the Western World*, vol. 19, ed. Robert M. Hutchins (Chicago: University of Chicago, 1952), 531.

14. St. Thomas Aquinas, *The Summa Theologica, vol. 2*, in *Great Books of the Western World*, vol. 20, ed. Robert M. Hutchins (Chicago: University of Chicago, 1952), 220.

15. Quentin Skinner, "Machiavelli," in *Great Political Thinkers*, ed. Keith Thomas (Oxford: Oxford University Press, 1992), 38ff.

16. Niccolò Machiavelli, *The Prince*, trans. W. K. Marriott (London: J. M. Dent and Sons, 1931), 97.

17. Francis Bacon, *Novum Organum*, in vol. 28, *Great Books of the Western World*, ed. Mortimer J. Adler (Chicago: University of Chicago, 1990), 107.

18. Ibid., 126, 127, 129, 130, and 132 respectively.

19. For a subtle and thorough reading of Bacon on this score, see Evelyn Fox Keller, "Baconian Science: The Arts of Mastery and Obedience," in her *Reflections on Gender and Science* (New Haven: Yale University Press, 1985), 33–42.

20. Thomas Hobbes, *Leviathan*, ed. C. B. MacPherson (New York: Pelican, 1977), 161.

21. Michael Lessnof, "Introduction," in *Social Contract Theory*, ed. Michael Lessnof (Oxford: Basil Blackwell, 1990), 10.

22. John Locke, in *Social Contract Theory*, 85–89, 95.

23. Jean-Jacques Rousseau, *The Social Contract*, trans. G. D. H. Cole (London: Campbell Publishers, 1993), 190–91.

24. Edmund Burke, *Reflections on the Revolution in France*, vol. 4 in *The Works of Edmund Burke* (London: Oxford University Press, n.d.), 49.

25. Particularly important to my view, besides my own reading of Nietzsche, is the interpretation of Walter Kaufmann in *Nietzsche: Philosopher, Psychologist, Antichrist* (Princeton: Princeton University Press, 1974).

26. Friedrich Nietzsche, *Twilight of the Idols* and the *Antichrist*, trans. R. J. Hollingdale (New York: Penguin, 1982), 115.

27. Kaufmann, *Nietzsche*, 360.

28. Friedrich Nietzsche, *On the Genealogy of Morals*, trans. Walter Kaufmann and R. J. Hollingdale (New York: Vintage Books, 1969), 117–18.

29. Nietzsche, *Twilight of the Idols*, 42.

30. Nietzsche, *On the Genealogy of Morals*, 125.

31. Nietzsche, *Twilight of the Idols*, 94.

32. Nietzsche, *On the Genealogy of Morals*, 150, 152–53.

33. Nietzsche, *Twilight of the Idols*, 156.

34. Michel Foucault, *Discipline and Punish: The Birth of the Prison* (New York: Vintage Books, 1979), 22–23.

35. Michel Foucault, *Power/Knowledge. Selected Interviews and Other Writings, 1972–77*, ed. Colin Gordon (New York: Pantheon Books, 1980), 61.

36. Foucault, *Discipline and Punish*, 215–16.

37. Foucault, *Power/Knowledge*, 96.

38. Hans Bertens, *The Idea of the Postmodern: A History* (London: Routledge, 1995), 7–8.

39. Gerda Lerner, *The Creation of Patriarchy* (New York: Oxford University Press, 1986), 1:220.

40. Brochure from Divinity Forum, University of Cambridge, 31 October 1996.

41. Linda Boynton Arthur, "Clothing, Control, and Women's Agency: The Mitigation of Patriarchal Power," in *Negotiating at the Margins: The Gendered Discourses of Power and Resistance*, ed. Sue Fisher and Kathy Davis (New Brunswick: Rutgers University Press, 1993), 81–82.

42. Nancy Hartsock, *Money, Sex, and Power: Toward a Feminist Historical Materialism* (New York: Longman, 1983).

43. Sue Fisher and Nancy Davis, *Negotiating at the Margins: The Gendered Discourses of Power and Resistance* (New Brunswick: Rutgers University Press, 1993), 8.

44. Nancy Hartsock, "Foucault on Power: A Theory for Women?" in *Feminism/Postmodernism*, ed. Linda J. Nicholson (New York: Routledge, 1990), 169.

45. Fisher and Davis, *Negotiating at the Margins*, 4.

46. Ben Agger, *Gender, Culture and Power: Toward a Feminist Postmodern Critical Theory* (Westport, Conn.: Praeger, 1993), 4.

Chapter 3. The Anabaptist Revolt and Political and Religious Power

1. On anticlericalism in the Reformation, see Hans-Jürgen Goertz, *Pfaffenhaß und gross Geschrei: Die reformatorischen Bewegungen in Deutschland, 1517–1529* (Munich: Beck, 1987), and *Antiklerikalismus und Reformation. Sozialgeschichtliche Untersuchungen* (Göttingen: Vandenhoeck and Ruprecht, 1995); *Anticlericalism in Late Medieval and Early Modern Europe*, ed. Peter A. Dykema and Heiko A. Oberman (Leiden: Brill, 1993); Geoffrey Dipple, *Antifraternalism and Anticlericalism in the German Reformation. Johann Eberlin von Günzburg and the Campaign against the Friars* (Scolar Press: Aldershot, 1996); James M. Stayer, "Anticlericalism: A Model for a Coherent Interpretation of the Reformation," in *Special Volume: The Reformation in Germany and Europe: Interpretations and Issues*, ed. Hans R. Guggisberg and Gottfried G. Krodel (Gütersloh: Gütersloher Verl.-Haus, 1993), 39–47.

2. Bernd Moeller, "Piety in Germany around 1500," in *The Reformation in Medieval Perspective*, ed. Steven E. Ozment (Chicago: Quadrangle Books, 1971), 50–75.

3. Heiko A. Oberman, "The Gospel of Social Unrest," in *The German Peasant War 1525: New Viewpoints*, ed. Robert W. Scribner and Gerhard Benecke (London: Allen and Unwin, 1979), 44–46.

4. Peter Blickle, *The Revolution of 1525: The German Peasants' War from a New Perspective*, trans. by Thomas A. Brady Jr. and H. C. Erik Midelfort (Baltimore: Johns Hopkins University Press, 1981).

5. James M. Stayer, *The German Peasants' War and Anabaptist Community of Goods* (Montreal: McGill-Queen's University Press, 1991), 3–92, 174–200.

6. Blickle, *Revolution*, 195–96.

7. Oberman, "Social Unrest," 47–48.

8. Victor D. Thiessen, *"To the Assembly of Common Peasantry:* The Case of the Missing Context," *Archiv für Reformationsgeschichte* 86 (1995): 175–98.

9. Hans-Jürgen Goertz, *Thomas Müntzer: Apocalyptic Mystic and Revolutionary* (Edinburgh: T. & T. Clark, 1993), 177.

10. Stayer, *Peasants' War*, 61–92, 186–200.

11. *The Sources of Swiss Anabaptism: The Grebel Letters and Related Documents*, Classics of the Radical Reformation, vol. 4, ed. Leland Harder (Scottdale, Pa.: Herald Press, 1985), 290, 293.

12. James M. Stayer, *Anabaptists and the Sword* (Lawrence, Kans.: Coronado, 1976), 103–7.

13. Harder, *Sources of Swiss Anabaptism*, 448.

14. Robert C. Walton, "Was There a Turning Point of the Zwinglian Reformation?" *Mennonite Quarterly Review* 42 (1968): 45–56; C. Arnold Snyder, "Word and Power in Reformation Zurich," *Archiv für Reformationsgeschichte* 81 (1990): 263–85.

15. Scott A. Gillies, "Huldrych Zwingli and the Zurich Origins of the Covenant, 1524–1527," Master's thesis, Queen's University, Kingston, Canada, 1996.

16. Werner O. Packull, *Hutterite Beginnings: Communitarian Experiments During the Reformation* (Baltimore and London: Johns Hopkins University Press, 1995), 15–32.

17. *Quellen zur Geschichte der Täufer in der Schweiz* [hereafter QGTS], vol. 1, *Zürich*, ed. Leonhard von Muralt and Walter Schmid (Zurich: Theologischer Verlag, 1952), 49–50, 216.

18. Ibid., 171–72.

19. James M. Stayer, "Reublin and Brötli: The Revolutionary Beginnings of Swiss Anabaptism," in *The Origins and Characteristics of Anabaptism*, ed. Marc Lienhard (The Hague: Nijhoff, 1977), 83–102.

20. Werner O. Packull, *Mysticism and the Early South German–Austrian Anabaptist Movement, 1525–1531* (Scottdale, Pa.: Herald Press, 1977), 62–117, 199–214.

21. C. Arnold Snyder, *Anabaptist History and Theology. An Introduction* (Kitchener, Ont.: Pandora Press, 1995), 101–13, esp. 107.

22. Heinold Fast, "Hans Krüsis Buchlein über Glauben und Taufe," *Zwingliana* 11 (1959–63): 456–75.

23. Stayer, *Anabaptists and the Sword*, 154.

24. C. Arnold Snyder, "The Schleitheim Articles in Light of the Revolution of the Common Man: Continuation or Departure?" *Sixteenth Century Journal* 16 (1985): 419–30.

25. Original text in QGTS 2: *Ostschweiz*, ed. Heinold Fast (Zurich: Theologischer Verlag, 1973), 26–36 ; English translation in *The Legacy of Michael Sattler*, Classics of the Radical Reformation, vol. 1, ed. John H. Yoder (Scottdale, Pa.: Herald Press, 1973), 34–43.

26. Yoder, *Legacy of Michael Sattler*, 66–85.

27. Claus-Peter Clasen, *Anabaptism: A Social History, 1525–1618: Switzerland, Austria, Moravia and South and Central Germany* (Ithaca: Cornell University Press, 1972), 370–86, 419–22.

28. Hans-Jürgen Goertz, *Die Täufer. Geschichte und Deutung* (Munich: Beck, 1988), 121–36.

29. Stayer, *Peasants' War*, 95–163, 200–219.

30. Stayer, *Anabaptists and the Sword*, 189–201, esp. 190–93.

31. Hans-Peter Jecker, "Die Basler Täufer," *Basler Zeitschrift für Geschichte und Altertumskunde* 80 (1980): 6–131.

32. Packull, *Hutterite Beginnings*, 66–76.

33. Ibid., 33–53.

34. Ibid., 161–213; Wolfgang Lassmann, "Möglichkeiten einer Modellbildung zur Verlaufsstruktur des tirolischen Anabaptismus," in *Anabaptistes et dissidents au XVIe siècle*, ed. Jean-Georges Rott and Simon L. Verheus (Baden-Baden and Bouxwiller: V. Koerner, 1987), 297–309.

35. Stayer, *Anabaptists and the Sword*, 107–8.

36. An English translation is in *Balthasar Hubmaier: Theologian of Anabaptism*, Classics of the Radical Reformation, vol. 5, eds. H. Wayne Pipkin and John H. Yoder (Scottdale, Pa.: Herald Press, 1989), 492–523; original text in *Quellen zur Geschichte der Täufer*, 9: *Balthasar Hubmaier Schriften*, eds., Gunnar Westin and Torsten Bergsten (Gütersloh: Gerd Mohn, 1962), 434–57.

37. Stayer, *Anabaptists and the Sword*, 162–66.

38. Ibid., 160; Ray C. Gingerich, "The Legacy of Hans Hut: From the Augsburg Synod (August 1527) to his Death (December 1527)," unpublished ms. delivered at 1995 Anabaptist Colloquium, Goshen, Indiana. Gingerich argues that Hut evolved toward nonresistance in the course of his Anabaptist career and that the statements made in his Augsburg interrogation were simply unreliable. This is one way to look at the historical evidence, but it seems less probable because of similar statements by Hut's followers. (See also Ray C. Gingerich, "The Mission Impulse of Early Swiss and South German–Austrian Anabaptism" [Ph.D. diss., Vanderbilt University, 1980].)

39. Packull, *Hutterite Beginnings*, 54–66, 100–106.

40. Ibid., 106–19; ms. copy of Adler's "Judgement," as yet unpublished and unedited, at Mennonite Historical Library, Goshen, Ind.

41. James M. Stayer, "Wilhelm Reublin: A Picaresque Journey Through Early

Anabaptism," in *Profiles of Radical Reformers: Biographical Sketches from Thomas Müntzer to Paracelsus*, ed. Hans-Jürgen Goertz (Scottdale, Pa.: Herald Press, 1982), 107–17, esp. 115.

42. Original text photographically reproduced in Hans J. Hillerbrand, "An Early Treatise on the Christian and the State," *Mennonite Quarterly Review* 32 (1958): 34–47; edited in *Flugschriften vom Bauernkrieg zum Täuferreich (1526–1535)*, vol. 2, ed. Adolf Laube (Berlin: Akademie Verlag, 1992), 1019–45.

43. Walter Klaassen, "Investigation into the Authorship and the Historical Background of the Anabaptist Tract 'Aufdeckung der Babylonischen Hurn'," *Mennonite Quarterly Review* 61 (1987): 251–61.

44. Stayer, *Anabaptists and the Sword*, 170–72; Packull, *Hutterite Beginnings*, 133–38, 357–59.

45. Packull, *Hutterite Beginnings*, 214–302, 377–401.

46. Stayer, *Peasants' War*, 139–59, 213–18.

47. Peter Riedemann, *Account of Our Religion, Doctrine, and Faith* . . . (Bungay, 1950), 105–7, 113, 217–20; *Die älteste Chronik der Hutterischen Brüder*, ed. A. J. F. Zieglschmid (Ithaca, N.Y.: Cayuga, 1943), 296–308, trans. *The Chronicle of the Hutterian Brethren*, 2 vols. (Rifton, N.Y.: Plough, 1987), I: 276–86; *Quellen zur Geschichte der Täufer*, 12: *Glaubenzeugnisse oberdeutscher Taufgesinnter*, 2, ed. Robert Friedmann (Gutersloh: Gerd Mohn, 1967), 230–98.

48. Werner O. Packull, "The Origins of Peter Riedemann's *Account of Our Faith*," *Sixteenth Century Journal* 30 (1999): 61–69.

49. Stayer, *Peasants' War*, 149–50.

50. Packull, *Hutterite Beginnings*, 89–98, 287–89, 348–52, 397–98.

51. Ibid., 139–46, 360–61.

52. Stayer, *Anabaptists and the Sword*, 127–29; Martin Haas, "The Path of the Anabaptists into Separation: The Interdependence of Theology and Social Behaviour," in *The Anabaptists and Thomas Müntzer*, ed. James M. Stayer and Werner O. Packull (Dubuque, Iowa: Kendall/Hunt, 1980), 72–84.

53. Klaus Deppermann, *Melchior Hoffman: Social Unrest and Apocalyptic Visions in the Age of Reformation*, trans. Malcolm Wren (Edinburgh: T. & T. Clark, 1987).

54. Stayer *Anabaptists and the Sword*, xxv–xxvii, 211–26.

55. Stayer, *Peasants' War*, 123–32, 208–12; James M. Stayer, "Was Dr. Kuehler's Conception of Early Dutch Anabaptism Historically Sound? The Historical Discussion of Münster 450 Years Later," *Mennonite Quarterly Review* 60 (1986): 261–88.

56. Martin Brecht, "Die Theologie Bernhard Rothmanns," *Jahrbuch für Westfälische Kirchengeschichte* 78 (1985): 49–85.

57. Taira Kuratsuka, "Gesamtgilde und Täufer. Der Radikalisierungsprozess in der Reformation Münsters: Von der reformatorischen Bewegung zum Täuferreich 1533/34," *Archiv für Reformationsgeschichte* 76 (1985): 231–70; Karl-Heinz Kirchhoff, "Was There a Peaceful Anabaptist Congregation in Münster in 1534?" trans. Elizabeth Bender, *Mennonite Quarterly Review* 44 (1970): 357–70.

58. Günter Vogler, "Das Täuferreich zu Münster als Problem der Politik im Reich," *Mennonitische Geschichtsblätter* 42 (1985): 7–23.

59. Lammert G. Jansma, "De chiliastische beweging der Wederdopers (1530–1535)," *Doopsgezinde Bijdragen* n.s. 5 (1979): 41–55.

60. Stayer, *Peasants' War*, 132–8, 212–13; Karl-Heinz Kirchhoff, *Die Täufer in Münster 1534/35* (Münster: Aschendorff, 1973).

61. Richard van Dülmen, *Reformation als Revolution. Soziale Bewegung und religiöser Radikalismus in der deutschen Reformation* (Munich: Deutscher Taschenbuch Verlag, 1977), 322–28.

62. Stayer, *Anabaptists and the Sword*, 238–52.

63. Ibid., 283–97.

64. Gary K. Waite, *David Joris and Dutch Anabaptism, 1524–1543* (Waterloo, Ont.: Wilfrid Laurier University Press, 1990); Samme Zijlstra, *Nicolaas Meyndertz van Blesdijk. Een bijdrage tot de geschiedenis van het Daridjorisme* (Assen: Van Gorcum, 1983).

65. Snyder, *Anabaptist History and Theology*, 159–76, isolates a distinct apocalyptic hermeneutic, "prophetic spirit and prophetic letter," from more typical Anabaptist hermeneutics assigning priority to letter over spirit, or to spirit over letter.

66. Stayer, *Anabaptists and the Sword*, 309–28; Christoph Bornhäuser, *Leben und Lehre Menno Simons'* (Neukirchen-Vluyn: Neukirchner Verlag, 1973); translated statements of Menno Simons on government and nonresistance, in *Anabaptism in Outline. Selected Primary Sources*, ed. Walter Klaassen (Scottdale, Pa.: Herald Press, 1981), 255–57, 275–77, 280–81.

67. *Bibliotheca Reformatoria Neerlandica — Geschriften uit den tijd der Hervorming in de Nederlanden*, vol. 2, ed. Samuel Cramer (The Hague: Nijhoff, 1910).

68. W. J. Kühler, *Geschiedenis der Nederlandsche doopsgezinden in de zestiende eeuw* (Haarlem: Willink, 1961), 339–42.

69. J. J. Woltjer and M. E. H. N. Mont, "Settlements: The Netherlands," in *Handbook of European History, 1400–1600*, ed. Thomas A. Brady Jr., Heiko A. Oberman, and James D. Tracy (Leiden: E. J. Brill, 1995), 2:401–8, esp. 406: "The Mennonites were especially numerous in Frisia and Holland where they fiercely competed with the Reformed church. From time to time Calvinist ministers asked for a banning order, but the authorities were never willing to comply and protected the Mennonites."

70. Alastair Duke, *Reformation and Revolt in the Low Countries* (London: Hambledon Press, 1990).

71. Karel Vos, "Revolutionary Reformation," in *Anabaptists and Thomas Müntzer*, 91.

72. *QGTS*, 1: *Zürich*, 24.

73. Ibid., 216.

74. James M. Stayer, "The Passing of the Radical Moment in the Radical Reformation," *Mennonite Quarterly Review* 71 (1997): 151–52.

75. Late sixteenth-century Anabaptism is less studied than Anabaptist begin-

nings, and during this period we know more about the Mennonites and the Hutterites than about the Swiss Brethren. There is some evidence of a less austere version of nonresistance in a statement by Swiss Brethren from Bern in 1590. Although the different behavior of Christians and rulers is stressed in the manner of the Schleitheim Articles, the Brethren caution that they do not mean to imply that the government comes from the devil. Their stress is that the government should not coerce people's consciences (drawing on statements from Luther's *On Temporal Authority* of 1523), nor should rulers claim a special role in the Christian community by virtue of their secular authority. But a concession that carries them far from Michael Sattler states: "If a ruler possesses the virtues of a reborn Christian, then we believe that a ruler can be a Christian and a Christian a ruler, just so long as he lives and behaves according to the Gospel, as was the case with the New Testament Christians who held offices, like the centurion, Cornelius, Sergius Paulus, Erastus and the jailer, who were all officials of the Roman Empire." Thanks to Arnold Snyder, who provided me with a transcription of this source. Snyder thinks he sees influence of the Marpeck brotherhood in this document, and its tone is more akin to Marpeck's statements against Schwenckfeld than to earlier Swiss Brethren formulations of nonresistance. See Codex 628, Berner Burgerbibliothek.

Chapter 4. Power and Authority in Mennonite Theological Development

1. An acknowledgment of diversity in the historical origins of Anabaptism in recent years has contributed to an acknowledgment of diversity in theological development within Mennonite writings. For a historical analysis, see James M. Stayer, Werner O. Packull, and Klaus Deppermann, "From Monogenesis to Polygenesis: The Historical Discussion of Anabaptist Origins," *Mennonite Quarterly Review* 49 (April, 1975): 83–121. For an overview of the diverse approaches to theology among contemporary Mennonites, see A. James Reimer, "Anabaptist-Mennonite Systematic Theology," *Ecumenist* 21, no. 4 (May/June, 1983): 68–72.

2. This term is used by the philosopher Wittgenstein in delineating his notion of "language-games." See Ludwig Wittgenstein, *Philosophical Investigations*, 3rd edition, trans. G. E. M. Anscomb (New York: Macmillan, 1968), part I, par. 67ff. See also Anthony C. Thiselton, *The Two Horizons* (Grand Rapids, Mich.: Eerdmans, 1980), 373–79, and Alan Keightley, *Wittgenstein, Grammar and God* (London: Epworth Press, 1976), 31–40.

3. The reinterpretation of the sacraments during the Reformation is one illustration of the debate surrounding the relationship of spirit and matter. See John D. Rempel, *The Lord's Supper in Anabaptism* (Waterloo, Ont.: Herald Press, 1993).

4. See Helmut Isaac, "Menno's Vision of the Anticipation of the Kingdom of God in His Early Writings," in *Menno Simons: A Reappraisal*, ed. Gerald R. Brunk (Harrisonburg, Va.: Eastern Mennonite College, 1992), 57–72.

5. Ibid., 70.

6. *Complete Writings of Menno Simons*, trans. Leonard Verduin, ed. J. C. Wenger (Scottdale, Pa.: Mennonite Publishing House, 1984), 554–56.

7. Ibid., 562.

8. Menno followed Melchoir Hoffman in a spiritualistic Christology in which Jesus received his flesh directly from God and became human "in Mary," not "of Mary."

9. *Complete Writings*, 93.

10. Ibid., 967–68.

11. C. Arnold Snyder discusses variations of this view of the church as sacrament in the various Anabaptist groups. See *Anabaptist History and Theology: An Introduction* (Kitchener, Ont.: Pandora Press, 1995), 251–364.

12. *The Complete Writings*, 129.

13. Ibid., 202.

14. Hans-Jürgen Goertz, "The Confessional Heritage in Its New Mold: What Is Mennonite Self-Understanding Today?" in *Mennonite Identity: Historical and Contemporary Perspectives*, ed. Calvin Wall Redekop and Samuel J. Steiner (Lanham, Md.: University Press of America, 1988), 1.

15. For a discussion of women in Anabaptism, see C. Arnold Snyder and Linda Huebert Hecht, eds., *Profiles of Anabaptist Women: Sixteenth Century Reforming Pioneers*, Studies in Women and Religion, vol. 3 (Waterloo, Ont.: Wilfrid Laurier Press, 1996); for a discussion of economic sharing, see James M. Stayer, *The German Peasants' War and Anabaptist Community of Goods* (Montreal: McGill-Queen's University Press, 1991); for the movement toward a more egalitarian *Gemeindetheologie*, see Walter Klaassen, *Anabaptism: Neither Catholic nor Protestant* (Waterloo, Ont.: Conrad Press, 1973).

16. Balthasar Hubmaier, "A Christian Instruction," in *Anabaptism in Outline: Selected Primary Sources*, ed. Walter Klaassen (Kitchener, Ont.: Herald Press, 1981), 214.

17. Note the development of elements of church order and structure in the quotations of Anabaptists in ibid., 118–39.

18. Snyder, *Anabaptist History and Theology*, 299–303.

19. *Anabaptism in Outline*, 211.

20. *Complete Works*, 193.

21. Ibid., 198.

22. Snyder, *Anabaptist History and Theology*, 181–83.

23. See Chapter 3.

24. Howard John Loewen, *One Lord, One Church, One Hope, and One God* (Elkhart, Ind.: Institute of Mennonite Studies, 1985), 81.

25. *Complete Works*, 198.

26. Loewen, *One Lord, One Church*, 44.

27. Goertz, "The Confessional Heritage," 4–5.

28. See Harold S. Bender, *The Anabaptist Vision* (Scottdale, Pa.: Herald Press, 1944).

29. Ibid., 34.

30. "Living Between the Times: 'The Anabaptist Vision and Mennonite Reality' Revisited," in *Refocusing a Vision*, ed. John D. Roth (Goshen, Ind.: Mennonite Historical Society, 1995), 51. The focus in this paper is on those Mennonites primarily affected by the recovery of the "Anabaptist Vision" symbolized by Bender's influential essay. This would include the General Conference Mennonite Church and the Mennonite Church. See *The Recovery of the Anabaptist Vision*, ed. Guy F. Hershberger (Scottdale, Pa.: Herald Press, 1967) and the evaluation of this recovery fifty years later in *Conrad Grebel Review* 12, nos. 3 and 4 (1994 and 1995).

31. J. R. Burkholder speaks about the importance of Hershberger's works by suggesting that all denominational resolutions and position statements from the 1940s to the 1960s reflect the Hershberger consensus "with no significant deviations" (John Richard Burkholder, ed., *Mennonite Peace Theology: A Panorama of Types* [Akron, Pa.: Mennonite Central Committee, 1991], 10).

32. Guy F. Hershberger, *War, Peace, and Nonresistance* (Scottdale, Pa.: Herald Press, 1969), 266.

33. Ibid., 1.

34. Ibid., 187.

35. Guy F. Hershberger, *The Way of the Cross in Human Relations* (Scottdale, Pa.: Herald Press, 1958), 43.

36. Hershberger, *War, Peace, and Nonresistance*, 53.

37. Ibid., 169.

38. Hershberger, *Way of the Cross*, 348.

39. Ibid., 353.

40. See H. Richard Niebuhr, *Christ and Culture* (New York: Harper and Row, 1951), esp. chap. 2.

41. John H. Yoder, *The Politics of Jesus: Vicit Agnus Noster* (Grand Rapids, Mich.: Eerdmans, 1994).

42. Ibid., 134–61.

43. Ibid., 145.

44. Ibid., 157.

45. John H. Yoder, *The Royal Priesthood: Essays Ecclesiological and Ecumenical* (Grand Rapids, Mich.: Eerdmans, 1994), 10.

46. Yoder, *Politics of Jesus*, 162–93.

47. Ibid., 180.

48. Ibid., 209.

49. John H. Yoder, *The Priestly Kingdom* (Notre Dame: University of Notre Dame Press, 1984), 155–66.

50. Ibid., 157.

51. Yoder, *The Royal Priesthood*, 146–47.

52. See Leo Driedger and Donald B. Kraybill, *Mennonite Peacemaking: From Quietism to Activism* (Scottdale, Pa.: Herald Press, 1994) for a more sociological analysis of the changes occurring in the Mennonite community amidst the vagaries

of time and place. See particularly 87–107, where the debate between responsible engagement with society and separatist approaches are described.

53. Howard J. Loewen, "Peace in the Mennonite Tradition: Toward a Theological Understanding of a Regulative Concept," in *Baptism, Peace and the State in the Reformed and Mennonite Traditions*, ed. Ross T. Bender and Alan P. F. Sell (Waterloo, Ont.: Wilfrid Laurier Press, 1991), 106–12.

54. Gordon Kaufman, *Nonresistance and Responsibility and Other Mennonite Essays* (Newton, Kans.: Faith and Life Press, 1979), 52.

55. Loewen, "Peace in the Mennonite Tradition," 111.

56. This critical stance can be seen in his article "Anabaptist Vision and Mennonite Reality," in *Consultation on Anabaptist-Mennonite Theology*, ed. A. J. Klassen (Fresno, Calif.: Council of Mennonite Seminaries, 1970), 1–46.

57. Several conferences have been organized by Mennonite women around the theme "Women Doing Theology" in the last few years. These witness both to the sense that women have had of being the "other" and to the growing acceptance by women of the responsibility of articulating publicly their own theology. See *Conrad Grebel Review* 10 (Winter 1992); *Mennonite Quarterly Review* 65 (April 1994); and *Conrad Grebel Review* 14 (Spring, 1996) for the published papers of these conferences.

58. See John Esau, "Recovering, Rethinking, and Re-imagining: Issues in a Mennonite Theology for Christian Ministry," in *Understanding Ministerial Leadership* (Elkhart, Ind.: Institute of Mennonite Studies, 1995), 1–26.

59. Waldemar Janzen, "A Canonical Rethinking of the Anabaptist-Mennonite New Testament Orientation," in *The Church as Theological Community*, ed. Harry Huebner (Winnipeg, Man.: CMBC Publications, 1990), 94–5.

60. J. Lawrence Burkholder, *The Problem of Social Responsibility from the Perspective of the Mennonite Church* (Elkhart, Ind.: Institute of Mennonite Studies, 1989); Gordon Kauffman, *In Face of Mystery: A Constructive Theology* (Cambridge: Harvard University Press, 1993). The writings of both of these theologians have been marginalized in Mennonite institutions because of their deviation from the accepted norm.

Chapter 5. The Abuse of Power among Mennonites in South Russia, 1789–1919

1. D. H. Epp, *Johann Cornies. Zuege aus seinem Leben und Wirken* (Berdjansk: Der Botschafter, 1909), 133; James Urry, *None but Saints. The Transformation of Mennonite Life in Russia 1789–1889* (Winnipeg: Hyperion Press, 1989), 93.

2. P. Hildebrand, *Erste Auswanderung der Mennoniten aus dem Danziger Gebiet nach Suedrussland* (Halbstadt: A. Neufeld, 1888), 68ff.

3. Epp, *Johann Cornies,*131–34; George K. Epp, "Mennonite-Ukraine Relations," *Journal of Mennonite Studies* 7 (1989): 133–34.

4. James M. Stayer, *Anabaptists and the Sword* (Lawrence, Kans.: Coronado Press, 1972), 172.

5. D. G. Rempel "The Mennonite Commonwealth in Russia: A Sketch of Its Founding and Endurance, 1789–1919," *Mennonite Quarterly Review* 47 and 48 (1973, 1974): 259–308; 5–54.

6. John B. Toews, *Czars, Soviets and Mennonites* (Newton, Kans.: Faith and Life Press, 1982), 33; John B. Toews, "The Russian Origins of the Mennonite Brethren: Some Observations," in *Pilgrims and Strangers: Essays in Mennonite Brethren History*, ed. Paul Toews (Fresno, Calif.: CMBS, 1977), 88.

7. Urry, *None But Saints*, 60; Harvey Dyck, "Landlessness in the Old Colony: The *Judenplan* Experiment, 1850–1880," in *Mennonites in Russia, 1788–1988: Essays in Honour of Gerhard Lohrenz*, ed. John Friesen, (Winnipeg: CMBC Publications, 1989), 187.

8. C. Henry Smith, *The Story of the Mennonites*, 5th ed. (Newton: Faith and Life Press, 1981); *Mennonite Encyclopedia* (Scottdale, Pa.: Mennonite Publishing House, 1956), 2:187; 4:389.

9. James Urry, "Mennonite Economic Development in the Russian Mirror," in *Mennonites in Russia*, 107; James Urry, "The Closed and the Open: Social and Religious Change Amongst the Mennonites in Russia, 1789–1889" (Ph.D. diss., Oxford University, 1978), 144.

10. Frank H. Epp, *Mennonite Exodus* (Altona, Man.: D. W. Friesen and Sons, 1962), 24; James Urry, "Through the Eye of a Needle: Wealth and the Mennonite Experience in Imperial Russia," *Journal of Mennonite Studies* 3 (1985): 24; Urry, "Mennonite Economic Development," 106–7.

11. Calvin Redekop, personal communication.

12. "Aus den Kolonien: Wahlprojeckt," *Odessaer Zeitung*, 26 October 1863, 974–75; "Die gegenseitigen Verhaeltnisse der Landbesitzenden und Landlosen Molotschner Mennoniten," *Odessaer Zeitung*, 10 January 1864, 26; Cornelius Krahn, "Some Social Attitudes of Mennonites in Russia," *Mennonite Quarterly Review* 9 (1935): 171.

13. James Urry and Lawrence Klippenstein, "Mennonites and the Crimean War, 1854–1856," *Journal of Mennonite Studies* 7 (1989): 12–13, 19.

14. *Odessaer Zeitung*, 26 October 1863, 974–75; 10 January 1864, 26.

15. Al Reimer, "The Mennonite *Gutsbesitzertum* in Russia," Paper read at the Symposium on the Bicentennial of Mennonites in Russia, Winnipeg, Manitoba, November 9–11, 1989, 2.

16. Ibid., 6; J. C. Toews, "Das Mennonitische Gutsbesitzertum in Russland," *Der Bote* 15 September 1954, 4.

17. Krahn, "Some Social Attitudes of Mennonites in Russia,"170.

18. D .G. Rempel, "The Mennonite Colonies in Russia: A Study of Their Settlement and Economic Development from 1789 to 1914" (Ph.D. diss., Stanford University, 1933), 91; Toews, "Das Mennonitsche Gutsbesitzertum in Russland,"

Der Bote, 21 July 1954, 3; Reimer, "The Mennonite *Gutbesitzertum* in Russia," 9; Urry, "Through the Eye of a Needle," 25.

19. Toews, "Das Mennonitische Gutbesitzertum in Russland," *Der Bote,* 11 August 1954, 45.

20. Reimer, "The Mennonite *Gutsbesitzertum* in Russia," 17.

21. Krahn, "Some Social Attitudes of Mennonites in Russia," 169.

22. Adolf Ehrt, *Das Mennonitentum in Russland von seiner Einwanderung bis zur Gegenwart* (Berlin: Verlag von Julius Beltz, 1932), 17–18.

23. Urry, "Mennonite Economic Development," 113; 102.

24. Ehrt, *Das Mennonitentum in Russland,* 92; Urry, "Through the Eye of a Needle," 12.

25. See the list in Urry, "Through the Eye of a Needle," 2.

26. Toews, *Czars, Soviets and Mennonites,* 6.

27. Urry, "Mennonite Economic Development," 119; Urry, "Through the Eye of a Needle," 18.

28. Ehrt, *Das Mennonitentum in Russland,* 91–92; Toews, "Das Mennonitsche Gutsbesitzertum in Russland"; Urry, "Through the Eye of a Needle," 12–13.

29. Urry, "Through the Eye of a Needle," 21.

30. Ehrt, *Das Mennonitentum in Russland,* 88.

31. Urry, "Mennonite Economic Development," 116.

32. Ehrt, *Das Mennonitentum in Russland,* 93–96.

33. Urry, "Through the Eye of a Needle," 19.

34. Ibid., 24.

35. Ibid., 26–28.

36. Toews, "Das Mennonitische Gutsbesitzertum in Russland," *Der Bote,* 11 August 1954, 4–5.

37. Toews, *Czars, Soviets and Mennonites,* 9–11.

38. Urry, "The Closed and the Open," 183.

39. Peter M. Friesen, *The Mennonite Brotherhood in Russia (1789–1910)* (Fresno, Calif.: Board of Christian Literature, 1980), 193.

40. Frank H. Epp, *Mennonites in Canada, 1786–1920* (Toronto: Macmillan of Canada, 1974), 166; Ehrt, *Das Mennonitentum in Russland,* 39; Heinrich Goerz, *Die Molotschnaer Ansiedlung. Entstehung, Entwicklung und Untergang* (Steinbach, Man.: Echo Verlag, 1950), 34.

41. Epp, *Johann Cornies. Zuege aus seinem Leben und Wirken,* 18–19.

42. Horst Penner, *Weltweite Bruderschaft: Ein Mennonitsches Geschichtsbuch* (Karlsruhe: Verlag Heinrich Schneider, 1955), 130.

43. Krahn, "Some Social Attitudes of Mennonites in Russia," 171.

44. John B. Toews, *Perilous Journey: The Mennonite Brethren in Russia 1860–1910* (Winnipeg: Kindred Press, 1988), 19.

45. Urry, *None But Saints,* 149.

46. Calvin Redekop, "The Mennonite Transformation from Gelassenheit to

Capitalism," in *Visions and Realities*, ed. Harry Loewen and Al Reimer (Winnipeg: Hyperion Press, 1985), 99–103.

47. Franz Isaak, *Die Molotschnaer Mennoniten* (Halbstadt: Kommissionsverlag und Druck von H. J. Braun, 1908), 276; Epp, *Mennonite Exodus*, 211.

48. Urry and Klippenstein, "Mennonites and the Crimean War," 14.

49. Ehrt, *Das Mennonitentum in Russland*, 39.

50. Jacob John Toews, "Cultural Background of the Mennonite Brethren Church" (master's thesis, University of Toronto, 1951), 206; Robert Kreider, "The Anabaptist Conception of the Church in the Russian Mennonite Environment 1789–1870," *Mennonite Quarterly Review* 25 (1951): 25; Epp, *Mennonite Exodus*, 24.

51. Kreider, "The Anabaptist Conception of the Church," 27.

52. John B. Toews, "The Origins and Activities of the Mennonite *Selbstschutz* in the Ukraine (1918–1919)," *Mennonite Quarterly Review* 46 (1972): 15; Reimer, "The Mennonite *Gutsbesitzertum* in Russia,"17; Toews, "Das Mennonitische Gutsbesitzertum in Russland," *Der Bote*, 1 September 1954, 3.

53. Toews, "Origins and Activities of the *Selbstschutz*," 15; John B. Toews, *Lost Fatherland: The Story of the Mennonite Emigration from Soviet Russia, 1921–1927* (Scottdale, Pa.: Herald Press, 1967), 26; Colin P. Neufeld, *The Fate of the Mennonites in Soviet Ukraine and the Crimea During the Soviet Collectivization and the Famine (1928–1933)* (Coaldale, Alta.: Colin P. Neufeld, 1989), 13.

54. Neufeld, "The Fate of the Mennonites,"15; Bernard J. Dick, "Something About the *Selbstschutz* of the Mennonites in South Russia (July 1918–March 1919)," *Journal of Mennonite Studies* 4 (1986): 137.

55. Toews, *Lost Fatherland*, 26.

56. Dick, "Something About the *Selbstschutz*," 135.

57. Toews, "Origins and Activities of the Mennonite *Selbstschutz*," 15–16; Adolf A. Reimer, "Wie es kam," *Der Rundschau Kalender IV* (1930): 42.

58. Dick, "Something About the *Selbstschutz*," 136.

59. Ehrt, *Das Mennonitentum in Russland*, 114.

60. Harry Loewen and James Urry, "Protecting Mammon: Some Dilemmas of Mennonite Non-resistance in Late Imperial Russia and the Origins of the *Selbstschutz*," *Journal of Mennonite Studies* 9 (1991): 42–43, 48–49.

61. *Mennonite Encyclopedia* (Scottdale, Pa.: Mennonite Publishing House, 1960), 2:158; Friesen, *Mennonite Brotherhood in Russia*.

62. *Mennonite Encyclopedia* 2:811; *Mennonitisches Lexicon*, ed. Christian Hege and Christian Neff (Weierhof, 1937), 2:346.

63. Isaak, *Die Molotschnaer Mennoniten*, 114–21.

64. Rempel, "Mennonite Commonwealth in Russia"; Urry, "The Closed and the Open," 169.

65. Isaak, *Die Molotschnaer Mennoniten*, 114–21.

66. See Al Reimer, *My Harp Is Turned to Mourning* (Winnipeg: Hyperion Press Limited, 1985), 75–77.

67. Urry, "The Closed and the Open," 206–7; Urry, *None But Saints*, 74–79.

68. Ibid., 206–7.

69. Toews, *Perilous Journey*, 12.

70. Ehrt, *Das Mennonitentum in Russland*, 50.

71. Urry, *None But Saints*, 79; Lawrence Klippenstein, "Mennonite Pacifism and State Service in Russia: A Case Study in Church-State Relations, 1789–1936" (Ph.D. diss., University of Minnesota, 1984), 75–93; C. F. Plett, *The Story of the Krimmer Mennonite Brethren Church* (Winnipeg: Kindred Press, 1985), 6.

72. Goerz, *Die Molotschnaer Ansiedlung*, 57.

73. Urry, "The Closed and the Open," 69.

74. Toews, *Perilous Journey*, 18; Urry and Klippenstein, "Mennonites and the Crimean War," 21.

75. Klippenstein, "Mennonite Pacifism and State Service in Russia," 22; Isaak, *Die Molotschnaer Mennoniten*, 116.

76. Isaak, *Die Molotschnaer Mennoniten*, 276; Epp, *Mennonite Exodus*, 211; Goerz, *Die Molotschnaer Ansiedlung*, 95; Epp, *Johann Cornies*, 85.

77. "Tagebuch gefuehrt von David Epp in Chortitz," 20 September 1838, Mennonite Heritage Centre Archives, Winnipeg, 1017:56; Harvey Dyck, trans. and ed., *A Mennonite in Russia: The Diaries of Jacob D. Epp 1851–1880* (Toronto: University of Toronto Press, 1991), 14.

78. A. H. Unruh, *Die Geschichte der Mennoniten-Bruedergemeinde 1860–1954* (Hillsboro, Kans.: General Conference of the Mennonite Brethren Church of North America, 1954), 39; D. H. Epp, *Die Chortitzer Mennoniten: Versuch einer Darstellung des Entwicklungsganges derselben* (Steinbach, Man.: Die Mennonitische Post, 1984), 71.

79. Isaak, *Die Molotschnaer Mennoniten*, 122–23; Epp, *Die Chortitzer Mennoniten*, 71.

80. Isaak, *Die Molotschnaer Mennoniten*, 102–7, 145–49.

81. Ibid., 176–80.

82. Friesen, *Mennonite Brotherhood in Russia*, 348.

83. Toews, *Czars, Soviets and Mennonites*, 33.

84. Isaak, *Die Molotschnaer Mennoniten*, 238.

85. Harry Loewen, "Echoes of Drumbeats: The Movement of Exuberance Among the Mennonite Brethren," *Journal of Mennonite Studies* 3 (1985): 120–24; Friesen, *Mennonite Brotherhood in Russia*, 268–70.

86. Ibid.; Peter M. Hamm, *Continuity and Change Among Canadian Mennonite Brethren* (Waterloo, Ont.: Wilfrid Laurier University Press, 1987), 49; John A. Toews, *A History of the Mennonite Brethren Church* (Fresno, Calif.: General Conference of the Mennonite Brethren Church, 1975), 61–62.

87. Friesen, *Mennonite Brotherhood in Russia*, 401–6.

88. Epp, *Die Chortitzer Mennoniten*, 74–75.

89. Dyck, *A Mennonite in Russia*, 204.

90. Isaak, *Die Molotschnaer Mennoniten*, 54–56.

91. Ibid., 63–65.

92. A. A. Klaus, *Unsere Kolonien. Studien und Materialien zur Geschichte und Statistik der auslaendischen Kolonisation in Russland*, trans. Jacob Toews (Odessa, 1887), 270.

93. The Epp diaries, seemingly written by grandfather, father, and son, were translated and edited by Harvey Dyck, *A Mennonite in Russia: The Diaries of Jacob D. Epp, 1851–1880* (Toronto: University of Toronto Press, 1991).

94. Loewen, "Echoes of Drumbeats," 120; Jacob P. Bekker, *Origin of the Mennonite Brethren Church* (Hillsboro, Kans.: Mennonite Brethren Publishing House, 1973), 37.

95. This is a "skeleton in the closet" of one of the author's own family.

Chapter 6. Power under the Cover of Tradition: A Case Study of a "Plain Community"

1. From this point on, all discussions about "community" will be with reference to Oak Tree, Sarah's community. Other than minimal contact with Aaron's immediate family, I had no contact with Aaron's home community.

2. These are the words used by Sarah's mother during the early period of this experience to explain the basis of the emotional dilemma she faced when attempting to deal with the sudden appearance of HIV/AIDS in her life.

3. In fact, the bishop attempted to contact me twice, but I was not at home either time, and the outgoing message on my answering machine obviously confounded him because he left no messages for me. He did not try again. But evidently he was so distraught about the situation that his wife took it upon herself to contact me. I happened to be at home when she called, and we made arrangements for me to visit them in their home. It seems significant within the context of the situation that in both instances the initiative for contacting me was made by women.

4. Fears, specific and generalized, in many instances based on misconceptions and misinformation propagated in the larger society as well as through the religious literature previously referred to, dominated much of the thinking and considerations throughout the duration of this incident. The information I provided to the bishop and the Burkholder family seemed to allay some of these fears in the early stages of the events described here; but the fears remained in the consciousness of many people and surfaced periodically. When Aaron later became seriously ill with AIDS-related complications, these fears dominated people's thinking and behavior both within the Anabaptist community and in the surrounding non-Anabaptist society. Many Oak Tree people worked in the surrounding area. Some of the men, particularly those who were known to have had personal contact with Aaron, had their employment terminated. Many of the Anabaptist women who regularly did cleaning and other household work, or provided child care for non-Anabaptist families, were also fired.

5. After Aaron became terminally ill with AIDS complications, a member of Sarah's family phoned this practitioner and confronted him about his claims that Aaron had tested negative for the HIV virus. He denied making any such claims; he insisted that Aaron and Sarah had obviously misunderstood him. He insisted that from the beginning he claimed only to be able to help Aaron remain healthier longer, that he never claimed to be able to cure HIV disease, nor did he claim to have tested Aaron for his HIV condition or make any recommendations about having unprotected conjugal relations. He suggested that the couple had been untruthful in their reporting of the situation.

6. At this time there was still a considerable lack of definitive information about HIV/AIDS among local medical practitioners. The rural physician who delivered Sarah's child took blood from the baby as well as from Sarah for the purpose of HIV testing. Both samples tested positive, but in the case of the baby it was a "false positive" because the test was based not on the presence of the virus itself, but on the presence of HIV antibodies. Since the antibodies can much more easily traverse the placenta than can the HIV virus, the test results reflect the presence of the mother's antibodies. The physician should have waited until the baby was 8 to 10 months old—time enough for the mother's antibodies to have dissipated. At my suggestion, the baby was retested at about one year of age with a negative result. However, because Sarah believed—on the basis of the initial test—that the baby was already HIV-positive, she breast-fed the child. Subsequent testing indicated that the child had become HIV-positive, probably a result of the long-term breast feeding.

7. Calvin Redekop, "Power," in *Dictionary of Pastoral Care and Counseling*, ed. Rodney J. Hunter (Nashville, Tenn.: Abingdon Press, 1990), 931–33.

8. Donald B. Kraybill, *The Riddle of Amish Culture* (Baltimore: Johns Hopkins University Press, 1989), 73.

9. John A. Hostetler and Gertrude Enders Huntington, *The Hutterites in North America* (New York: Holt, Rinehart, and Winston, 1980), 35–36.

10. Georges Balandier, *Political Anthropology* (London: Allen Lane, 1970), 36.

Chapter 7. Mennonite Culture Wars:
Power, Authority, and Domination

The work for this chapter was supported by a generous grant from the Lilly Endowment (grant 900760).

1. There are, of course, distinctions to be made between pacifism and nonresistance. Guy Hershberger's concise summary of Anabaptist criticisms of pacifism in the *Mennonite Encyclopedia* offers just one example. See Guy Hershberger, "Pacifism," *Mennonite Encyclopedia* (Scottdale, Pa.: Mennonite Publishing House, 1959), 4:104–5. See also his *War, Peace, and Nonresistance* (Scottdale, Pa.: Herald Press, 1944).

2. Paul Harrison, *Authority and Power in the Free Church Tradition: A Social Case*

Study of the American Baptist Convention (Princeton: Princeton University Press, 1959), 53.

3. Calvin Redekop, *Mennonite Society* (Baltimore: Johns Hopkins University Press, 1989), 65.

4. Harold Bender, "The Church," *Mennonite Encyclopedia* (Scottdale, Pa.: Mennonite Publishing House, 1955), 1:594.

5. Ibid., 597.

6. Don Kraybill, "Yieldedness and Accountability in Traditional Anabaptist Communities," in *Anabaptist Currents: History in Conversation with the Present*, ed. Carl Bowman and Stephen Longenecker (Bridgewater, Va.: Forum for Religious Studies, 1995), 269.

7. Robert Friedmann, "Gelassenheit," *Mennonite Encyclopedia* (Scottdale, Pa.: Mennonite Publishing House, 1956), 2:448. Friedmann notes that Pietism gave *Gelassenheit* a somewhat more mystical quality, suggesting the goal of "unperturbed calmness of the soul."

8. Cal Redekop argues that the centrality of the *Martyr's Mirror* in Mennonite family life for centuries points to the continued importance of the concept (*Mennonite Society*, 92). Robert Friedmann, however, concluded his entry on *Gelassenheit* in the *Mennonite Encyclopedia* by noting that "present-day Mennonitism [circa 1956] has lost the idea of *Gelassenheit* nearly completely; yet with the recovery of the ideal of discipleship also *Gelassenheit* may be revived" (2: 449).

9. Sandra Cronk, "Gelassenheit: The Rites of the Redemptive Process in Old Order Amish and Old Order Mennonite Communities," *Mennonite Quarterly Review* 55 (1981): 5–44.

10. Although it must be added that Schlabach's own work moves us far along in that regard. See Theron Schlabach, *Peace, Faith, Nation: Mennonites and Amish in Nineteenth Century America* (Scottdale, Pa.: Herald Press, 1988), 29.

11. Ibid., 88.

12. Ibid., 96.

13. Peter Berger and Brigette Berger, *Sociology: A Biographical Approach* (New York: Basic Books, 1975), 303–4.

14. Ibid., 279.

15. Thomas Wartenberg, *The Forms of Power: From Domination to Transformation* (Philadelphia: Temple University Press, 1990).

16. Berger and Berger, *Sociology*.

17. Dennis Wrong, *Power: Its Forms, Bases, and Uses* (New York: Harper, 1979), 49, 231ff.

18. See, for example, Peter Berger, *Invitation to Sociology* (New York: Doubleday, 1963).

19. John Hostetler and Gertrude Enders Huntington, *The Hutterites in North America* (New York: Holt, Rinehart, and Winston, 1967), 112. I would note that Hostetler and Huntington do allow for the role of power, albeit limited. They suggest that families sometimes contest leadership roles in the community. They do

not develop the implications for this by way of the leadership's role in setting community standards.

20. Schlabach, *Peace, Faith, Nation*, 104.

21. Calvin Redekop, *The Old Colony Mennonites: Dilemmas of Ethnic Minority Life* (Baltimore: Johns Hopkins University Press, 1969), 100.

22. Quoted in Bender, "The Church," 595.

23. Ibid.

24. *New York Times*, 7 December 1991, 10.

25. James Davison Hunter, *Culture Wars: The Struggle to Define America* (New York: Basic Books, 1991), 52.

26. Ibid., 60.

27. Sue Curry Jansen, *Censorship: The Knot that Binds Power and Knowledge* (New York: Oxford University Press, 1991), 7.

28. Wartenberg, *Forms of Power*.

29. George Marsden, *Fundamentalism and American Culture: The Shaping of Twentieth-Century Evangelicalism, 1870–1980* (New York: Oxford University Press, 1980), 4.

30. Paul Toews, "Fundamentalist Conflict in Mennonite Colleges: A Response to Cultural Transitions?" *Mennonite Quarterly Review* 57 (1983): 241–56.

31. This is not to say that they were anti-education. It was not education per se that bothered many fundamentalists, but rather a certain type of education.

32. James Juhnke, *Vision, Doctrine, War: Mennonite Identity and Organization in America, 1980–1930* (Scottdale, Pa.: Herald Press, 1989), 259.

33. Norman Kraus, "American Mennonites and the Bible, 1750–1950," *Mennonite Quarterly Review* 41 (1967): 309–29.

34. Juhnke, *Vision, Doctrine, War*, 262.

35. Ibid., 171.

36. For histories of Goshen College, see Susan Fisher Miller, *Culture for Service: A History of Goshen College, 1894–1994* (Goshen, Ind.: Goshen College, 1994); John Umble, *Goshen College, 1894–1954* (Goshen, Ind.: Goshen College, 1955). The Elkhart Institute opened its doors in 1894, moving to Goshen during the 1903–04 academic year. While the Elkhart Institute was originally more vocationally oriented, it moved in the direction of a liberal arts curriculum. A program of high school study continued for a time at Goshen in the form of the Goshen Academy. See Miller, *Culture for Service*, 34ff.

37. The latter notion was particularly controversial since many church leaders were opposed to the formal training of the ministry. See Stephen Ainlay, "The 1920 Seminary Movement: A Failed Attempt at Formal Theological Education in the Mennonite Church," *Mennonite Quarterly Review* 64 (1990): 325–51.

38. Miller, *Culture for Service*, 60.

39. Goshen's second through sixth presidents were: J. E. Hartzler, George Lapp, H. F. Reist, I. R. Detweiller, and Daniel Kauffman. The colleges of the (Old) Mennonite Church were not alone in facing difficulties. Bethel (General Confer-

ence Mennonite) and Tabor (Mennonite Brethren) were also battlefields of the culture war. See Toews, "Fundamentalist Conflict in Mennonite Colleges."

40. Miller, *Culture for Service*, 88.

41. The discourse around the closing of the college was given to the language of extremes. Opponents tended to vilify one another. Miller notes that "while today we can charge the anti-Goshenites with having carelessly applied 'liberal' and 'modernist' labels, we can also now recognize that the more reckless members of the besieged Goshen faction could rather indiscriminately paint the brethren on the board [of education] and in key Indiana-Michigan conference positions who tried to influence Goshen's course as political maneuverers" (*Culture for Service*, 96).

42. Miller, *Culture for Service*, 105.

43. Richard Brown, *Knowledge Is Power: The Diffusion of Information in Early America, 1700–1865* (New York: Oxford University Press, 1989). Equally instructive is the work of anthropologists like Lamont Lindstrom, *Knowledge and Power in a South Pacific Society* (Washington, D.C.: Smithsonian Institution Press, 1990).

44. John A. Hostetler, *God Uses Ink: The Heritage and Mission of the Mennonite Publishing House After Fifty Years* (Scottdale, Pa.: Herald Press, 1958), 10–11.

45. Juhnke, *Vision, Doctrine, War*, 42.

46. Ibid., 124ff.

47. The title was a combination of *The Gospel Witness*, which had been published in Scottdale, Pennsylvania, and Funk's *Herald of Truth*.

48. Juhnke, *Vision, Doctrine, War*, 267.

49. Juhnke, *Vision, Doctrine, War*, 312. The masthead on the *Sword and Trumpet* read "Devoted to the Defense of a Full Gospel, With Especial Emphasis upon Neglected Truths, and to an Active Opposition of the Various Forms of Error that Contribute to the Religious Drift of the Times."

50. Harold S. Bender, "Sword and Trumpet," *Mennonite Encyclopedia*, 4:677.

51. Juhnke, *Vision, Doctrine, War*, 268.

52. There certainly were ties between the *Exponent* and "old Goshen"—a reference to some of the faculty, administrators, and students who were seen as allied with the pre-closing Goshen College. See Juhnke, *Vision, Doctrine, War*, 267.

53. John Graybill, "The Search for Truth: A Study of the *Christian Exponent* and Its Place Within the Conservative-Progressive Conflict in the Mennonite Church in the 1920s" (Unpublished paper, Goshen College Library, 1982), 6.

54. *Sword and Trumpet* 2, no. 4 (October 1930): 7.

55. Lester Hostetler, "The 'Why' of the *Exponent*," *Christian Exponent* 1, no. 1 (January 4, 1924): 5–6.

56. See the brief review of his situation in Juhnke, *Vision, Doctrine, War*, 265.

57. Robert Dahl, "A Critique of the Ruling Elite Model," *American Political Science Review* 52 (June 1958): 463–69.

58. J. C. Wenger, *The Mennonites in Indiana and Michigan* (Scottdale, Pa.: Herald Press, 1961), 104.

59. J. C. Wenger, *Separated Unto God* (Scottdale, Pa.: Mennonite Publishing House, 1959), ix.

60. Nicholas Abercrombie, Stephen Hill, and Bryan Turner, *The Dominant Ideology Thesis* (London: Allen and Unwin, 1980).

61. The Concern Movement was a renewal movement composed of highly educated young church leaders who attempted to bring the Mennonite church more in line with what they considered to be "authentic" Anabaptism. Clearly the Concern Movement itself was a cultural elite with a stake in Mennonite culture wars. For more on the movement, see J. Lawrence Burkholder, "Concern Pamphlets Movement," *Mennonite Encyclopedia* (Scottdale, Pa.: Herald Press, 1990), 5:177–80.

62. Redekop, *Mennonite Society*, 304–6.

Chapter 8. Power and Authority in Mennonite Ecclesiology: A Feminist Perspective

1. Rosemary Radford Ruether, "Differing Views of the Church," in *Authority, Community and Conflict*, ed. Madonna Kolbenschlag (Kansas City: Sheed and Ward, 1986), 105.

2. Talcott Parsons and A. M. Henderson, eds., *Max Weber: The Theory of Social and Economic Organization* (New York: Free Press, 1965), 152. Weber defined power thus: "Macht bedeutet jede Chance innerhalb einer sozialen Beziehung den eigenen Willen auch gegen Widerstreben durchzusetzen gleichviel worauf diese Chance beruht" (*Wirtschaft und Gesellschaft: Grundriss der Sozialokonomik* [Tübingen: Verlag von J. C. B. Mont Paul Siebeck, 1925], 28). For an overview of various translations of this passage, see Isidor Walliman, Howard Rosenbaum, Nicholas Tatsis, and George Zito, "Misreading Weber: The Concept of Macht," *Sociology* 14, no. 2 (May 1980): 260–75.

3. Jean Baker Miller quoted in Gloria Durka, "Women and Power: Leadership in Religious Organization," *Journal of Pastoral Counseling* 17, no. 1 (1982): 73.

4. Elisabeth Schüssler Fiorenza, *Jesus: Miriam's Child, Sophia's Prophet* (New York: Continuum, 1994), 14, 62, 196.

5. Julia Kasdorf, "Bakhtin, Boundaries, and Bodies," *Mennonite Quarterly Review* 71 (1997): 186–87.

6. S. Loren Bowman, "The Balance of Power," in *Power and Polity Among the Brethren: A Study of Church Governance* (Elgin, Ill.: Brethren Press, 1987), 7ff.

7. Gordon Zook, "Current Patterns of Shared Leadership in Mennonite Church Congregations" (D.Min. thesis, Lancaster Theological Seminary, 1989), 5.

8. Lois Yvonne Barrett, "Wreath of Glory: Ursula's Prophetic Visions in the Context of Reformation and Revolt in Southwestern Germany 1524–1530" (Ph.D. diss., Union Institute, Cincinnati, 1992).

9. Joyce Irwin, "Society and the Sexes," in *Reformation Europe: A Guide to Research*, ed. Steven Ozment (St. Louis: Center for Reformation Research, 1982), 343–59.

10. Keith L. Sprunger, "God's Powerful Army of the Weak: Anabaptist Women

of the Radical Reformation," in *Triumph over Silence*, ed. Richard L. Greaves (Westport, Conn.: Greenwood Press, 1985), 45–74.

11. Linda Huebert Hecht, "Women and Religious Change: The Significance of Anabaptist Women in the Tirol, 1527–29," *Studies in Religion* 21, no. 1 (1992): 59.

12. Ibid., 61.

13. Linda Huebert Hecht, "An Extraordinary Lay Leader: The Life and Work of Helene of Freyberg, Sixteenth Century Noblewoman and Anabaptist from the Tirol," *Mennonite Quarterly Review* 63, no. 3 (1992): 312–41.

14. Ernst Troeltsch, *The Social Teaching of the Christian Churches* (New York: Macmillan, 1931).

15. C. Arnold Snyder, "The Believers' Church Heritage of Ministry," in *Servants of the World: Ministry in the Believers Churches*, ed. David B. Eller (Elgin, Ill.: Brethren Press, 1990), 150.

16. Harold S. Bender, "The Church," *Mennonite Encyclopedia* (Scottdale, Pa.: Mennonite Publishing House, 1960), 2:597. Calvin Redekop states, "Unquestionably the body of believers or the 'priesthood of the laity' gave the Mennonite tradition a starting point" (*Mennonite Society* [Baltimore: Johns Hopkins University Press, 1989], 65).

17. Stephen Ainlay and Fred Kniss, "Mennonites and Conflict: Reexamining Mennonite History and Contemporary Life," paper presented at the Conference on Mennonites and Conflict: New Directions in Scholarship, Goshen College, Goshen, Indiana, 1996, 3.

18. Elisabeth Schüssler Fiorenza, *Discipleship of Equals: A Critical Feminist Ekklesia-logy of Liberation* (New York: Crossroad, 1993), 301.

19. Quoted in Paul A. Lacey, *Quakers and the Use of Power* (Wallingford, Pa.: Pendle Hill Pamphlet # 241, 1981), 30.

20. Rodney Sawatsky, *Authority and Identity: The Dynamics of the General Conference Mennonite Church* (North Newton, Kans.: Bethel College, 1987), 61.

21. Snyder, "The Believers' Church," 144.

22. Ruether, "Differing Views of the Church," 106.

23. Judith Plaskow, "Transforming the Nature of Community," in *After Patriarchy: Feminist Transformations of the World*, ed. Paula M. Cooey, William R. Eakin, and Jay B. McDaniel (New York: Orbis Books, 1991), 98.

24. Letty M. Russell, *Church in the Round: Feminist Interpretation of the Church* (Louisville, Ky.: Westminster/John Knox Press, 1993), 52–53.

25. Ibid., 56–58, 64.

26. Snyder, "The Believers' Church," 146, 152–58.

27. Gene Sharp, *The Role of Power in Nonviolent Struggle* (Cambridge, Mass.: Albert Einstein Institute, 1990), 3.

28. Carter Heyward, *Our Passion for Justice: Images of Power, Sexuality, and Liberation* (New York: Pilgrim Press, 1984), 119.

29. Nina L. Colwill, *The New Partnership: Women and Men in Organizations* (Palo Alto, Calif.: Mayfield Publishers, 1982), 104.

30. Walliman, Rosenbaum, Tatsis, and Zito, "Misreading Weber," 269.

31. Thomas E. Wartenberg, *The Forms of Power: From Domination to Transformation* (Philadelphia: Temple University Press, 1990).

32. Michel Foucault, *Discipline and Punish: The Birth of the Prison* (New York: Pantheon Books, 1979), 194.

33. Ibid., 27.

34. Mary Daly, *Gyn/ecology : The Metaethics of Radical Feminism* (Boston: Beacon Press, 1990).

35. See, for example, Audre Lorde, "An Open Letter to Mary Daly," in *Sister Outsider* (Freedom, Calif.: Crossing Press, 1984).

36. Guida West and Rhoda Lois Blumberg, "Reconstructing Social Protest from a Feminist Perspective," in *Women and Social Protest*, ed. West and Blumberg (Oxford: Oxford University Press, 1990), 8.

37. Elaine L. Graham, "Gender, Personhood and Theology," *Scottish Journal of Theology* 48, 3 (1995): 343–44.

38. Durka, "Women and Power: Leadership in Religious Organization," 72.

39. Russell, *Church in the Round*, 25–7, 35–6.

40. Ibid., 42, 187.

41. Colwill, "Power," 106.

42. Lacey, *Quakers and the Use of Power*, 26.

43. Lois Janzen Preheim, "Power: One Woman's Perspective," *In Search* (Elkhart, Ind.: Mennonite Board of Missions, December 1991).

44. Colwill, "Power," 93–96.

45. Sally Brown Geis, "Church Perceptions of Power," *Quarterly Review* 15, no. 2, (1995): 214–17.

46. Rebecca Slough, "Changes Created by Women's Participation," MCC Women's Concerns *Report*, July-August 1996, 6.

47. Mary E. Hunt, "'Re-Imagining' Backlash," in *Feminist Theology in Different Contexts*, ed. Elizabeth Schüssler Fiorenza and Mary S. Copeland (New York: Orbis, 1996), 49.

48. Pamela Dickey Young, *Feminist Theology/Christian Theology: In Search of Method* (Minneapolis: Fortress Press, 1990), 108.

49. Russell, *Church in the Round*, 106.

50. Ibid., 125.

Chapter 9. Power in the Anabaptist Community

1. As Bertrand Russell puts it, "The love of power is an essential part of human nature . . . The love of power, like lust, is such a strong motive that it influences most men more then they think it should" (*Power* [London: Routledge, 1992], 179–81).

2. For a wide-ranging discussion of the nature and history of power, see Bertrand De Jouvenel, *On Power* (Boston: Beacon Press, 1962).

3. See Russell's chapter on "The Ethics of Power" in *Power*, for expanded anal-

ysis of the ethical dimensions of power. Though there is great variation in the Christian interpretation of power, most traditions would accept the view that Christ taught the rejection of power for selfish ends and instead taught that self-denying service to fellow humans was the ideal. This is the argument of Walter Wink, *Engaging the Powers* (Minneapolis: Fortress Press, 1992).

4. Max Weber, *From Max Weber: Essays in Sociology*, ed. H. H. Gerth and C. Wright Mills (New York: Oxford University Press, 1946), 180.

5. Ibid., 294–96.

6. Ibid., 294.

7. Social science has predominantly taken the "value neutral" position due to its positivist/empiricist philosophy. Until fairly recently the discussion of power among social scientists remained basically descriptive without concerns about asymmetry, control, or abuse of power.

8. The prevalence and centrality of power in political institutions is illustrated by Harold D. Lasswell and Abraham Kaplan, *Power and Society* (New Haven: Yale University Press, 1950), in their analysis of power as expressed in political institutions.

9. See Russell, "Economic Power," chap. 8 in *Power*.

10. Russell discusses the major forms of power, including intellectual and academic power, which is not often discussed by academics (ibid., 30ff.).

11. See for example *KIT*, a monthly journal published by ex-Bruderhof members, which contains innumerable accounts of abuse of power in the Bruderhofs. The literature describing the violation of human rights and oppression of individuals in utopian and sectarian groups, including the so-called cults, is voluminous.

12. For an extended analysis of the role of women in Mennonite society, see my *Mennonite Society* (Baltimore: Johns Hopkins University Press, 1989), especially 169ff. See also Linda Boynton Arthur, "Clothing, Control, and Women's Agency: The Mitigation of Patriarchal Power," in *Negotiating at the Margins: The Gendered Discourses of Power and Resistance*, ed. Sue Fisher and Nancy Davis (New Brunswick: Rutgers University Press, 1993), 66–84.

13. Fred Belk, *The Great Trek of the Russian Mennonites to Central Asia, 1880–1884*, (Scottdale, Pa.: Herald Press, 1976). See also Dallas Wiebe, *Our Asian Journey* (Waterloo, Ont.: Wilfrid Laurier University Press, 1997) for a fictionalized account of the power of individual charisma and group psychology.

14. Herbert C. Kelman, "Further Thoughts on the Processes of Compliance, Identification, and Internalization," in *Perspectives on Social Power*, ed. James T. Tedeschi (Chicago: Aldine Publishing Co., 1974), 125ff.

15. As indicated in note 7 above, the positivistic/empiricist philosophy on which social science is based does not acknowledge a transcendent reality or moral basis.

16. This discussion derives from my own interpretation of the philosophical and theological values of the Anabaptist/Mennonite tradition regarding the use of power. Little overt discussion of power in Anabaptist writings exists, hence I feel emboldened to take this step.

17. Augustine, *The City of God* (Chicago: Encyclopedia Britannica, 1952), bk. 19, chap. 14, 520. See also Chapter 2 in the present volume. The Anabaptists may not have read Augustine extensively, though Menno Simons cites him often. The idea of two kingdoms was, of course, central to Anabaptist thinking.

18. The Anabaptist theological system placed highest significance on Christ and his teachings, so Jesus' statements regarding violence had implicit as well as explicit normativity, particularly in relation to power understood as the exercise of physical force. But his strictures on power generally, as expressed for example in wealth, have rarely been expressed or explicated in Mennonite life.

19. Kenneth Scott LaTourette, *A History of Christianity* (New York: Harper, 1953), 258, 261. Not all agree with this assessment. Andrew Rule proposes that "although Christian leaders and organizations have abused power, sought alliances with centers of power which were not enlightened by love and justice, [and] failed to make a fully constructive use of power, still its record is much better than that of any other" ("Christianity and the Problem of Power," in *New 20th Century Encyclopedia of Religious Knowledge*, ed. J. D. Douglass [Grand Rapids: Baker, 1991], 661).

20. Klaus Hemmerle, "Power," in *Encyclopedia of Theology*, ed. Karl Rahner (Boston: Seabury, 1975), 1264.

21. For an earlier application of this idea to Anabaptism, see my "Institutions, Power and the Gospel" in *Kingdom, Cross and Community*, ed. J. Richard Burkholder and Calvin Redekop (Scottdale, Pa.: Herald Press, 1976).

22. The Apostle Paul also echoes the "being" status of members of the kingdom: "Therefore if anyone is in Christ, he is a new creation" (2 Cor. 5:17).

23. Emil Brunner, *The Misunderstanding of the Church* (Philadelphia: Westminster Press, 1953), 77.

24. Another way of addressing the "power of pure being" is to describe it as individual autonomy and freedom, whether in religious or secular contexts. As has been implied above, Anabaptism was one of the major forces to introduce the idea of individual freedom to believe during the Reformation.

25. This dynamic was undoubtedly operative in other "dissident" groups anticipating and during the Reformation period, such as the Apostolic Brethren, Waldensians, the Hussites, and the Huguenots. Ernst Troeltsch, referring to pre-Reformation groups, states: "People do not want to be ruled; they desire the freedom and equality of the Primitive State" (*The Social Teachings of the Christian Churches* [New York: Harper Torchbooks, 1960], 356ff.).

26. John H. Yoder, *The Politics of Jesus* (Grand Rapids: Eerdmans, 1972), 147. Yoder states that the question ultimately goes to the source of the social order itself, which theologically is God's work. From a social-scientific perspective the social order is constructed by humans themselves, so the derivation of power is a subset of the question of the creation of society itself. For an important treatment of this topic, see Peter L. Berger and Thomas Luckman, *The Social Construction of Reality* (Garden City, N.Y.: Doubleday Anchor, 1966).

27. "The Schleitheim Confession," in Howard John Loewen, *One Lord, One*

Church, One Hope, and One God (Elkhart, Ind.: Institute of Mennonite Studies, 1985), 80.

28. This interpretation has recently been strongly affirmed by Gerald Biesecker-Mast in "Anabaptist Separation and Arguments Against the Sword in the *Schleitheim Brotherly Union*," *Mennonite Quarterly Review* 74 (July 2000): 396–98, in which he states that the problem with state power is its legitimacy, not the issue of power itself.

29. James W. McClendon, *Systematic Theology: Ethics* (Nashville, Tenn.: Abingdon, 1986), 164.

30. Ibid., 166.

31. "Game theory" as used here is not totally aligned with the philosophical and sociological theory, which is based on mathematical analysis of chance and rational decision making. We are using the concept more as a heuristic device. McClendon's and our definition of the nature of the game, however, closely follows the theoretical discussion. See Oskar Morgenstern, "Game Theory," in *Dictionary of the History of Ideas*, ed. Philip Wiener (New York: Scribner's, 1973), 2:263–75.

32. "Schleitheim Confession," 80.

33. Quoted in Walter Klaassen, *Anabaptism in Outline* (Scottdale, Pa.: Herald Press, 1981), 299.

34. Menno Simons, *The Complete Writings of Menno Simons*, ed. J. C. Wenger (Scottdale, Pa.: Herald Press, 1956), 551.

35. Ibid., 551–52.

36. See Russell, *Power*, chap. 6, "Naked Power." As Russell puts it, "The power of the Catholic Church over Catholics is traditional, but its power over heretics which are persecuted is naked" (ibid., 57).

37. Roland Bainton, "The Anabaptist Contribution to History," in *The Recovery of the Anabaptist Vision*, ed. Guy F. Hershberger (Scottdale, Pa.: Herald Press, 1957), 317.

38. Ernest A. Payne, "The Anabaptist Impact on Western Christendom," in *Recovery of the Anabaptist Vision*, 311.

39. Yoder, *Politics of Jesus*, 153.

40. No concerted treatment of this issue exists, but J. Lawrence Burkholder's *The Problem of Social Responsibility from the Perspective of the Mennonite Church* (Elkhart, Ind.: Institute of Mennonite Studies, 1989) discusses the way institutions have arrogated to themselves the power that belongs in the congregations. See especially chapter 5.

41. See Marlin Jeschke, "Church Discipline," *Mennonite Encyclopedia* (Scottdale, Pa.: Herald Press, 1990), 5:239–40.

42. The oppression of women in Anabaptist/Mennonite communities has been largely ignored or repressed. Feminists maintain that until the asymmetry of power between men and women is rectified no truly healthy society can exist. This position can also be applied to the Anabaptist/Mennonite case. But this issue is so large that it would require a separate treatment.

43. For brief analysis and bibliography of these two Mennonite "common-wealths," see Redekop, *Mennonite Society*, chap. 6.

44. See Calvin Redekop, "The MCC Ethos and the Organizational Revolution," *Mennonite Quarterly Review* 70, no. 1 (1996): 107–33 for a review of the literature.

45. David Kipnis, "The Powerholder," in *Perspectives on Social Power*, 86.

46. Despite the presence of a few rather vague qualifications, this appears to be the perspective advanced in Rodney Sawatsky, "Leadership, Power, and Authority," *Mennonite Quarterly Review* 71, no. 4 (July 1997): 429–52.

47. Here again I refer to the view advanced by Sawatsky, ibid.

48. We maintain that this is the blind spot in Mennonite identity. Most Anabaptist/Mennonites maintain that nonresistance and pacifism is the unique credo—love of the enemy. But the issue of love in domestic life has not received nearly the same moral or ethical scrutiny or status.

49. Richard A. Schermerhorn, *Society and Power* (New York: Random House, 1961).

50. For a recent empirical and very helpful study, see J. Howard Kauffman, "Power and Authority in Mennonite Families," *Mennonite Quarterly Review* 64, no. 4 (1994), 501–23. One finding indicates that 6.2 percent of the female spouses had been abused one or more times (520). The communal Anabaptists, that is, the Hutterites, are probably the best illustration of the asymmetry principle. Almost immediately power began to express itself unequally in the Hutterite communities. See Werner Packull, *Hutterite Beginnings* (Baltimore: Johns Hopkins University Press, 1995).

51. For an extended analysis, see Redekop, *Mennonite Society*, especially chapter 5, "The Religious Base of the Mennonite Community." For the most recent and important study of power in Mennonite congregational and community life, see Fred Kniss, *Disquiet in the Land: Cultural Conflict in American Mennonite Communities* (New Brunswick: Rutgers University Press, 1997).

52. See Calvin Redekop, Stephen C. Ainlay, and Robert Siemens, *Mennonite Entrepreneurs* (Baltimore: Johns Hopkins University Press, 1995). Reinhold Niebuhr states that "the power which creates privilege need not be economic but usually is" (*Moral Man and Immoral Society* [New York: Scribner's, 1960], 114). See his chapter "Attitudes of Privileged Classes" for analysis of how wealth and privilege is the basis for power misuse.

53. However, in recent times the structural restraints in "domestic" Anabaptism are being addressed. Thus, for example, a conference entitled "Consultation on Issues of Power and Authority in the Mennonite Church" was held at Rockway Mennonite Collegiate, Kitchener, Ontario, in May 1997. The proceedings were published under the title given above (n.d., n.p.). A follow-up conference entitled "Power and Authority in the Mennonite Church, Consultation II" was held the following year in Waterloo, Ontario. Both conferences dealt with the implications of the application of power and authority in church and domestic life.

Bibliography

Abercrombie, Nicholas, Stephen Hill, and Bryan Turner. *The Dominant Ideology Thesis.* London: Allen and Unwin, 1980.

Agger, Ben. *Gender, Culture and Power: Toward a Feminist Postmodern Critical Theory.* Westport, Conn.: Praeger, 1993.

Ainlay, Stephen. "The 1920 Seminary Movement: A Failed Attempt at Formal Theological Education in the Mennonite Church." *Mennonite Quarterly Review* 64 (1990): 325–51.

Ainlay, Stephen, and Fred Kniss. "Mennonites and Conflict: Reexamining Mennonite History and Contemporary Life." *Mennonite Quarterly Review* 72 (1998), 121–40.

Aristotle. *The Politics.* Translated by Carnes Lord. Chicago: University of Chicago Press, 1984.

———. *The Politics.* Edited by Stephen Everson. Cambridge: Cambridge University Press, 1996.

Arthur, Linda Boynton. "Clothing, Control, and Women's Agency: The Mitigation of Patriarchal Power." In *Negotiating at the Margins: The Gendered Discourses of Power and Resistance,* edited by Sue Fisher and Kathy Davis. New Brunswick: Rutgers University Press, 1993.

Augustine, Saint. *Confessions. The City of God.* Vol. 16 in *Great Books of the Western World.* Edited by Mortimer J. Adler. Chicago: University of Chicago Press, 1990.

Bacon, Francis. *Novum Organum.* Vol. 28 in *Great Books of the Western World,* edited by Mortimer J. Adler. Chicago: University of Chicago Press, 1990.

Bainton, Roland. "The Anabaptist Contribution to History." In *The Recovery of the Anabaptist Vision,* edited by Guy F. Hershberger. Scottdale, Pa.: Herald Press, 1957.

Balandier, Georges. *Political Anthropology.* London: Allen Lane, 1970.

Barbe, Dominique. *A Theology of Conflict.* Maryknoll, N.Y.: Orbis Books, 1989.

Barnard, Chester L. *The Functions of the Executive.* Cambridge: Harvard University Press, 1964.

Barrett, Lois Yvonne. "Wreath of Glory: Ursula's Prophetic Visions in the Context of Reformation and Revolt in Southwestern Germany, 1524–1530." Ph.D. dissertation, Cincinnati Union Institute, 1992.

Bekker, Jacob P. *Origin of the Mennonite Brethren Church.* Hillsboro, Kans.: Mennonite Brethren Publishing House, 1973.

Belk, Fred. *The Great Trek of the Russian Mennonites to Central Asia, 1880–1884.* Scottdale, Pa.: Herald Press, 1976.

Bender, Harold S. *The Anabaptist Vision.* Scottdale, Pa.: Herald Press, 1944.

Bender, Ross T., and Alan P. F. Sell. *Baptism, Peace and the State in the Reformed and Mennonite Traditions.* Waterloo, Ont.: Wilfrid Laurier Press, 1991.

Berger, Peter. *Invitation to Sociology.* New York: Doubleday, 1963.

Berger, Peter, and Thomas J. Luckman. *The Social Construction of Reality.* Garden City, N.Y.: Doubleday/Anchor, 1966.

Berger, Peter, and Brigette Berger. *Sociology: A Biographical Approach.* New York: Basic Books, 1975.

Bertens, Hans. *The Idea of the Postmodern: A History.* London: Routledge, 1995.

Bierstedt, Robert. *Power and Progress.* New York: McGraw-Hill, 1974.

Blickle, Peter. *The Revolution of 1525. The German Peasants' War from a New Perspective.* Translated by Thomas A. Brady Jr. and H. C. Erik Midelfort. Baltimore: Johns Hopkins University Press, 1981.

Bornhäuser, Christoph. *Leben und Lehre Menno Simons'.* Neukirchen-Vluyn: Neukirchner Verlag, 1973.

Bowman, Carl, and Stephen Longenecker, eds. *Anabaptist Currents: History in Conversation with the Present.* Bridgewater, Va.: Forum for Religious Studies, 1995.

Bowman, S. Loren. *Power and Polity Among the Brethren: A Study of Church Governance.* Elgin, Ill.: Brethren Press, 1987.

Brady Jr., Thomas A., Heiko A. Oberman, and James D. Tracy, eds. *Handbook of European History, 1400–1600.* Leiden: E. J. Brill, 1995.

Brecht, Martin. "Die Theologie Bernhard Rothmans." *Jahrbuch für Westfälische Kirchengeschichte* 78 (1985): 49–85.

Brown, Richard. *Knowledge Is Power: The Diffusion of Information in Early America, 1700–1865.* New York: Oxford University Press, 1989.

Brunk, Gerald R., ed. *Menno Simons: A Reappraisal.* Harrisonburg, Va.: Eastern Mennonite College, 1992.

Brunner, Emil. *The Misunderstanding of the Church.* Philadelphia: Westminster Press, 1953.

Burke, Edmund. *Reflections on the Revolution in France.* Vol. 4 in *The Works of Edmund Burke.* London: Oxford University Press, undated.

Burkholder, J. Lawrence. *The Problem of Social Responsibility from the Perspective of the Mennonite Church.* Elkhart, Ind.: Institute of Mennonite Studies, 1989.

Burkholder, J. Richard, ed. *Mennonite Peace Theology: A Panorama of Types.* Akron, Pa.: Mennonite Central Committee, 1991.

Burkholder, J. Richard, and Calvin Redekop, eds. *Kingdom, Cross and Community.* Scottdale, Pa.: Herald Press, 1976.

Bush, Perry. *Two Kingdoms, Two Loyalties: Mennonite Pacifism in Modern America.* Baltimore: Johns Hopkins University Press, 1998.

Champlin, John R., ed. *Power.* New York: Atherton Press, 1971.

The Chronicle of the Hutterian Brethren. Rifton, N.Y.: Plough Publishing House, 1987.

Clark, Kenneth B. *The Pathos of Power.* New York: Harper and Row, 1974.

Clasen, Claus-Peter. *Anabaptism: A Social History, 1525–1618. Switzerland, Austria, Moravia and South and Central Germany.* Ithaca: Cornell University Press, 1972.

Colwill, Nina L. *The New Partnership: Women and Men in Organizations.* Palo Alto, Calif.: Mayfield Publishers, 1982.

Cooey, Paula M., William R. Eakin, and Jay B. McDaniel, eds. *After Patriarchy: Feminist Transformation of the World Religions.* New York: Orbis Books, 1991.

Coser, Lewis A. "Class." In *Dictionary of the History of Ideas,* vol. 1. Edited by Philip P. Wiener. New York: Scribner's, 1973.

Cramer, Samuel, ed. *Bibliotheca Reformatoria Neerlandica-Geschriften uit den tijd der Hervorming in de Nederlanden.* The Hague: Nijhoff, 1910.

Cronk, Sandra. "Gelassenheit: The Rites of Redemptive Process in Old Order Amish and Old Order Mennonite Communities." *Mennonite Quarterly Review* 55 (1981): 5–44.

Dahl, Robert. "A Critique of the Ruling Elite Model." *American Political Science Review* 52 (June 1958): 463–69.

Daly, Mary. *Gyn/ecology: The Metaethics of Radical Feminism.* Boston: Beacon Press, 1990.

De Jouvenel, Bertrand. *On Power.* Boston: Beacon Press, 1962.

Deppermann, Klaus. *Melchior Hoffman: Social Unrest and Apocalyptic Visions in the Age of Reformation.* Translated by Malcolm Wren. Edinburgh: T. and T. Clark, 1987.

Dick, Bernard J. "Something About the *Selbstschutz* of the Mennonites in South Russia (July 1918–March 1919)." *Journal of Mennonite Studies* 4 (1986), 135–42.

Dipple, Geoffry. *Antifraternalism and Anticlericalism in the German Reformation. Johann Eberlin von Günzburg and the Campaign against the Friars.* Aldershot: Scolar Press, 1996.

Driedger, Leo, and Donald B. Kraybill, eds. *Mennonite Peacemaking: From Quietism to Activism.* Scottdale, Pa.: Herald Press, 1994.

Duke, Alastair C. *Reformation and Revolt in the Low Countries.* London: Hambledon Press, 1990.

Durka, Gloria. "Women and Power: Leadership in Religious Organization." *Journal of Pastoral Counseling* 17:1 (1982): 69–74.

Dyck, Harvey. "Landlessness in the Old Colony: The *Judenplan* Experiment 1850–1880." In *Mennonites in Russia, 1788–1988: Essays in Honour of Gerhard Lohrenz,* edited by John Friesen. Winnipeg, Man.: CMBC Publications, 1989.

Dyck, Harvey, trans. and ed. *A Mennonite in Russia: The Diaries of Jacob D. Epp 1851–1880.* Toronto: University of Toronto Press, 1991.

Dykema, Peter A., and Heiko A. Oberman, eds. *Anticlericalism in Late Medieval and Early Modern Europe.* Leiden: Brill, 1993.

Ehrt, Adolf. *Das Mennonitentum in Russland von seiner Einwanderung bus zur Gegenwart* Berlin: Verlag von Julius Beltz, 1932.

Eller, David. B., ed. *The Servants of the Word: Ministry in the Believers Churches.* Elgin, Ill.: Brethren Press, 1990.

Epp, D. H. *Johann Cornies. Züge aus seinem Leben und Wirken.* Berdjansk: Der Botschafter, 1909.

———. *Die Chortitzer Mennoniten: Versuch einer Darstellung des Entwicklungsganges derselben.* Steinbach, Man.: Die Mennonitische Post, 1984.

Epp, Frank H. *Mennonite Exodus.* Altona, Man.: D. W. Friesen and Sons, 1962.

———. *Mennonites in Canada, 1786–1920.* Toronto: Macmillan of Canada, 1974.

Epp, George K. "Mennonite-Ukraine Relations." *Journal of Mennonite Studies* 7 (1989): 133–44.

Esau, John. "Recovering, Rethinking, and Re-imagining: Issues in a Mennonite Theology for Christian Ministry." In *Understanding Ministerial Leadership.* Elkhart, Ind.: Institute of Mennonite Studies, 1995.

Fast, Heinold. "Hans Krüsis Buchlein über Glauben und Taufe." *Zwingliana* 11 (1959–63): 456–75.

———, ed. *Quellen zur Geschichte der Täufer in der Schweiz, 2. Ostschweiz.* Zurich: Theologischer Verlag, 1973.

Feuerbach, Ludwig. *The Essence of Christianity.* New York: Harper Torchbooks, 1957.

Fiorenza, Elisabeth Schüssler. *Discipleship of Equals: A Critical Ekklesia-logy of Liberation.* New York: Crossroad, 1993.

———. *Jesus: Miriam's Child, Sophia's Prophet.* New York: Continuum. 1994.

Fiorenza, Elisabeth Schüssler, and Mary S. Copeland, eds. *Feminist Theology in Different Contexts.* New York: Orbis Books, 1996.

Fisher, Sue, and Kathy Davis, eds. *Negotiating at the Margins: The Gendered Discourses of Power and Resistance.* New Brunswick: Rutgers University Press, 1993.

Foucault, Michel. *Discipline and Punish: The Birth of the Prison.* New York: Vintage Books, 1979.

———. *Power/Knowledge: Selected Interviews and Other Writings.* Edited by Colin Gordon. New York: Pantheon Books, 1980.

Friedmann, Robert, ed. *Quellen zur Geschichte der Täufer, 12. Glaubenszeugnisse oberdeutscher Taufgesinnter, 2.* Gutersloh: Gerd Mohn, 1967.

Friesen, John, ed. *Mennonites in Russia, 1788–1988. Essays in Honour of Gerhard Lohrenz.* Winnipeg, Man.: CMBC Publications, 1989.

Friesen, Peter M. *The Mennonite Brotherhood in Russia 1789–1910.* Fresno, Calif.: Board of Christian Literature, 1980.

Geis, Sally Brown. "Church Perceptions of Power." *Quarterly Review* 15:2 (1995): 213–24.

Gillies, Scott A. "Huldrich Zwingli and the Zürich Origins of the Covenant 1524–1527." Master's thesis, Queen's University, Ontario, 1996.

Bibliography

Gingerich, Ray C. "The Mission Impulse of Early Swiss and South German–Austrian Anabaptism." Ph.D. dissertation, Vanderbilt University, 1980.

———. "The Legacy of Hans Hut: From the Augsburg Synod (August 1527) to His Death (December 1527)." Paper presented to Anabaptist Colloquium, Goshen, Indiana, 1995.

Girard, Rene. *Violence and the Sacred.* Baltimore: Johns Hopkins University Press, 1977.

Goertz, Hans-Jürgen. *Die Täufer: Geschichte und Deutung.* Munich: Beck, 1980.

———, ed. *Profiles of Radical Reformers: Biographical Sketches from Thomas Münzter to Paracelsus.* Scottdale, Pa.: Herald Press, 1982.

———. *Pfaffenhaß und gross Geschrei: Die reformatorischen Bewegungen in Deutschland, 1517–1529.* Munich: Beck, 1987.

———. "The Confessional Heritage in Its New Mold: What Is Mennonite Self-Understanding Today?" In *Mennonite Identity: Historical and Contemporary Perspectives,* edited by Calvin Redekop and Samuel J. Steiner. Lanham, Md.: University Press of America, 1988.

———. *Thomas Müntzer: Apocalyptic Mystic and Revolutionary.* Edinburgh: T and T Clark, 1993.

———. *Antiklerikalismus und Reformation: Sozialgeschichtliche Untersuchungen.* Göttingen: Vandenhoeck und Ruprecht, 1995.

Goerz, Heinrich. *Die Molotschnaer Ansiedlung: Entstehung, Entwicklung und Untergang.* Steinbach, Man.: Echo Verlag, 1950.

Graham, Elaine L. "Gender, Personhood and Theology." *Scottish Journal of Theology* 48, no. 3 (1995): 341–58.

Graybill, John. "The Search for Truth: A Study of the *Christian Exponent* and Its Place Within the Conservative-Progressive Conflict in the Mennonite Church in the 1920s." Research paper, Goshen College Library, 1982.

Greaves, Richard L., ed. *Triumph over Silence.* Westport, Conn.: Greenwood Press, 1985.

Guggisberg, Hans R., and Gottfried G. Kroedel, eds. *Special Volume. The Reformation in Germany and Europe: Interpretation and Issues.* Gutersloh: Verl-Haus, 1993.

Hamm, Peter M. *Continuity and Change Among Canadian Mennonite Brethren.* Waterloo, Ont.: Wilfrid Laurier University Press, 1987.

Harder, Leland, ed. *The Sources of Swiss Anabaptism: The Grebel Letters and Related Documents.* Scottdale, Pa.: Herald Press, 1985.

Harrison, Paul M. *Authority and Power in the Free Church Tradition: A Social Case Study of the American Baptist Convention.* Princeton: Princeton University Press, 1959.

Hartsock, Nancy. *Money, Sex, and Power: Toward a Feminist Historical Materialism.* New York: Longman, 1983.

———. "Foucault on Power: A Theory for Women?" In *Feminism/Postmodernism,* edited by Linda J. Nicholson. New York: Routledge, 1990.

Haas, Martin. "The Path of the Anabaptists into Separation: The Interdependence of Theology and Social Behavior." In *The Anabaptists and Thomas Müntzer*, edited by James M. Stayer and Werner O. Packull. Dubuque, Iowa: Kendall/Hunt, 1980.

Hecht, Linda Huebert. "Women and Religious Change: The Significance of Anabaptist Women in the Tirol, 1527–1529." *Studies in Religion* 21:1 (1992): 57–66.

———. "An Extraordinary Lay Leader: The Life and Work of Helene of Freyberg, Sixteenth Century Noblewoman and Anabaptist from the Tirol." *Mennonite Quarterly Review* 63:3 (1992): 312–41.

Hemmerle, Klaus. "Power." *Encyclopedia of Theology*, edited by Karl Rahner. Boston: Seabury, 1975.

Hershberger, Guy F. *War, Peace and Nonresistance*. Scottdale, Pa.: Herald Press, 1944, 1969.

———. *The Way of the Cross in Human Relations*. Scottdale, Pa.: Herald Press, 1958.

———. *The Recovery of the Anabaptist Vision*. Scottdale, Pa.: Herald Press, 1967.

Heyward, Carter. *Our Passion for Justice: Images of Power, Sexuality, and Liberation*. New York: Pilgrim Press, 1984.

Hildebrand, P. *Erste Auswanderung der Mennoniten aus dem Danziger Gebiet nach Südrussland*. Halbstadt: A. Neufeld, 1888.

Hillerbrand, Hans J. "An Early Treatise on the Christian and the State." *Mennonite Quarterly Review* 32 (1958): 34–47.

Hobbes, Thomas. *Leviathan*. Edited by C. B. MacPherson. New York: Pelican, 1977.

Homans, George C. *The Human Group*. New York: Harcourt, Brace and Co., 1950.

Hostetler, John A. *God Uses Ink: The Heritage and Mission of the Mennonite Publishing House After Fifty Years*. Scottdale, Pa.: Herald Press, 1958.

Hostetler, John A., and Gertrude Enders Huntington. *The Hutterites in North America*. New York: Holt, Rinehart, and Winston, 1980.

Hostetler, Lester. "The 'Why' of *The Christian Exponent*." *Christian Exponent*, 4 January 1924, 5–6.

Huebner, Harry, ed. *The Church as Theological Community*. Winnipeg, Man.: CMBC Publications, 1990.

Hunt, Mary E. "'Re-Imagining' Backlash." In *Feminist Theology in Different Contexts*, edited by Elizabeth Schüssler Fiorenza and Mary S. Copeland. New York: Orbis Books, 1996.

Hunter, James Davison, *Culture Wars: The Struggle to Define America*. New York: Basic Books, 1991.

Irwin, Joyce. "Society and the Sexes." In *Reformation Europe: A Guide to Research*, edited by Steven Ozment. St. Louis: Center for Reformation Research, 1982.

Isaac, Helmut. "Menno's Vision of the Anticipation of the Kingdom of God in His Early Writings." In *Menno Simons: A Reappraisal*, edited by Gerald R. Brunk. Harrisonburg, Va.: Eastern Mennonite College, 1992.

Isaak, Franz. *Die Molotschnaer Mennoniten*. Halbstadt: Kommissonsverlag und Druck von H. J. Braun, 1908.

Bibliography

Jansen, Sue Curry. *Censorship: The Knot that Binds Power and Knowledge.* New York: Oxford University Press, 1991.

Jansma, Lammert G. "De chiliastische beweging der Wederdopers (1530–1535)." *Doopsgezinde Bijdragen* n. s. 5. (1979): 41–55.

Janzen, Waldemar. "A Canonical Rethinking of the Anabaptist-Mennonite New Testament Orientation." In *The Church as Theological Community,* edited by Harry Huebner. Winnipeg, Man.: CMBC Publications, 1990.

Jecker, Hans-Peter. "Die Basler Täufer." *Basler Zeitschrift für Geschichte und Altertumskunde* 80 (1980): 6–131.

Juhnke, James. *Vision, Doctrine, War: Mennonite Identity and Organization in America, 1880–1930.* Scottdale, Pa.: Herald Press, 1989.

Kasdorf, Julia. "Bakhtin, Boundaries, and Bodies." *Mennonite Quarterly Review* 71 (1997), 169–88.

Kauffman, J. Howard. "Power and Authority in Mennonite Families." *Mennonite Quarterly Review* 68 (1994): 501–23.

Kaufman, Gordon. *Nonresistance and Responsibility and Other Mennonite Essays.* Newton, Kans.: Faith and Life Press, 1979.

———. *In Face of Mystery: A Constructive Theology.* Cambridge: Harvard University Press, 1993.

Kaufmann, Walter. *Nietzsche: Philosopher, Psychologist, Antichrist.* Princeton: Princeton University Press, 1974.

Keightley, Alan. *Wittgenstein, Grammar and God.* London: Epworth Press, 1976.

Keller, Evelyn Fox. *Reflections on Gender and Science.* New Haven: Yale University Press, 1985.

Kelman, Herbert C. "Further Thoughts on the Process of Compliance, Identification and Internalization." In *Perspectives on Social Power,* edited by James T. Tedeschi. Chicago: Aldine, 1974.

Kipnis, David. "The Powerholder." In *Perspectives on Social Power,* edited by James T. Tedeschi. Chicago: Aldine, 1974.

Kirchhoff, Karl-Heinz. "Was There a Peaceful Anabaptist Congregation in Muenster in 1534?" Translated by Elizabeth Bender. *Mennonite Quarterly Review* 44 (1970): 357–70.

———. *Die Täufer in Münster, 1534/35.* Münster: Aschendorff, 1973.

Klaassen, Walter. *Anabaptism: Neither Catholic nor Protestant.* Waterloo, Ont.: Conrad Press, 1973.

———, ed. *Anabaptism in Outline: Selected Primary Sources.* Scottdale, Pa.: Herald Press, 1981.

———. "Investigation into the Authorship and the Historical Background of the Anabaptist Tract 'Aufdeckung der Babylonischen Hurn.'" *Mennonite Quarterly Review* 61 (1987): 251–61.

Klapp, Orin E. *Models of Social Order.* Palo Alto, Calif.: National Press Books, 1973.

Klassen, A. J. *Consultation on Anabaptist-Mennonite Theology.* Fresno, Calif.: Council of Mennonite Seminaries, 1970.

Klaus, A. A. *Unsere Kolonien. Studien und Materiallien zur Geschichte und Statistik der ausländischen Kolonisation in Russland.* Translated by Jacob Toews. Odessa, 1887.

Klippenstein, Lawrence. "Mennonite Pacifism and State Service in Russia: A Case Study in Church-State Relations, 1789–1936." Ph.D. dissertation, University of Minnesota, 1984.

Kniss, Fred. *Disquiet in the Land: Cultural Conflict in American Mennonite Communities.* New Brunswick: Rutgers University Press, 1997.

Kolbenschlag, Madonna, ed. *Authority, Community and Conflict.* Kansas City: Sheed and Ward, 1986.

Krahn, Cornelius. "Some Social Attitudes of Mennonites in Russia." *Mennonite Quarterly Review* 9 (1935): 165–71.

Kraus, Norman. "American Mennonites and the Bible, 1750–1950." *Mennonite Quarterly Review* 41 (1967): 309–29.

Kraybill, Donald B. *The Riddle of Amish Culture.* Baltimore: Johns Hopkins University Press, 1989.

———. "Yieldedness and Accountability in Traditional Anabaptist Communities." In *Anabaptist Currents: History in Conversation with the Present,* edited by Carl Bowman and Stephen Longenecker. Bridgewater, Va.: Forum for Religious Studies, 1995.

Kreider, Robert. "The Anabaptist Conception of the Church in the Russian Mennonite Environment 1789–1870." *Mennonite Quarterly Review* 25 (1951): 17–33.

Kühler, W. J. *Geschiedenis der Nederlandsche doopsgezinden in de zestiende eeuw.* Haarlem: Willink, 1961.

Kuratsuka, Taira. "Gesamtgilde und Täufer. Der Radikalisierungsprozess in der Reformation Münsters: Von der reformatorischen Bewegung zum Täuferreich 1533–34. *Archiv für Reformationsgeschichte* 76 (1985), 231–70.

Lacey, Paul. *Quakers and the Use of Power.* Wallingford, Pa.: Pendle Hill, 1981.

Lassmann, Wolfgang. "Möglichkeiten einer Modellbildung zur Verlaufsstruktur des tirolischen Anabaptismus." In *Anabaptistes et disidents au XVIe siècle,* edited by Jean-Georges Rott and Simon L. Verheus. Baden-Baden: V. Koerner, 1987.

Lasswell, Harold, and Abraham Kaplan. *Power and Society.* New Haven: Yale University Press, 1950.

LaTourette, Kenneth Scott. *A History of Christianity.* New York: Harper, 1953.

Laube, Adolf. ed. *Flugschriften vom Bauernkrieg zum Täuferreich (1526–1535),* vol. 2. Berlin: Akademie Verlag, 1992.

Leinhard, Mark. ed. *The Origins and Characteristics of Anabaptism.* The Hague: Nijhoff, 1977.

Lerner, Gerda. *The Creation of Patriarchy,* vol. 1. New York: Oxford University Press, 1986.

Lindstrom, Lamont. *Knowledge and Power in a South Pacific Society.* Washington: Smithsonian Institution Press, 1990.

Locke, John. *Social Contract Theory*. Edited by Michael Lessnof. Oxford: Basil Blackwell, 1990.

Loewen, Harry. "Echoes of Drumbeats: The Movement of Exuberance Among the Mennonite Brethren." *Journal of Mennonite Studies* 3 (1985): 118–27.

Loewen, Harry, and Al Reimer, eds. *Visions and Realities*. Winnipeg, Man.: Hyperion Press, 1985.

Loewen, Harry, and James Urry. "Protecting Mammon: Some Dilemmas of Mennonite Non-resistance in Late Imperial Russia and the Origins of the *Selbstschutz*." *Journal of Mennonite Studies* 9 (1991): 34–53.

Loewen, Howard John. *One Lord, One Church, One Hope and One God*. Elkhart, Ind.: Institute of Mennonite Studies, 1985.

———. "Peace in the Mennonite Tradition: Toward a Theological Understanding of a Regulative Concept." In *Baptism, Peace and the State in the Reformed and Mennonite Traditions*, edited by Ross T. Bender and Alan P. F. Sell. Waterloo, Ont.: Wilfrid Laurier University Press, 1991.

Loewen, Jacob A., and Wesley J. Prieb. *Only the Sword of the Spirit*. Winnipeg, Man.: Kindred Press, 1998.

Lorde, Audre. *Sister Outsider: Essays and Speeches*. Trumansburg, Pa.: Crossing Press, 1984.

Machiavelli, Niccolò. *The Prince*. Translated by W. K. Marriott. London and Toronto: J. M. Dent and Sons, 1931.

Marsden, George. *Fundamentalism and American Culture: The Shaping of Twentieth-Century Evangelicalism, 1870–1980*. New York: Oxford University Press, 1980.

McClellan, Charles A. "Power and Influence." In *Power*, edited by John Champlin. New York: Atherton Press, 1971.

McClendon, James W. *Systematic Theology: Ethics*. Nashville, Tenn.: Abingdon, 1986.

McGuire, Meredith B. "Discovering Religious Power." *Sociological Analysis* 44:1 (1983): 1–9.

The Mennonite Encyclopedia, vols. 1–4. Scottdale, Pa.: Mennonite Publishing House, 1955–59; 1960.

The Mennonite Encyclopedia, vol. 5. Scottdale, Pa.: Herald Press, 1990.

Mennonitisches Lexicon. Edited by Christian Hege and Christian Neff. Weierhof, 1937.

Miller, Keith Graber. *Wise as Serpents, Innocent as Doves: American Mennonites Engage Washington*. Knoxville: University of Tennessee Press, 1996.

Miller, Susan Fisher. *Culture for Service: A History of Goshen College, 1894–1994*. Goshen: Goshen College, 1994.

Mills, C. Wright. *The Power Elite*. Oxford: Oxford University Press, 1959.

Moeller, Bernd. "Piety in Germany Around 1500." In *The Reformation in Medieval Perspective*, edited by Steven E. Ozment. Chicago: Quadrangle Books, 1971.

———. "The Gospel of Social Unrest." In *The German Peasants War 1525: New*

Viewpoints, edited by Robert W. Scribner and Gerhard Benecke. London: Allen and Unwin, 1979.

Morgenstern, Oskar. "Game Theory." In *Dictionary of the History of Ideas,* vol. 2, edited by Philip P. Wiener. New York: Scribner's, 1973.

Muralt, Leonhard von, and Walther Schmid, eds. *Quellen zur Geschichte der Täufer in der Schweiz, 1: Zürich.* Zürich: Theologischer Verlag, 1952.

Nafziger-Leis, Cheryl. *Consultation on Issues of Power and Authority in the Mennonite Church.* Kitchener, Ont.: Rockway Collegiate, 1997.

Neufeld, Colin. *The Fate of the Mennonites in Soviet Ukraine and the Crimea During the Soviet Collectivization and the Famine (1928–1933).* Coaldale, Alta.: Colin P. Neufeld, 1989.

Niebuhr, H. Richard. *Christ and Culture.* New York: Harper and Row, 1951.

Niebuhr, Reinhold. *Moral Man and Immoral Society.* New York: Scribner's, 1960.

Nietzsche, Friedrich. *On the Genealogy of Morals.* Translated by Walter Kaufmann and R. J. Hollingdale. New York: Vintage Books, 1969.

———. *Twilight of the Idols* and *The Antichrist.* Translated by R. J. Hollingdale. New York: Penguin, 1982.

Oberman, Heiko A. "The Gospel of Social Unrest." In *The German Peasants War, 1525: New Viewpoints,* edited by Robert Scribner and Gerhard Benecke. London: Allen and Unwin, 1979.

Ozment, Stephen E., ed. *The Reformation in Medieval Perspective.* Chicago: Quadrangle Books, 1971.

———, ed. *Reformation Europe: A Guide to Research.* St. Louis: Center for Reformation Research, 1982.

Packull, Werner O. *Mysticism and the Early South German–Austrian Anabaptist Movement, 1525–1531.* Scottdale, Pa.: Herald Press, 1977.

———. *Hutterite Beginnings: Communitarian Experiments during the Reformation.* Baltimore: Johns Hopkins University Press, 1995.

———. "The Origins of Peter Riedemann's *Account of Our Faith.*" *Sixteenth Century Journal* 30 (1999): 61–69.

Parsons, Talcott. *The Social System.* Glencoe, Ill.: Free Press, 1951.

Parsons, Talcott, and A. M. Henderson, eds. *Max Weber: The Theory of Social and Economic Organization.* New York: Free Press, 1965.

Payne, Ernest A. "The Anabaptist Impact on Western Christendom." In *The Recovery of the Anabaptist Vision,* edited by Guy F. Hershberger. Scottdale, Pa.: Herald Press, 1957.

Penner, Horst. *Weltweite Bruderschaft. Ein Mennonitisches Geschichtsbuch.* Karlsruhe: Verlag Heinrich Schneider, 1955.

Pipkin, H. Wayne, and John H. Yoder, eds. *Balthasar Hubmaier: Theologian of Anabaptism.* Scottdale, Pa.: Herald Press, 1989.

Plaskow, Judith. "Transforming the Nature of Community." In *After Patriarchy: Feminist Transformation of the World Religions.* Edited by Paula M. Cooey, William R. Eakin, and Jay B. McDaniel. New York: Orbis Books, 1991.

Bibliography

Plato. *The Republic of Plato.* Translated by Francis Macdonald Cornford. Oxford: At the Clarendon Press, 1948.

Plett, C. F. *The Story of the Krimmer Mennonite Brethren Church.* Winnipeg, Man.: Kindred Press, 1985.

Pope, Liston. *Millhands and Preachers.* New Haven: Yale University Press, 1942.

Preheim, Lois Janzen. "Power: One Woman's Perspective." *In Search* (December 1991).

Presthus, Robert V. *Men at the Top: A Study in Community Power.* New York: Oxford University Press, 1964.

Redekop, Calvin W. *The Old Colony Mennonites: Dilemmas of Ethnic Minority Life.* Baltimore: Johns Hopkins University Press, 1969.

———. "Institutions, Power and the Gospel." In *Kingdom, Cross and Community,* edited by J. Richard Burkholder and Calvin Redekop. Scottdale, Pa.: Herald Press, 1976.

———. "The Mennonite Transformation from Gelassenheit to Capitalism." In *Visions and Realities,* edited by Harry Loewen and Al Reimer. Winnipeg: Hyperion Press, 1985.

———. *Mennonite Society.* Baltimore: Johns Hopkins University Press, 1989.

———. "Power." In *Dictionary of Pastoral Care and Counseling,* edited by Rodney J. Hunter. Nashville, Tenn.: Abingdon Press, 1990.

———. "The MCC Ethos and the Organizational Revolution." *Mennonite Quarterly Review* 70 (1996): 107–33.

Redekop, Calvin W., and Samuel J. Steiner, eds. *Mennonite Identity: Historical and Contemporary Perspectives.* Lanham, Md.: University Press of America, 1988.

Redekop, Calvin W., Stephen C. Ainlay, and Robert Siemens. *Mennonite Entrepreneurs.* Baltimore: Johns Hopkins University Press, 1995.

Reimer, A. James. "Anabaptist-Mennonite Systematic Theology." *Ecumenist* 21, no. 4 (May-June 1983): 68–72.

Reimer, Al. *My Harp Is Turned to Mourning.* Winnipeg, Man.: Hyperion Press, 1985.

———. "The Mennonite *Gutsbesitzer* in Russland." Paper presented at the Symposium on the Bicentennial of Mennonites in Russia, Winnipeg, Man., 1989.

Rempel, D. G. "The Mennonite Colonies in Russia: A Study of Their Settlement and Economic Development from 1789 to 1914." Ph.D. dissertation, Stanford University, 1933.

———. "The Mennonite Commonwealth in Russia: A Sketch of Its Founding and Endurance, 1789–1919." *Mennonite Quarterly Review* 47 (1973): 259–308; 48 (1974): 5–54.

Rempel, John D. *The Lord's Supper in Anabaptism.* Waterloo, Ont.: Herald Press, 1993.

Riedemann, Peter. *Account of Our Religion, Doctrine, and Faith.* Bungay, 1950.

Rose, Arnold M. *The Power Structure.* New York: Oxford University Press, 1967.

Rousseau, Jean-Jacques. *The Social Contract.* Translated by G. D. H. Cole. London: Campell Publishers, 1993.

Ruether, Rosemary Radford. "Differing Views of the Church." In *Authority, Community and Conflict*, edited by Madonna Kolbenschlag. Kansas City: Sheed and Ward, 1986.

Rule, Andrew. "Christianity and the Problem of Power." In *New 20th Century Encyclopedia of Religious Knowledge*, edited by J. D. Douglass. Grand Rapids: Baker, 1991.

Russell, Bertrand. *Power.* London: Routledge, 1992.

Russell, Letty M. *Church in the Round: Feminist Interpretation of the Church.* Louisville, Ky.: Westminster/John Knox Press, 1993.

Sawatsky, Rodney. *Authority and Identity: The Dynamics of the General Conference Mennonite Church.* North Newton, Kans.: Bethel College, 1987.

———. "Leadership, Power and Authority." *Mennonite Quarterly Review* 71 (July 1997): 429–52.

Sawatsky, Rodney J., and Scott Holland, eds. *The Limits of Perfection: Conversations with J. Lawrence Burkholder.* Waterloo, Ont.: Institute of Anabaptist-Mennonite Studies, 1993.

Schermerhorn, Richard A. *Society and Power.* New York: Random House, 1961.

Schlabach, Theron. *Peace, Faith, Nation: Mennonites and Amish in Nineteenth Century America.* Scottdale, Pa.: Herald Press, 1988.

Schoenherr, Richard A. "Power and Authority in Organized Religion: Disaggregating the Phenomenological Core." *Sociological Analysis* 47 (March 1987): 52–71.

Scribner, Robert W., and Gerhard Benecke. *The German Peasants War 1525: New Viewpoints.* London: Allen and Unwin, 1979.

Sharp, Gene. *The Role of Power in Nonviolent Struggle.* Cambridge: Albert Einstein Institute, 1990.

Skinner, Quentin. "Machiavelli." In *Great Political Thinkers*, edited by Keith Thomas. Oxford: Oxford University Press, 1992.

Slough, Rebecca. "Changes Created by Women's Participation," MCC *Women's Concerns Report* (July-August 1966).

Smith, C. Henry. *The Story of the Mennonites*, 5th ed., Newton, Kans.: Faith and Life Press, 1981.

Snyder, C. Arnold. "The Schleitheim Articles in Light of the Revolution of the Common Man: Continuation or Departure?" *Sixteenth Century Journal* 16 (1985): 419–30.

———. "Word and Power in Reformation Zurich." *Archiv für Reformationsgeschichte* 81 (1990): 263–85.

———. "The Believers' Church Heritage of Ministry." In *Servants of the Word: Ministry in the Believers' Church*, edited by David B. Eller. Elgin, Ill.: Brethren Press, 1990.

———. *Anabaptist History and Theology. An Introduction.* Kitchener, Ont.: Pandora Press, 1995.

Snyder, C. Arnold, and Linda A. Hecht, eds. *Profiles of Anabaptist Women: Sixteenth*

Century Reforming Pioneers. Waterloo, Ont.: Wilfrid Laurier University Press, 1996.

Sprunger, Keith. "God's Powerful Army of the Weak: Anabaptist Women of the Radical Reformation." In *Triumph over Silence,* edited by Richard L. Greaves. Westport, Conn.: Greenwood Press, 1985.

Stayer, James M. *Anabaptists and the Sword.* Lawrence, Kans.: Coronado Press, 1972, 1976.

———. "Reublin and Brötli: The Revolutionary Beginnings of Swiss Anabaptism." In *The Origins and Characteristics of Anabaptism,* edited by Mark Lienhard. The Hague: Nijhoff, 1977.

———. "Wilhelm Reublin: A Picaresque Journey Through Early Anabaptism." In *Profiles of Radical Reformers: Biographical Sketches from Thomas Müntzer to Paracelsus,* edited by Hans-Jürgen Goertz. Scottdale, Pa.: Herald Press, 1982.

———. "Was Dr. Kuehler's Conception of Early Dutch Anabaptism Historically Sound? The Historical Discussion of Münster 450 Years Later." *Mennonite Quarterly Review* 60 (1986): 261–88.

——— "Anticlericalism: A Model for a Coherent Interpretation of the Reformation." In *Special Volume: The Reformation in Germany and Europe: Interpretations and Issues,* edited by Hans R. Guggisberg and Gottfried G. Krodel. Gütersloh: Gütersloher Verl.-Haus, 1993.

———. *The German Peasants' War and Anabaptist Community of Goods.* Montreal: McGill-Queen's University Press, 1991.

———. "The Passing of the Radical Moment in the Radical Reformation." *Mennonite Quarterly Review* 71 (1997): 147–52.

Stayer, James M., Werner O. Packull, and Klaus Deppermann. "From Monogenesis to Polygenesis: The Historical Discussion of Anabaptist Origins." *Mennonite Quarterly Review* 49 (April 1975): 83–121.

Stayer, James M., and Werner O. Packull. *The Anabaptists and Thomas Müntzer.* Dubuque, Iowa: Kendall/Hunt, 1980.

Tedeschi, James T. *Perspectives on Social Power.* Chicago: Aldine, 1974.

Thiessen, Victor D. "*To the Assembly of Common Peasantary:* The Case of the Missing Context." *Archiv für Reformationsgeschichte* 86 (1995): 175–98.

Thiselton, Anthony C. *The Two Horizons: New Testament Hermeneutics and Philosophical Description with Special Reference to Heidegger, Bultmann, Gadamer, and Wittgenstein.* Grand Rapids: Eerdmans, 1980.

Thomas Aquinas, Saint. *The Summa Theologica.* Vols. 19 and 20 in *Great Books of the Western World,* edited by Robert M. Hutchins. Chicago: University of Chicago Press, 1952.

Tillich, Paul. *Love, Power, and Justice.* New York: Oxford University Press, 1954.

Toews, J. C. "Das Mennonitische Gutsbesitzertum in Russland." *Der Bote,* 15 September 1954.

Toews, Jacob John. "Cultural Background of the Mennonite Brethren Church." Master's thesis, University of Toronto, 1951.

Toews, John A. *A History of the Mennonite Brethren Church*. Fresno, Calif.: General Conference of the Mennonite Brethren Church, 1975.

Toews, John B. *Lost Fatherland: The Story of the Mennonite Emigration from Soviet Russia, 1921–1927*. Scottdale, Pa.: Herald Press, 1967.

———. "The Origins and Activities of the Mennonite *Selbstschutz* in the Ukraine (1918–1919)." *Mennonite Quarterly Review* 46 (1972): 5–40.

———. "The Russian Origins of the Mennonite Brethren: Some Observations." In *Pilgrims and Strangers: Essays in Mennonite Brethren History*, edited by Paul Toews. Fresno: CMBS, 1977.

———. *Czars, Soviets and Mennonites*. Newton, Kans.: Faith and Life Press, 1982.

———. *Perilous Journey: The Mennonite Brethren in Russia, 1860–1910*. Winnipeg, Man.: Kindred Press, 1988.

Toews, Paul, ed. *Pilgrims and Strangers: Essays in Mennonite Brethren History*. Fresno, Calif.: CMBS, 1977.

———. "Fundamentalist Conflict in Mennonite Colleges: A Response to Cultural Transitions?" *Mennonite Quarterly Review* 57 (1983): 241–56.

Toffler, Alvin. *Power Shift*. New York: Bantam Books, 1990.

Troeltsch, Ernst. *The Social Teachings of the Christian Churches*. New York: Macmillan, [1931], 1960.

Umble, John. *Goshen College, 1984–1954*. Goshen, Ind.: Goshen College, 1955.

Unruh, A. H. *Die Geschichte der Mennoniten-Brüdergemeinde 1860–1954*. Hillsboro, Kans.: General Conference of the Mennonite Brethren Church of North America, 1954.

Urry, James. "The Closed and the Open: Social and Religious Change Amongst the Mennonites in Russia, 1789–1889." Ph.D. dissertation, Oxford University, 1978.

———. "Through the Eye of a Needle: Wealth and the Mennonite Experience in Imperial Russia." *Journal of Mennonite Studies* 3 (1985): 7–35.

———. *None But Saints. The Transformation of Mennonite Life in Russia, 1789–1889*. Winnipeg, Man.: Hyperion Press, 1989.

——— "Mennonite Economic Development in the Russian Mirror." In *Mennonites in Russia, 1788–1988: Essays in Honour of Gerhard Lohrenz*, edited by John Friesen. Winnipeg, Man.: CMBC Publications, 1989.

Urry, James, and Lawrence Klippenstein. "Mennonites and the Crimean War, 1854–1856." *Journal of Mennonite Studies* 7 (1989): 9–32.

Van Dülmen, Richard. *Reformation als Revolution. Soziale Bewegung und religiöser Radikalismus in der deutschen Reformation*. Munich: Deutscher Taschenbuch Verlag, 1977.

Vogler, Günter. "Das Täuferreich zu Münster als Problem der Politik im Reich." *Mennonitische Geschichtsblätter* 42 (1985): 7–23.

Von Muralt, Leonard, and Walter Schmid, eds. *Quellen zur Geschichte der Täufer in der Schweiz. 1. Zürich*. Zurich: Theologischer Verlag, 1952.

Vos, Karel. "Revolutionary Reformation." In *The Anabaptists and Thomas Müntzer*, edited by James M. Stayer and Werner O. Packull. Dubuque, Iowa: Kendall/ Hunt, 1980.

Wach, Joachim. *Sociology of Religion*. Chicago: University of Chicago Press, 1944.

———. *Types of Religious Experience: Christian and Non-Christian*. Chicago: University of Chicago Press, 1951.

Waite, Gary K. *David Joris and Dutch Anabaptism, 1524–1543*. Waterloo, Ont.: Wilfrid Laurier University Press, 1990.

Walliman, Isidor, Howard Rosenbaum, Nicholas Tatsis, and George Zito. "Misreading Weber: The Concept of Macht," *Sociology* 14, no. 2 (May 1980): 260–75.

Walton, Robert C. "Was There a Turning Point of the Zwinglian Reformation?" *Mennonite Quarterly Review* 42 (1968): 45–56.

Wartenberg, Thomas. *The Forms of Power: From Domination to Transformation*. Philadelphia: Temple University Press, 1990.

Weber, Max. *Wirtschaft und Gesellschaft: Grundriß der Sozialokonomik*. Tübingen: Verlag von J. C. B. Mont Paul Siebeck, 1925.

———. *From Max Weber: Essays in Sociology*. Edited by H. H. Gerth and C. Wright Mills. New York: Oxford University Press, 1946.

———. *The Sociology of Religion*. Boston: Beacon Press, 1963.

Wenger, J. C. *Separated unto God*. Scottdale, Pa.: Mennonite Publishing House, 1959.

———. *The Mennonites in Indiana and Michigan*. Scottdale, Pa.: Herald Press, 1961.

———, ed. *The Complete Writings of Menno Simons*. Translated by Leonard Verduin. Scottdale, Pa.: Herald Press, 1956, 1984.

West, Guida, and Rhoda Lois Blumberg. *Women and Social Protest*. Oxford: Oxford University Press, 1990.

Westin, Gunnar, and Torsten Bergsten. *Quellen zur Geschichte der Täufer 9: Balthasar Hubmaier Schriften*. Gütersloh: Gerd Mohn, 1962.

Wiebe, Dallas. *Our Asian Journey*. Waterloo: Wilfrid Laurier University Press, 1997.

Wink, Walter. *Engaging the Powers*. Minneapolis: Fortress Press, 1992.

Wittgenstein, Ludwig. *Philosophical Investigations*. trans. G. E. M. Anscomb. New York: Macmillan Publishing Co., 1968.

Woltjer, J. J., and M. E. H. N. Mont, "Settlements: The Netherlands." In *Handbook Of European History, 1400–1600*, vol. 2, edited by Thomas A. Brady, Jr., Heiko A. Oberman, and James D. Tracy. Leiden: E. J. Brill, 1995.

Yinger, J. Milton. *Religion and the Struggle for Power*. Durham: Duke University Press, 1946.

Yoder, John Howard. "Anabaptist Vision and Mennonite Reality." In *Consultation on Anabaptist-Mennonite Theology*, edited by A. J. Klassen. Fresno, Calif.: Council of Mennonite Seminaries, 1970.

———. *The Politics of Jesus*. Grand Rapids, Mich.: Eerdmans, 1972, 1994.

————, ed. *The Legacy of Michael Sattler.* Scottdale, Pa.: Herald Press, 1973.

————. *The Priestly Kingdom: Social Ethics as Gospel.* Notre Dame: University of Notre Dame Press, 1984.

————. *The Royal Priesthood: Essays Ecclesiological and Ecumenical.* Grand Rapids, Mich.: Eerdmans, 1994.

Young, Pamela Dickey. *Feminist Theology/Christian Theology: In Search of Method.* Minneapolis: Fortress Press, 1996.

Ziegelschmid, A. J. F., ed. *Die älteste Chronik der Hutterischen Brüder.* Ithaca: Cayuga, 1943.

Zilstra, Samme. *Nicolaas Meyndertz van Blesdijk: Een bijdrage tot de geschiedenis van het Daridjorisme.* Assen: Van Gorcum, 1983.

Zook, Gordon. *Current Patterns of Shared Leadership in Mennonite Church Congregations.* D. Min. thesis, Lancaster Theological Seminary, 1989.

Contributors

Stephen C. Ainlay is Vice President for Academic Affairs and Dean at the College of the Holy Cross, Worcester, Massachusetts. He received his Ph.D. degree from Rutgers University. He has taught courses in the sociology of knowledge, sociology of religion, and the sociology of aging, and has published books and articles in each of these areas. His publications include *Mennonite Entrepreneurs* (coauthored with Calvin Redekop and Robert Siemens, Johns Hopkins University Press, 1995); *Day Brought Back My Night: Aging and New Vision Loss* (Routledge, 1989); and *Making Sense of Modern Times: Peter L. Berger and the Vision of Interpretive Sociology* (coedited with James Davison Hunter, Routledge, 1986).

J. Lawrence Burkholder is a Mennonite churchman, philosopher, and theologian who was introduced to issues concerning power, justice, ambiguity, and complexity when he served as post–World War II administrator of relief programs in China with the Mennonite Central Committee, Church World Service, and the United Nations. After graduate studies at Princeton Theological Seminary, he taught at Goshen College and Harvard University. He served as President of Goshen College from 1971 to 1984. He is the author of *Sum and Substance* (1986); *The Problem of Social Responsibility from the Perspective of the Mennonite Church* (Institute of Mennonite Studies, 1989); and *The Limits of Perfection* (Institute of Mennonite Studies, 1993).

Lydia Neufeld Harder received a Th.D. from the Toronto School of Theology in 1994 and was Director of the Toronto Mennonite Theological Centre for five years. She currently teaches courses in ecclesiology and biblical hermeneutics at the Toronto School of Theology and Conrad Grebel College, Waterloo, Ontario. She has published several articles and chapters on Mennonite topics, including "Menno's View of Jesus," in *Discipleship in Context*, ed. Hoekma and Kuitze (Institute of Mennonite Studies, 1997). Her research on issues of power and authority has been published in *Obedience, Suspicion, and the Gospel of Mark: A Mennonite-Feminist Exploration of Biblical Authority* (Wilfrid Laurier Press, 1998).

Joel Hartman is Associate Professor Emeritus of Rural Sociology at the University of Missouri. He has received awards for distinguished teaching, including the William T. Kemper Fellowship for Excellence in Teaching in 1996. He has been a frequent consultant to healthcare organizations and public health agencies on working with Amish and Plain Mennonite communities.

Jacob A. Loewen served as a Mennonite Brethren missionary in Colombia from 1947 through 1957. He received a Ph.D. in linguistics from the University of Washington in 1958. He has taught at Tabor College in Hillsboro, Kansas, and worked as a translation consultant in South America and Africa, encountering more than two hundred different cultures and languages. His books include *Culture and Human Values* (William Carey Library, 1975); *Only the Sword of the Spirit* (coauthored with Wesley Prieb, Kindred Press, 1997); and *The Bible in Cross-Cultural Perspective* (William Carey Library, 1996).

Dorothy Yoder Nyce received an M.Div. from the Associated Mennonite Biblical Seminaries in 1981 and a D.Min. from Western Theological Seminary in 1997. Dr. Nyce is author and editor of numerous publications. Recent publications include: coeditor of *Mission Today: Challenges and Concerns* (Chennai, India, 1998); editor of *Rooting and Branching: Women Worldwide* (Goshen, Indiana, 1998); and author of "Interreligious Dialogue: From Principle to Praxis," in *Studies in Interreligious Dialogue* (1998). She has had assignments in India seven times, carried pastoring roles, and worked for justice in areas of women's issues and human sexuality.

Lynda Nyce received a Ph.D. in sociology from the University of Notre Dame (2000), with an emphasis in the sociology of sex and gender. She is Assistant Professor of Sociology at Bluffton College, Ohio. Her areas of research and writing include sex and gender, qualitative research methods, urban studies, and nonprofit organizations. Dr. Nyce is active in consulting for nonprofit housing organizations and is currently a researcher in the Coalition for Christian Colleges and Universities' Faithful Change project.

Wesley Prieb (now deceased) received his M.A. in English from the University of Kansas in 1950. He served as Dean and Acting President of Tabor College, Hillsboro, Kansas, during a long career of teaching and administration there. He was Director of the Center for Mennonite Brethren Studies from 1977 to 1990 and served as Chairman of the Mennonite Brethren Board of Publications. His publications include *P. C. Hiebert: He Gave Them Bread* (Center for Mennonite Brethren Studies, 1990), and *Only the Sword of the Spirit* (coauthored with Jacob Loewen, Kindred Press, 1997). Shortly before his death, Prieb served a term as Scholar in Residence at the Young Center for Anabaptist and Pietist Studies, Elizabethtown College, Pennsylvania (1995).

Benjamin W. Redekop received a Ph.D. in history from the University of British Columbia in 1996. He has taught courses in intellectual history and the history of science at the University of British Columbia and Trinity Western University, and he is currently Assistant Professor of Social Science at Kettering University. He has published journal articles on Mennonite history and on the German and Scottish

Enlightenments and is the author of *Enlightenment and Community: Lessing, Abbt, Herder, and the Quest for a German Public* (McGill-Queen's University Press, 2000) and coeditor of *Entrepreneurs in the Faith Community: Profiles of Mennonites in Business* (Herald Press, 1996). From 1996 to 1998 he was Senior Research Fellow at Wolfson College, University of Cambridge.

Calvin W. Redekop received an M.A. in history from the University of Minnesota in 1954 and a Ph.D. in anthropology and sociology from the University of Chicago in 1959. He has taught in several Mennonite colleges as well as the University of Waterloo, Canada. His major research has focused on ethnicity, minorities, and sociology of religion, having done research in Canada, Mexico, and Paraguay on these topics. He has also conducted research on religion and economics. His publications include *The Old Colony Mennonites* (Johns Hopkins University Press, 1969), *Mennonite Society* (Johns Hopkins University Press, 1989), and *Mennonite Entrepreneurs* (coauthored with Stephen C. Ainlay and Robert Siemens, Johns Hopkins University Press, 1995).

James M. Stayer is Professor of History at Queen's University, Ontario. He has been occupied with the topic of Anabaptism and power throughout his career. His Ph.D. dissertation (Cornell, 1964) was entitled "The Doctrine of the Sword in the first Decade of Anabaptism," and an expanded version of the work was published in 1972 as *Anabaptists and the Sword* (Coronado Press, 1972, 1976). He has published widely in the field of Anabaptist studies, including *The German Peasants' War and Anabaptist Community of Goods* (McGill-Queen's University Press, 1991) and articles in *The New Cambridge Modern History* (1990) and *The Encyclopedia of the Reformation* (1996).

Index

Other Books in the Series

Carl F. Bowman, *Brethren Society: The Cultural Transformation of a "Peculiar People"*

Perry Bush, *Two Kingdoms, Two Loyalties: Mennonite Pacifism in Modern America*

John A. Hostetler, ed., *Amish Roots: A Treasury of History, Wisdom, and Lore*

Donald B. Kraybill, *The Riddle of Amish Culture*, rev. ed.

Donald B. Kraybill, ed., *The Amish and the State*

Donald B. Kraybill and Carl F. Bowman, *On the Backroad to Heaven: Old Order Hutterites, Mennonites, Amish, and Brethren*

Donald B. Kraybill and Steven M. Nolt, *Amish Enterprise: From Plows to Profits*

Lucian Niemeyer and Donald B. Kraybill, *Old Order Amish: Their Enduring Way of Life*

Werner O. Packull, *Hutterite Beginnings: Communitarian Experiments during the Reformation*

Calvin Redekop, Stephen C. Ainlay, and Robert Siemens, *Mennonite Entrepreneurs*

Calvin Redekop, ed., *Creation and the Environment: An Anabaptist Perspective on a Sustainable World*

Steven D. Reschly, *The Amish on the Iowa Prairie, 1840 to 1910*

Diane Zimmerman Umble, *Holding the Line: The Telephone in the Old Order Mennonite and Amish Life*